# Performance Management in the Public Sector

In times of rising expectations and decreasing resources for the public sector, performance management is high on the agenda. Increasingly, the value of performance management systems themselves is under scrutiny, with more attention being paid to the effectiveness of performance management in practice. This new edition of *Performance Management in the Public Sector* explores performance, as well as performance measurement, and making performance information useful for management. The book:

- situates performance in some of the current public management debates, including some emerging discussions on the new public governance and neo-Weberianism;
- discusses the many definitions of performance and how it has become one of the most contested agendas of public management;
- examines the use as well as the non-use of performance information;
- conveys a nuanced discussion of the so-called perverse effects of using performance indicators;
- discusses the technicalities of performance measurement in a five-step process: prioritizing measurement, indicator development, data collection, analysis and reporting; and
- explores the challenges and future directions of performance management.

*Performance Management in the Public Sector*, 2nd edition, offers clear insight into a complex theme for practitioners and students alike. For scholars, the book directs attention to key research issues, most pressingly the use of performance information.

**Wouter Van Dooren** is Associate Professor of Public Administration at the research group Public Administration & Management of the Department of Political Science, University of Antwerp, Belgium. Research interests include performance measurement and management, the political dimensions of public administration, accountability and participation.

**Geert Bouckaert** is Professor at the Public Governance Institute of the KU Leuven, Belgium, and Visiting Professor at the University of Potsdam, Germany. He is President of the International Institute of Administrative Sciences (IIAS) (2013–16) and was the President of the European Group for Public Administration (EGPA) (2004–10).

**John Halligan** is Professor of Public Administration, Institute for Governance and Policy Analysis, University of Canberra, Australia. His research interests are comparative public governance and management, performance management and public sector reform.

D0145564

# ROUTLEDGE MASTERS IN PUBLIC MANAGEMENT

*Edited by Stephen P. Osborne*

**Routledge Masters in Public Management** series is an integrated set of texts. It is intended to form the backbone for the holistic study of the theory and practice of public management, as part of

- a taught Master's, MBA or MPA course at a university or college;
- a work-based, in-service programme of education and training; or
- a programme of self-guided study.

Each volume stands alone in its treatment of its topic, whether it be strategic management, marketing or procurement, and is co-authored by leading specialists in their field. However, all volumes in the series share both a common pedagogy and a common approach to the structure of the text. Key features of all volumes in the series include:

- a critical approach to combining theory with practice which educates its reader, rather than solely teaching him/her a set of skills;
- clear learning objectives for each chapter;
- the use of figures, tables and boxes to highlight key ideas, concepts and skills;
- an annotated bibliography, guiding students in their further reading; and
- a dedicated case study in the topic of each volume, to serve as a focus for discussion and learning.

# Performance Management in the Public Sector

## Second Edition

Wouter Van Dooren,
Geert Bouckaert and
John Halligan

LONDON AND NEW YORK

First published 2010

Second Edition 2015
by Routledge
2 Park Square, Milton Park, Abingdon, Oxon OX14 4RN

and by Routledge
711 Third Avenue, New York, NY 10017

*Routledge is an imprint of the Taylor & Francis Group, an informa business*

*British Library Cataloguing in Publication Data*
A catalogue record for this book is available from the British Library

*Library of Congress Cataloging-in-Publication Data*
Dooren, Wouter van.
    Performance management in the public sector / Wouter van Dooren,
    Geert Bouckaert, John Halligan.—Second edition.
    pages cm — (Routledge masters in public management)
    Includes bibliographical references and index.
    1. Government productivity—Evaluation. 2. Performance—
    Management. 3. Public administration. I. Bouckaert, Geert.
    II. Halligan, John. III. Title.
    JF1525.P67D66 2015
    352.6'6—dc23
    2014030159

ISBN: 978-0-415-73809-5 (hbk)
ISBN: 978-0-415-73810-1 (pbk)
ISBN: 978-1-315-81759-0 (ebk)

Typeset in Perpetua and Bell Gothic
by Florence Production Ltd, Stoodleigh, Devon, UK

# Contents

# Figures

# Tables

# Boxes

# Introduction

**LEARNING OBJECTIVES**

- To be able to position the performance debate in contemporary public administration, public sector reform, public management and public policy.
- To understand the controversy around performance management.

**KEY POINTS IN THIS CHAPTER**

- The concept of performance has many meanings, which can be classified based on the value judgements they imply.
- Performance is not only a concept, but also a contested agenda of change which calls for a balanced treatment of the issue.
- A clear distinction between measurement, incorporation and use of performance information is vital.
- Performance management is embedded in debates of reform, management and policy.

**DISCUSSION QUESTIONS**

- What does it mean when somebody claims an organization (e.g. a railway company, a municipality, a police department) as *performing*?
- Is performance the state of the art of public administration? Why then is it contested?

The subject of this book is the core of public management, certainly in its New Public Management (NPM) form: is it possible to envisage management in the public sector without due regard to the pursuit of performance? Nevertheless, performance management lacks a coherent treatment that explicates its significance, analyses its several dimensions as a working system, compares its application internationally and challenges its shortcomings. The purpose of this book is to develop this comprehensive understanding of performance management as a concept and phenomenon that has swept through OECD countries, in order to examine how it has been applied in practice and in order to review the relationship with public management and public policy.

The aim of this introductory chapter is to situate performance, performance measurement and performance management in some of the current debates in public management. We discuss the many meanings of the word 'performance' and how it has become one of the main, but contested, agendas in public administration. We also introduce the sequence of measurement, incorporation and use of performance information, which reflects the structure of the book. We finally argue that performance measurement has become pivotal not only in reform, but also in daily public management and policymaking. We end the chapter with an outline of the book and summaries of the chapters. The discussions are deliberately sketchy since we primarily want to outline the relevance of and controversies surrounding the performance debate. We will seek more definitional precision in the next chapter.

## 1 PERFORMANCE AS A CONCEPT

Performance can mean many things. Dubnick (2005) asserts that

> outside of any specific context, performance can be associated with a range of actions from the simple and mundane act of opening a car door, to the staging of an elaborate re-enactment of the Broadway musical 'Chicago'. In all these forms, performance stands in distinction from mere 'behaviour' in implying some degree of intent.
>
> (p. 319)

In science, connotations vary according to disciplines. For example, psychology, social sciences and managerial sciences use different definitions depending more on individual, societal, or organizational and system performance. Clearly, performance has many meanings, and our task is to characterize this variation.

From Dubnick's observations of car doors and musicals, we can infer a universal definitional ingredient. Performance is about intentional behaviour, which can be individual or organizational. Based on this understanding of performance as deliberate action, a classification of performance perspectives can be built. The

**Table 1.1** *Four perspectives on how performance is understood (based on Dubnick, 2005)*

| Does the perspective imply quality of actions? | Does the perspective imply quality of achievements? | |
| --- | --- | --- |
| | No | Yes |
| No | Performance as production (P1) | Performance as good results (P3) |
| Yes | Performance as competence/ capacity (P2) | Performance as sustainable results (P4) |

two dimensions of Table 1.1 reflect the importance that a perspective attaches to quality of performance; does a definition imply a statement on whether performance is good or bad? Quality is either (a) the quality of the actions being performed, or (b) the quality of what has been achieved because of those actions. This allows distinctions between four perspectives on performance that also help to organize the performance literature.

The first perspective of performance focuses the attention on tasks being carried out by the performing agent (P1). Performance then includes all actions that are performed. A police patrol, a vaccination campaign, a medical treatment, teaching a course, judging in courts: all are examples of performances, irrespective of whether they were successful. Performance is intentional behaviour of government actors. This conceptualization is relatively neutral in nature, but also very broad.

The other dimensions of the concept 'performance' contain a value judgement. Performance has a quality that can be either high or low. First, when performance is about the quality of the actions, and not as much about the quality of the achievements, performance is conceptualized as *competence* or *capacity* (P2). Under the assumption that a highly competent performer will be more likely to generate more and better quality output from an activity most of the time, performance becomes associated with the competence of the performing institution (Dubnick, 2005: p. 392).

There is substantial literature on high-performing public sector organizations and governments that roughly equates performance with superior capacity of the performing institutions. Using the metaphor of the galloping elephants, Rainey & Steinbauer (1999) explained in a seminal article what makes public bureaucracies perform: supportive behaviours from external stakeholders such as political authorities, agency autonomy in refining and implementing missions, high 'mission valence' (an attractive mission), a strong, mission-oriented culture, and certain leadership behaviours were found to drive motivation and performance. Another notable assessment of performance capacity was the 'Government Performance

Project', initiated by Syracuse University. It studied the performance of US states by measuring how well management capacity is developed (Maxwell School of Citizenship and Public Affairs, 2002).

Second, when performance is about the quality of the achievements and not as much about the quality of the actions, performance equals *results* (P3). The capacity of the organization is not the focus of this conceptualization. The opinion that only results matter is emblematic of this position (see Box 1.1 for a nice narrative reflecting this perspective). Below, it is argued that results may be both the outputs and the outcomes of the public sector. Many NPM texts see performance like this. As long as the results are proven, it does not really matter how they came about.

Finally, when performance is conceptualized with attention to both the quality of actions and the quality of achievements, it may be typified as *sustainable results*. Performance refers to the productive organization, that is, an organization that has the capacity to perform and converts this capacity into results – outputs and outcomes. Performance in this text refers to the last conceptualization. In our perspective performance indicators may cover the whole value chain from inputs over outputs to outcomes. We will study how measurement of both capacity and results is embedded in public organizations.

---

## BOX 1.1 ONLY RESULTS MATTER

A priest and a taxi driver both died and went to heaven. St Peter was at the Pearly Gates waiting for them.

'Come with me,' said St Peter to the taxi driver.

The taxi driver did as he was told and followed St Peter to a mansion. It had anything you could imagine from a bowling alley to an Olympic-size pool.

'Wow, thank you,' said the taxi driver.

Next, St Peter led the priest to a rugged old shack with a bunk bed and a little old television set.

'Wait, I think you are a little mixed up,' said the priest. 'Shouldn't I be the one who gets the mansion? After all, I was a priest, went to church every day, and preached God's word.'

'Yes, that's true. But during your sermons people slept. When the taxi driver drove, everyone prayed.'

*Lesson*: only results count.

*Source: taken from Hatry, 1999*

## 2 PERFORMANCE AS AN AGENDA

Performance is not only a concept, but also an agenda. The term 'performance' expresses a programme of change and improvement, which is promoted by a group of like-minded actors that is usually only loosely coupled. In chapter 3, these groups of actors sharing a performance agenda are called *performance movements*.

In western societies, the promise of increasing performance has been one of the dominant agendas in the public sector. Ingraham (2005) observes that 'for much of the twentieth century – and certainly for the last 25 years – performance has been a siren's song for nations around the world' (p. 390). The post-war expansion of the welfare state has raised expectations about the role of government. In the 1980s, this expansion was no longer supported (Pollitt & Bouckaert, 2011). Fiscal stress pressured the public budget and legitimacy crises pressured the politico-administrative system. In those days, US president Ronald Reagan marked government as the problem rather than the solution. As a response, governments pledged to do more with fewer resources – a government that works better and costs less (Gore, 1993).

Government across the globe reformed in the name of performance. In particular, in the UK and the USA, this led to cutback management and a reduction of the size of government (Dunleavy, 1986). Other countries followed other trajectories. Pollitt & Bouckaert (2011) identify four strategies: to minimize (privatize), to marketize (bringing private sector techniques and values into government), to modernize (changing public sector techniques and values) and to maintain (using the old techniques more intensely). The societal demand for a high-performing public sector still resonates today, and filters through to the organizational level.

## 3 A CONTESTED DEBATE

The roots of the performance agenda lie well beyond NPM. It should however not be forgotten that there are quite distinct, but maybe less eye-catching, agendas in public administration such as establishing the rule of law, eradicating corruption, safeguarding equity, transparency and democratization. One of the most persistent lines of attack on the performance agenda is that it does not take these other values into account. Performance may even be at cross-purposes with other values. As a result, positions on performance management have been quite polarized, with proponents contending against the dissenters who argued that the fundamental premises were wrong and produced dysfunctional behaviour.

With time and experience, attitudes have matured and some convergence is apparent. Yet performance management is at a turning point and is the object of close scrutiny and questioning by both external observers and practitioners, wrestling with the challenges in practice (Bouckaert & Halligan, 2008; Flynn, 2007; Moynihan, 2008).

A new generation of studies is addressing the age of performance characterized by its pervasive influence on governments wrestling with complexities. This growing middle ground of analysts sees the limitations of performance management, but believes there is something worthy of careful investigation by examining assumptions and exposing faulty thinking as a means of narrowing the gap between rhetoric and practice (Radin, 2006; Moynihan, 2008). The OECD (2009) has been exploring a range of performance questions as well. At the same time, more private debates have been occurring among officials in several jurisdictions about the efficacy of existing arrangements.

The fiscal crisis tested the performance agenda (Hood, 2013). Is performance management a fair-weather tool that only thrives in stable and affluent times? Or is the performance focus more pressing than ever, when budgets are cut? The abolition of the UK Audit Commission's indicators of local government performance is a high-profile example of a performance scheme in crisis. Michael O'Higgins, chairman of the Audit Commission, was surprised, stating that 'given the fiscal consolidation, if anything we anticipated there would be a bigger role for a body that focused on value for money and providing comparative examples of how you could do things better' (Timmins, 2012). The UK government however frames the decision as a move towards decentralization and savings. The press statement argues that the government will

> refocus audit on helping local people hold councils and local public bodies to account for local spending decisions. The changes will pass power down to people, replace bureaucratic accountability with democratic accountability and save the taxpayer £50 million a year.
>
> (GOV.UK, 2010)

Note that the message is not to curb performance management and accountability. Rather, the UK government is putting the responsibility for performance management in the hands of local governments. More critical voices argue that this strategy is also driven by the desire to transfer the UK government's responsibility for cutting public service budgets to the local governments, but also to make performance failure less visible.

While the story of the Audit Commission is a testimony to the tensions between centralized performance regimes, political accountability and public budgeting, we should not generalize what is happening in England too readily. Countries, as Pollitt (2009) notes, are not 'all in the same boat'. We may all be at sea in the same storm, but we are traveling in different kinds of vessel. The general impact of the fiscal crisis, if any, remains uncertain. Overall, it seems that performance management will continue to be central to the government, albeit in a different way. Several factors – institutional, cultural and administrative tradition – assist in accounting for different levels of commitment to performance management

(KPMG, 2008). Later in this book, we will argue that the shift from accountability to learning may be the most fundamental transformation.

## 4 MEASUREMENT, INCORPORATION AND USE OF PERFORMANCE INFORMATION

This book is structured around the notions of measurement, incorporation and use of performance (Bouckaert & Halligan, 2008). It is a logic sequence of collecting data, integrating data into the management systems, and finally, putting information at work. Measurement could also be seen as the supply side, whereas the envisaged use is the demand side. Supply and demand will not automatically adjust to each other. Hence, incorporation assures the link between both.

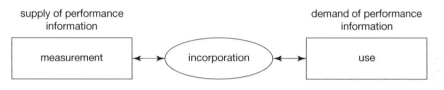

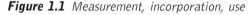

**Figure 1.1** *Measurement, incorporation, use*

Measuring performance is systematically collecting data by observing and registering performance-related issues for some performance purpose. There could be a causal reason, for example a law or a regulation which requires an organization to collect specific data. There could be an organizational objective, for example a need to use data for improvement.

Incorporating is intentionally importing performance-related data in documents, and includes procedures with the potential and purpose of using them. The purpose is to create the possibility of including performance-related information in the discourse and ultimately in the culture and the memory of the organization. Tools and techniques can be used to generate and anchor information in procedures, documents and organizations. Organizations may have a different incorporation capacity, which makes it possible to use performance information functionally. The capacity of anchoring instruments to institutionalize performance information will create the conditions for use. Examples of these tools and techniques could be in financial, personnel or organizational legislation, and related handbooks for implementation. So there are levels and degrees of incorporation.

Incorporated performance information can be used for designing policies; for deciding; for allocating resources, competencies and responsibilities; for controlling and redirecting implementation; for (self-)evaluating and assessing behaviour and results; and for substantiating reporting and accountability mechanisms. Incorporating performance data is necessary but not sufficient for using performance

**7**

information. There is a need for a *fit-for-purpose* data infrastructure (i.e. incorporation), and for an accommodating and motivating performance culture as suprastructure. In such a way, performance is fully institutionalized.

To the extent that information is available across organizations, benchmarking and *benchlearning* could be used to upgrade systems to specific standards (single loop learning), to adjust standards (double loop learning) or even to adjust systems constantly as learning how to learn (meta learning). Using also suggests abusing and misusing, and therefore there is a legitimate concern for increasing potential value added and for reducing possible dysfunctions (like new red tape or gaming), and for equilibrating costs and benefits. This results in looking at general and specific use (reporting, learning, accountability), but also at the costs (dysfunctions) and benefits (value added) of using incorporated performance information.

## 5 PERFORMANCE MEASUREMENT AND PUBLIC SECTOR REFORM

Performance measurement has played a pivotal role in reform initiatives. Box 1.2 includes a sample of some key texts that served as catalysts for public management reform with a performance agenda. England in particular witnessed a boost in indicators by the end of the 1980s. Reform initiatives such as the Financial Management Initiative, the Next Steps agenda, and the Citizen's Charter led to the creation of performance indicator systems for most public services, central and local. League tables were created for, amongst others, schools, hospitals, health trusts, ambulance services and local authorities. No other country went so far in the use of performance indicators in governance regimes. The intrusion of indicators in the fibres of the public sector has led Hood to conclude that it is English exceptionalism (Hood, 2007). Even Scotland and Wales opted for a softer approach.

In general, Continental Europe has not used performance indicators with the same intensity as the Anglo-Saxon world. Yet, there are considerable variations between countries. In Germany, the New Steering Model (*das Neues Steuerungsmodell*) stressed the importance of performance indicators (Naschold & Bogumil, 2000). However, the reform was only applied in some big cities, city-states and Länder. Nowadays, the reform enthusiasm seems to be over and there is increasing acknowledgement of reform fatigue. In France, the Loi Organique Relative aux Lois de Finances (LOLF) introduced a form of performance budgeting (Calmette, 2006). In Sweden, which has a highly decentralized public sector, performance measures mainly played a role in the steering of agencies. In Norway, the Management by Objectives and Results system has been widely adopted, albeit after a transformation and translation by the agencies (Laegreid *et al.*, 2008).

The country with the strongest tradition in performance measurement in Continental Europe is probably the Netherlands. The first initiatives were undertaken in the 1970s, and by the 1980s, several local governments implemented

## BOX 1.2 PERFORMANCE AND PUBLIC MANAGEMENT REFORM – SOME KEY TEXTS

This box presents some key texts that propagate reform and link it directly to performance. These are not academic texts, but policy documents by governments and their think tanks.

1   1993: US vice president Al Gore publishes the National Performance Review. The title is revealing: *From Red Tape to Results: Creating a Government That Works Better & Costs Less*. The report was accompanied by the Government Performance and Results Act (1993), which imposed performance plans and reports as a basis for managerial accountability in the federal government. It was strongly indebted to Osborne & Gaebler's *Reinventing Government* (1993).

2   1997: The OECD's Public Management Service (PUMA) publishes a study titled *In Search for Results, Performance Management Practices*. It is a case catalogue of performance-oriented reform practices in ten, mainly Anglo-Saxon and Scandinavian OECD countries. The performance practices are a blend of financial management, HRM and accountability reforms. The activities of PUMA were later critiqued for imposing a NPM framework, regardless of context (Premfors, 1998).

3   1999: The British PM Tony Blair launches Modernizing Government, a reform agenda which confirmed the use of targets and indicators in the British public service. In 2001, the publication *Choosing the Right FABRIC – A Framework for Performance Information* substantiated this agenda. It was issued jointly by the main players in the field of measurement: the Treasury, the Audit Commission, the National Audit Office, the Office for National Statistics and the Cabinet Office.

4   2003: the UK House of Commons' Public Administration Select Committee brings out a report titled *On Target? Government by Measurement*. The committee documented an overly strong focus on the performance measures at the expense of performance itself. The report proposes a shift from a measurement culture towards a performance culture.

5   2008: The election of the Rudd government in 2007 produced an agenda to improve budget transparency (termed Operation Sunlight) (Tanner, 2008). It critiqued the outcomes and outputs framework for being unable to shift the focus of financial reporting from inputs (programmes, expenses, and recipients) to outputs and outcomes, that

**9**

> is, actual results. Basic information on inputs was lost in the change-over, and reporting of outcomes was seriously inadequate.
>
> 6   President Obama signs the Government Performance and Results Modernization act. This GPRA modernisation act builds upon the 1993 act. Bill Clinton's National Performance Review (1993) intro-duced performance analysis for agencies in the US federal government. George W. Bush's President's Management Agenda (2001) shifted accountability requirements from agencies to programmes when introducing the Programme Assessment and Rating Tool. President Obama did not brand a new big initiative, but refocused on the use of performance information in learning networks (Kamensky, 2011).

NPM-like measurement-based reforms. The first large-scale implementations of performance-oriented reforms at a central level took place in the 1990s. The series of reforms culminated in 1999 with the VBTB initiative – an outcome-based budget structure. In 2006, inspired by the UK's Prime Minister's delivery unit, the Netherlands developed a monitor of 84 government objectives. The Rutte Cabinet (2010) replaced the VBTB performance budget with a new initiative called *Verantwoord begroten* (responsible and accountable budgeting). The new budget has (1) to link more closely to the concrete responsibilities of the ministers, rather than to elaborate on broad policies, (2) to provide more information on the costs of policy instruments, and (3) to reduce the burden of performance indicator reporting, while strengthening the linkages with policy evaluation (van Hofwegen & de Jong, 2012).

Bouckaert & Peters (2002) argue that performance measurement is the 'Achilles' heel' of many public sector reforms. The availability of performance information is a necessary but insufficient condition for the success of many reform initiatives – at least in the New Public Management form. Yet, often the availability of performance information is assumed. The presence of performance information is one of the most decisive and susceptible aspects of the recent tide of public management reforms. This observation legitimizes a scientific focus on measurement of performance. Yet, performance measurement goes beyond public sector reform. It is found in recurring activities in public management and public policy.

## 6 PERFORMANCE MEASUREMENT AND PUBLIC MANAGEMENT

Performance information is not only pivotal in public sector reform; it also plays a role in daily management practice. The Government Performance Project (GPP), a six-year research initiative evaluating the management capacity of federal, state and local government entities in the USA, has provided some insight into the role of performance information in organizations (Ingraham *et al.*, 2003). The most visible part of the project was the graded reports of the 50 states. The underlying model of the assessment identified four management subsystems that contribute to management capacity – defined as the potential for performance, financial management, human resources management, capital management and information technology management. The GPP identifies two crosscutting levers: leadership and information. First, leadership is the driver since leaders are able to make informed decisions, to provide guidance and direction, to develop the institution's mission, vision and values, to communicate these to the members and to coordinate organizational components. Second, information and a focus on results are connectors. Information connects the management subsystems with each other. It also connects the management system with the outside world through measurement of programme delivery and performance.

Besides performance information, other connectors in the management of organizations may be identified. The 60-year-old Friedrich–Finer debate on accountability systems points to an important addition (Bouckaert & Halligan, 2008). Finer championed a system based on objective accountability. He would support performance information for its integrative potential. Friedrich advocated a system based on professional 'fellowship' between practitioners. The pride-related arguments of these professionals allow for a subjective accountability mechanism derived from their values, which could also be seen as a connector between subsystems.

The Friedrich–Finer debate also reflects different views on human resources management: another large field of performance research. The main issue here is how to motivate individual employees through performance incentives. Finer's formal accountability schemes would champion schemes of performance pay based on tight performance indicators. Friedrich's professional accountability would propagate performance schemes that entice learning and improvement. The focus of this book is not on HRM strategies for performance. Our level of analysis is the organization as well as the political and policy context in which an organization operates. We will devote ample attention to how the leadership of the organization decides to use the information for decision-making. Yet, the behavioural logics of action such as Friedrich's professionalism or Finer's formal accountability are essentially the same as in the HRM literature.

## 7 PERFORMANCE MEASUREMENT AND POLICY EVALUATION

Performance measurement also plays a role in public policy. Performance measurement and policy evaluation are adjacent fields. Wholey (1994) sees a role for performance data in the evaluability study that may precede an evaluation.

## BOX 1.3 THE DIFFERENCE BETWEEN PERFORMANCE MEASUREMENT AND EVALUATION

McDavid & Hawthorn (2006: p. 293) point to seven differences.

1   performance measurement systems are ongoing while evaluation is episodic;
2   performance measurement addresses general issues while programme evaluation is issue specific;
3   performance measures are routinized while evaluation measures are customized for each evaluation;
4   performance measurement generally takes attribution for granted while for evaluation it is a central issue;
5   resources for performance measurement are usually part of the organizational infrastructure while resources for evaluation are targeted;
6   managers often play a key role in performance measurement while evaluators and managers are less connected;
7   the uses of performance information evolve over time while the intended purposes of programme evaluation are usually negotiated up front.

Weiss (1998) points to performance data as a data source for evaluators. Some authors go further and advocate an integration of performance measurement and evaluation. McDavid & Hawthorn (2006) assert that performance measurement may be seen as an approach to evaluation. The basic programme evaluation tools are also useful for performance measurement. They are complementary evaluation strategies. Yet, some important differences remain (see Box 1.3).

The evaluation community has critiqued the absence of intervention theories in performance management systems (McDavid & Hawthorn, 2006; Nielsen & Ejler, 2008). The general argument is that while performance management has more timely, but superficial, data on a routine basis, evaluation allows going into depth based on a more developed policy theory. While this complementarity may be a comforting perspective for the communities of practice in respectively performance and evaluation, the field of performance management should reflect on the implications of being only marginally theorized. In recent years, the performance communities of policy evaluation and performance management seem to have come closer to one another. The performance literature increasingly propagates the use of logic models to strengthen the theoretical foundations of performance measurement systems (Newcomer & Caudle, 2011). The high-priority goals of

President Obama's performance strategy are also calling for more policy evaluation in performance regimes (Joyce, 2011).

## 8 APPROACH AND OUTLINE OF THE BOOK

The book aspires to a deeper understanding of performance management, its strengths, its weaknesses and its context. Several choices have been made in writing this book:

1   Performance management is a contested field with advocates and opponents in both the academic and the practitioner community. This book assumes that it is not necessary to take sides. A combination of a critical attitude and openness towards the inherent potential of measurement is possible.
2   Key for critical believers of performance management is an understanding of the conditionality of successful performance management; what works when and under which circumstances? This text will pay ample attention to contextual variation.
3   A common but accurate saying states that there is nothing more practical than a good theory. More than how-to manuals of performance management, theories in the field of public administration are applied. The practical relevance of theoretical argumentation lies in the capacity to discover regularities in the relation between performance management and its context. The book does not envisage a grand theoretical scheme. Rather, middle-range theories are suggested when appropriate.
4   The book does not discuss the technicalities of measurement. Discussions on analysis techniques and ICT support are not included in this text. Performance management is seen as a social phenomenon in a political and administrative context. A strong focus on the use, users and non-use of performance information follows from this viewpoint.

The outline of the book is as follows:

Chapter 2 develops and extends the concepts. Key concepts are performance, performance measurement and performance management. Questions include: What is performance and how does it relate to public values? What is micro, meso and macro performance? What is performance measurement? Is everything measurable? What is performance management and what is it not?

Chapter 3 describes the history of performance management in the twentieth century. Several performance movements are identified. A chronological account of those movements is followed by a discussion of elements of change and continuity in performance management.

Chapter 4 is about performance *measurement*. The subsequent stages of deciding what to measure, identifying indicators, analysing, reporting and safeguarding quality are discussed in detail. This chapter deals with the major design parameters for a performance measurement system.

Chapter 5 discusses how performance information can be incorporated into policy and management. Policy and management cycles are the target for the incorporation of performance information. If successful, incorporation should bridge the gap between the provision of information through measurement (chapter 4) and its use (chapter 6).

Chapter 6 then deals with the use of performance information. Three modes of use are distinguished: learning, steering & control, and accountability. The chapter further argues that the design parameters of a measurement system (see chapter 4) need to vary according to the use that is envisaged.

Chapter 7 looks at performance information from the perspective of the users: public managers, politicians, citizens, oversight agencies, and media. The actor perspective on use is intensely intertwined with the thematic approach in chapter 6.

Chapter 8 reflects upon the observation that performance information is often not used. Several theories can explain why performance information is not always functional for management and policy. Besides insufficient quality of performance information, psychological, cultural and institutional barriers may inhibit use.

Chapter 9 discusses the effects of performance measurement: does performance measurement perform? Both the functional and dysfunctional effects are covered. The chapter concludes with some strategies to cope with dysfunctional effects of measurement effects.

Chapter 10 is titled 'The future of performance management'. Some slightly provocative statements are put forward in order to challenge thinking about performance management while using the concepts of the book. The chapter first outlines some paradoxes in measurement, after which a number of potential improvements in implementation are taken into consideration. Finally, three more fundamental departures from the current practice of performance management are discussed.

## 9 CONCLUSION

This introductory chapter has sketched the subject of the book in broad outlines. It is argued that performance is pivotal in contemporary public management. Performance permeates management, public sector reform and public policy. Performance however is not only a concept; it also suggests an agenda of change and improvement. As a result, performance is also heavily contested for being too one-sided. The core of the critique is a neglect of other values such as equity, openness and integrity.

Much of the controversy is about performance as an agenda (propagated by a performance movement) and not as much about performance as a concept.

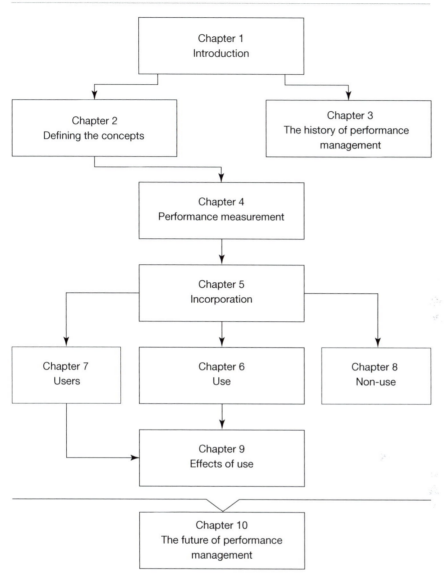

 **Figure 1.2** *Outline of the book*

Chapter 3 deals with the history of performance movements, which propagated often-contested performance agendas. Chapter 2 seeks more conceptual precision and suggests a framework to reconcile the performance concept and the concept of public values. This book further builds on the concepts, and not on the controversy around the performance agenda.

## FURTHER READING

A good start to situate the performance concepts is Dubnick's (2005) article on accountability and the promise of performance. Ingraham (2005) and Bouckaert & Halligan (2008) provide an overview of the performance agenda: where it came from, what it promised and where it is going. A good start to thinking about the state of the art of performance research is 'Performance Measurement: Building Theory, Improving Practice' by De Lancer Julnes & Holzer (2008). The controversy around performance management is best described by Radin's book *Challenging the Performance Movement* (Radin, 2006). It may also be useful to critically review some of the texts that advocate performance management, for example Gore's National Performance Review (1993) and Osborne & Gaebler's *Reinventing Government* (1993).

## REFERENCES

Bouckaert, G., & Halligan, J. (2008). *Managing Performance: International Comparisons*. London: Routledge.

Bouckaert, G., & Peters, B. G. (2002). 'Performance Measurement and Management: The Achilles' Heel in Administrative Modernization'. *Public Performance & Management Review*, 25, 359–62.

Calmette, J. F. (2006). 'La loi organique relative aux lois de finances (LOLF): un texte, un esprit, une pratique'. *Revue française d'administration publique*, 117, 43–55.

De Lancer Julnes, P., & Holzer, M. (2008). *Performance Measurement: Building Theory, Improving Practice*. Armonk, NY: M. E. Sharpe.

Dubnick, M. (2005). 'Accountability and the Promise of Performance: In Search of Mechanisms'. *Public Performance and Management Review*, 28, 376–417.

Dunleavy, P. (1986). 'Explaining the Privatization Boom: Public Choice versus Radical Approaches'. *Public Administration*, 64, 13–34.

Flynn, N. (2007). *Public Sector Management*. Thousand Oaks: Sage.

Gore, A. (1993). *From Red Tape to Results: Creating a Government That Works Better & Costs Less*. Report of the National Performance Review. Washington, DC: US Government Printing Office.

GOV.UK. (2010). 'Eric Pickles to Disband Audit Commission in New Era of Town Hall Transparency'. Retrieved 3 March 2014 from https://www.gov.uk/government/news/eric-pickles-to-disband-audit-commission-in-new-era-of-town-hall-transparency.

Hatry, H. P. (1999). *Performance Measurement: Getting Results*. Washington, DC: Urban Institute Press.

Hood, C. (2007). 'Public Service Management by Numbers: Why Does It Vary? Where Has It Come From? What Are the Gaps and the Puzzles?'. *Public Money and Management*, 27, 95–102.

—— (2013). 'Reflections on Public Service Reform in a Cold Fiscal Climate'. In Kippin, H., Stoker, G., & Griffiths, S. (eds). *Public Services: A New Reform Agenda*. London: Bloomsbury Academic.

Ingraham, P. W. (2005). 'Performance: Promises to Keep and Miles to Go'. *Public Administration Review*, 65, 390–5.

Ingraham, P. W., Joyce, P. G., & Donahue, A. K. (2003). *Government Performance: Why Management Matters*. Baltimore: Johns Hopkins University Press.

Joyce, P. G. (2011). 'The Obama Administration and PBB: Building on the Legacy of Federal Performance-Informed Budgeting?', *Public Administration Review*, 71(3), 356–67.

Kamensky, J. (2011). 'The Obama Performance Approach'. *Public Performance & Management Review*, 35(1), 133–48.

KPMG (2008). *Holy Grail or Achievable Quest? International Perspectives on Public Sector Performance Management*. Ottawa: CAPAM.

Laegreid, P., Roness, P. G., & Rubecksen, K. (2008). 'Performance Information and Performance Steering: Integrated System or Loose Coupling?' In Van Dooren, W., & Van de Walle, S. (eds) *Performance Information in the Public Sector: How It Is Used*. Basingstoke: Palgrave McMillan.

McDavid, J. C., & Hawthorn, L. R. L. (2006). *Program Evaluation and Performance Measurement: An Introduction to Practice*. Thousand Oaks: Sage.

Maxwell School of Citizenship and Public Affairs (2002). *Paths to Performance in State and Local Government: A Final Assessment of the Maxwell School of Citizenship and Public Affairs*. Syracuse: Maxwell School of Citizenship and Public Affairs.

Moynihan, D. P. (2008). *The Dynamics of Performance Management: Constructing Information and Reform*. Washington, DC: Georgetown University Press.

Naschold, F., & Bogumil, J. (2000). *Modernisierung des Staates: new public management in deutscher und internationaler Perspektive*. Leverkusen: Leske & Budrich.

Newcomer, K., & Caudle, S. (2011). 'Public Performance Management Systems'. *Public Performance & Management Review*, 35(1), 108–32.

Nielsen, S. B., & Ejler, N. (2008). 'Improving Performance? Exploring the Complementarities between Evaluation and Performance Management'. *Evaluation*, 14(2), 171–92.

OECD (2009). *Measuring Government Activity*. Paris: OECD.

Osborne, D., & Gaebler, T. (1993). 'Reinventing Government: How the Entrepreneurial Spirit Is Transforming the Public Sector from Schoolhouse to State House'. Reading, MA: Addison Wesley.

Pollitt, C. (2009). *Public Management Reform during Financial Austerity*. Presented at EUPAN Directors General meeting, Stockholm. 10 December.

**17**

Pollitt, C., & Bouckaert, G. (2011). *Public Management Reform: A Comparative Analysis*. Oxford: Oxford University Press.

Premfors, R. (1998). 'Reshaping the Democratic State: Swedish Experiences in International Perspective'. *Public Administration*, 76, 141–59.

Radin, B. A. (2006). *Challenging the Performance Movement: Accountability, Complexity, and Democratic Values*. Georgetown University Press.

Rainey, H. G., & Steinbauer, P. (1999). 'Galloping Elephants: Developing Elements of a Theory of Effective Government Organizations'. *Journal of Public Administration Research and Theory*, 9(1), 1–32.

Tanner (2008). *Operation Sunlight: Enhancing Budget Transparency*. Canberra: ALP.

Timmins, N. (2012). 'Audit Commission's Ex-head: Its Abolition Will Affect Public Services'. *Guardian*. 9 October. Retrieved from http://www.theguardian.com/society/2012/oct/09/audit-commission-chairman-abolition-value.

Van Hofwegen, J., & De Jong, M. (2012). 'Naar een verantwoorde begrotingspresentatie Over verantwoord omgaan met (on)zekerheden'. (Towards Accountable Budgeting: Dealing with Uncertainties.) In Ministerie van Financiën (ed.) *De toekomst van de financie_le functie van het Rijk: een beeld voor 2020* (*The Future of the Financial Function of the State: A Vision for 2020*) (pp. 75–90). Den Haag: Ministerie van Financiën.

Weiss, C. H. (1998). 'Have We Learned Anything about the Use of Evaluation?' *American Journal of Evaluation*, 19(1), 13–21.

Wholey, J. S. (1994). 'Assessing the Feasibility and Likely Usefulness of Evaluation'. In Wholey, J. S. *Handbook of Practical Program Evaluation* (pp. 15–39). New York: Wiley.

# Chapter 2

# Defining the concepts

## LEARNING OBJECTIVES

- To have a precise understanding of the distinct concepts of performance, performance measurement and performance management.
- To be able to recognize differences in measurability.
- To situate performance management vis-à-vis other management types.

## KEY POINTS IN THIS CHAPTER

- Performance can be operationalized using a production logic; a substantial definition of performance can build on public value theory.
- The unique characteristics of public sector performance compared to private sector performance warrant a distinct public administration approach.
- Performance measurement has to take measurability of organizations and issues into account.
- Performance management does not exist in its pure form; public management in practice is always a mixture of ideal typical management types.

## DISCUSSION QUESTIONS

- Apply the production model of performance to a policy field: higher education, urban renewal, mobility, etc. (and experience the confusion of applying a straightforward model).

- Are economic models useful for discussing public sector performance?
- Which public services are easy to measure, and which are not?
- What is the dominant management type in your organization (university, municipality, agency, etc.)?

Performance management has accumulated many meanings. Since virtually all NPM flavoured public administration practices are associated with performance management, the utility of the concept for analysis declines. In debates on performance management, people often feel they are talking at cross-purposes. In order to avoid such ambiguity in this text, more definitional precision is required. This chapter develops the definitions that will be used in further chapters.

*Performance* can be defined as outputs and outcomes. Yet, the output or outcome labels do not tell much about the substantive content of performance. Public value literature may help in making more sense of performance. *Performance measurement* is the bundle of activities aimed at obtaining information on performance. Besides traditional measurement, other more qualitative resources such as focus groups with citizens, expert advice and privileged witnesses may yield performance information. Besides this explicit information, people usually also have *tacit knowledge* of government performance built up through personal experience. As we will discuss in chapter 8, tacit knowledge and prior experience may play a vital role in explaining non-use. *Performance management* is a type of management that incorporates and uses performance information for decision-making.

# 1 PERFORMANCE

The conventional definition of performance uses the metaphor of the production process. Performances are the outputs and outcomes of activities. An alternative view sees performance as the realization of public values.

## 1.1 Performance as a result of a production process

The most widely used conception of performance follows a logic of production. A basic model, derived from the private sector, only looks at inputs, activities and outputs. A growing awareness of the inadequacies of this simple model for public and non-profit activities led several public administration scholars to redefine the model (see for instance Hatry, 1999; Poister, 2003; and Pollitt & Bouckaert, 2011). Policy evaluators generally use the same logic to assess programme performance (McDavid & Hawthorn, 2006). Figure 2.1 includes the most important elements of the extended production model of performance. Performance management can cover the whole chain from input to outcome. Bouckaert & Halligan (2008) refer to this dimension as the 'span of performance'.

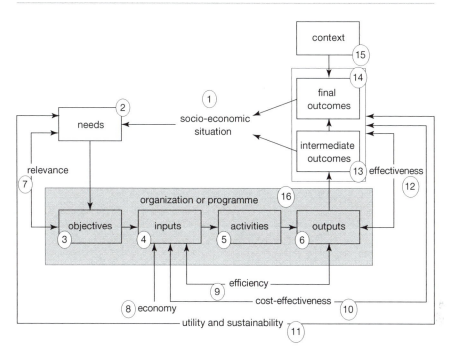

**Figure 2.1** *The production model of performance*

## Problems, needs and relevance

The starting point is the socio-economic situation. Socio-economic issues (1 in Figure 2.1) induce a need for action by the public sector (2). In accordance with the traditional politics–administration dichotomy, politicians are expected to define the societal needs. Agenda-setting research however demonstrates that not only politicians are involved in translating issues to problems and problems to policies. Civil servants, interest groups, media and chance events also play a role in formulating needs. However, the political system's unique role is to filter issues and to determine priorities. These priorities are, following the model, translated into objectives (3) of the organization or programme under review. The confrontation of the objectives of a policy with the needs allows assessing the relevance (7) of the pursued policies.

## Outputs and efficiency

Inputs (such as financial and human resources) (4) are allocated to organizations and programmes in order to stage activities (5) that yield outputs (6). Economy (8) is the ratio of a monetary input over another input (e.g. the cost of a computer). The ratio of the input over the outputs is efficiency (9). Economists make a

**21**

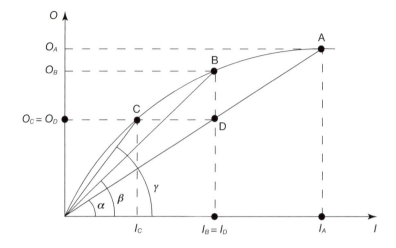

**Figure 2.2** *Productivity and efficiency*

distinction between efficiency and productivity. Figure 2.2 helps to define the concepts more precisely. On the X-axis are the inputs and on the Y-axis are the outputs. The organizations A, B and C are all efficient. No organization is able to produce the same level of output with fewer resources, or more output with the same resources. Organization D is inefficient. B is producing more with the same inputs and C is producing the same output with fewer inputs. Efficiency is thus defined as being on the production frontier. Productivity is defined as input over output and thus is the slope of the linear curve through the origin in Figure 2. Organization C has the steepest slope and the highest productivity. The enveloping curve around A, B and C assumes decreasing returns to scale.

Maximization of financial profit is not an objective of public sector organizations. However, public sector organizations should also evaluate their output mix. They should also consider whether they provide the right bundle of services. This assessment is intrinsically more complicated in the public sector. First, the definition of output in itself is more complex. The number of transactions between producers and consumers is not a valid way of defining public sector output. We need to consider the volume of services *provided*. For more information on the provision versus the transaction approach, see Box 2.1. Second, the criterion for determining optimal output levels should be societal profit instead of financial profit. A hospital that is routinely taking X-rays of all its patients is maximizing its output and in all probability will become technically efficient. However, it will not be allocative efficient.

Performance is thus, in economic parlance, about maximizing profit for society. Yet, it is far from clear what profit for society actually means. A complex and dynamic system of political representation, fuelled by interests, power, ideology

## BOX 2.1 OUTPUT AS TRANSACTION OR AS PROVISION

An important technical distinction is between output measures that capture transactions and those that reflect the provision of services. These approaches reflect the perspectives used traditionally in economics and public administration respectively.

In the economic notion, output is counted when the transaction is complete, that is, when the output is consumed. This transaction approach is used in many existing direct output measures of public services, for example number of pupils, prisoners, crimes, fires attended, etc. The Atkinson review (2005) provides an elaborate discussion of the uses and limitations of this approach.

The provision (public administration) approach sees output as products or services that come out of the production process, regardless of whether they are consumed or not. Instead of the number of pupils or prisoners, the number of teaching hours or the number of prison cells is defined as the output. This approach is more common in public administration because of the potential use of the data for holding people or entities to account. Public organizations that are providing services often have no impact on the level of consumption. For example, prisons cannot reasonably be held accountable for the low level of consumption of their services if, fortuitously, criminality decreases. Moreover, many of the non-market services of the public sector are non-transactional (e.g. typical public goods such as safety) (OECD, 2009).

and political judgement, determines what society values. As a result, there is no such thing as a single and definite allocative optimum for public services. There is a constant tension between increasing or decreasing public service provision and interference of government in the private sphere. Hence, economic models for understanding public administration often are deceitfully simple.

Outputs and efficiency are adequate conceptualizations of performance in the private sector, but unsatisfactory in the public sector. Both in public and in private organizations, outputs are expected to have effects in society. In the private sector, this effect is determined and valued by each individual consumption decision. When a customer buys a car, he or she devotes a significant share of income to the purchase and thus values it. The difference between sales price and production costs is the added value of the product. The aggregation of these individual added values is the main component of the total profit of the firm, and thus its outcome in society. Financial analysts speak of the bottom line of a firm.

**23**

It should be noted that the public/private distinction is not black and white. The private sector discusses its social role beyond individual consumption as well. The United Nations for instance has defined a triple bottom line (TBL), which is an expanded spectrum of values and criteria for measuring organizational success: profits, people and planet. The *people* concept refers to fair and beneficial business practices towards labour and the community in which a firm conducts its business. The *planet* concept refers to sustainable environmental practices. *Profit*, in the TBL definition, is the economic benefit of economic activity for society. It is the lasting economic impact the organization has on its economic environment. The TBL definition of profit is clearly broader than the conventional definition of internal profit discussed above. It remains to be seen whether efforts of private companies to reflect upon their social role imply a converging trend between public and private concerns, or whether TBL and other efforts are mainly cosmetic. The response of private corporations to the financial crisis may be a test: which bottom line will come under greatest pressure?

## Outcomes and effectiveness

The outcomes of public services are either collective or consist of externalities that are not taken into account by individual consumers. Unlike in market transactions, citizens do not directly attribute monetary values to services. Rather, and only in democratic societies, there is a remote and indirect assessment through political participation.

Public administration scholars have disentangled the outcome concept. Outcomes can be *intermediate* (usually but not always in the short term) (13 in Figure 2.1) or *final* (usually but not always in the long term) (14). The final outcomes in particular are influenced by the *context* (15) on which the organization or the programme has a limited or no impact. Such contextual factors can be encompassing socio-economic or ecological trends, but also policy measures from other governments. Agencies in European Union member states for instance are restrained by European regulation. The ratio of output over outcome is the *effectiveness* (12). The ratio of the input over the outcome is the *cost-effectiveness* (10). The outcomes of a programme or an organization have to address the needs of society. The confrontation of needs and outcomes allows assessment of the *sustainability and utility* (11) of the programme or organization. Box 2.2 applies the whole production logic to the issue of traffic casualties.

The metaphor of a production process is currently the dominant perspective on performance. It was initially launched by systems theorists such as David Easton (1965). Public administration in his view is an open system which converts inputs (demands as well as support) into outputs. Outputs of different other systems within (intra-societal environment) and outside (extra-societal environment) society are inputs for the political system. Outputs of the political system

## BOX 2.2 PRODUCTION MODEL OF PERFORMANCE APPLIED TO THE ISSUE OF TRAFFIC CASUALTIES

As an example, we apply the model to the issue of traffic casualties. Suppose that politicians formulate the need to reduce the number of traffic casualties. Typically, several interest groups and the (perceived) pressure from their constituencies influence politicians. The issue is also particularly susceptible to chance events such as accidents with children that put it all at once at the top of the agenda. A potential objective is to reduce the number of casualties to a number comparable to that of other developed countries. In order to attain this goal, government will use (financial and other) resources to build cycle tracks, to reconstruct crossroads and to install speed traps. The outputs then are the kilometres of new tracks, the new crossroads constructed and the number of vehicles controlled. To this point, government has a good grip on the chain of events. The decisive test however is the outcome in society. In the short run, it may be that more children cycle to school and that fewer drivers violate the speed limits. These are intermediate outcomes. Government however wants to reduce the numbers of casualties. The question then is whether the immediate outcomes lead to the final outcomes. Undoubtedly, environmental factors will interfere. For instance, a failure to reduce the number of casualties may be the result of bad weather conditions. In cold and rainy weather, there are usually fewer cyclists and pedestrians, which leads to motorists being less aware. Moreover, driving conditions are worse, and therefore there is a higher chance of accidents.

in turn influence the environment. In public administration practice, system thinking was a defining element of major reform packages such as the Planning Programming and Budgeting System (PPBS) (Schick, 1966). In order to provide more insight into performance, budgeting systems had to systematically account for planned outputs and outcomes instead of the traditional report on inputs spent.

Since performance is a ratio between inputs and outputs (or outcomes), different strategies to improve performance can be followed. Figure 2.3 graphically represents the ways to improve the ratio between inputs and outputs. The first scenario, *doing more with less*, has been the reform catchphrase in many countries. The US National Performance Review for instance promised a government that works better and costs less. Although the political salience of the first scenario stands out, other scenarios are conceivable. Governments can also do *much more*

**25**

*with some more* investments. New challenges such as immigration require more expenditures and investment in many countries. Yet, the pressure immigration puts on public services such as education and childcare typically requires more performance improvements than public money can buy in times of shrinking public budgets. Hence, much more performance is expected from a modest increase in resources. In a third scenario, *more output from the same input* is requested. This is also a quite common strategy in governments. Rather than cutting budgets, governments often aim at improving the fiscal balance by only allowing expenditures to grow with inflation. In this way public expenditure is reduced relative to GDP (with positive GDP growth). Yet, at the same time, a growing economy and society may also put new demands on public services. The fourth scenario attains the *same level of performance with fewer resources*. In practice, this scenario is often found. A complaint in decentralization programmes for instance is sometimes that budgets do not follow responsibilities. In the Netherlands for instance, the transfer of youth policies to local governments led to budget cuts between 4 per cent and 12.5 per cent (VNG, n.d.). The scenario of doing the same with less also applies when employees that are not available are not replaced. A soft approach to reducing the public workforce is not to replace retired employees. This gradual reduction in inputs is typically not matched by a reduction in tasks. In a fifth scenario, governments expect *less performance with much less* inputs. Drastic budget cuts are expected to only have minor consequences. It may be a politically safer bet to hold out diminishing performance rather than to promise more performance from fewer resources. The austerity rhetoric in countries such as Greece and Portugal is making exactly this promise. Increased activity in the private sector – both for and not for profit – is said to be the answer to an atrophying public sector that resorts to its core tasks of providing safety and a stable business climate. A decimated public budget therefore is nonetheless expected to provide for acceptable public performance. A final note on the scenarios is that countries develop *mixed strategies* for different policy sectors. Many countries for instance hope for a doing-much-more-with-more scenario when R&D is concerned. Infrastructure budgets on the contrary are often under pressure. In the short and mid-term, users are not aware of disinvestment in infrastructure maintenance, and hence the scenario appears to be one of doing the same with less. In the long term, costs may rise exponentially.

## 1.2 Performance and public values

The definition of performance as a production process leaves an important question unanswered: what are the defining characteristics of performance? Besides the process of getting to performance, we also need to conceptualize the substance of performance. In the performance measurement and management literature, little conceptual work has been done to describe the substance of performance. This also has an effect on the research that studies the determinants of performance.

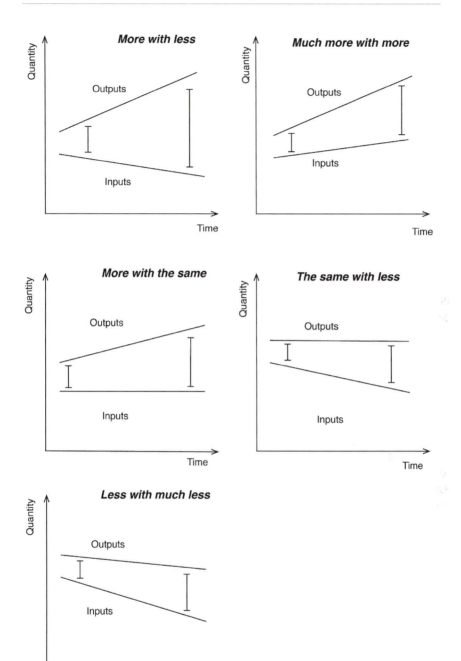

**Figure 2.3** *Performance strategies*

27

## BOX 2.3 INVENTORIES OF PUBLIC VALUES

Several studies attempted to clarify the concept of public value.

Moore (1995) draws a parallel with the private sector. Public value in the public and non-profit sector is the analogue of shareholder and user value in the private sector. Public value refers to the value created by government through services, laws, regulation and other actions. The public value concept is also used in practice. The UK Cabinet Office published a study on the concept (Kelly & Muers, 2002). In *Recognizing Public Value* Moore (2012) shows how public professionals manage for public value. He uses case narratives to elicit managerial strategies.

Jorgensen & Bozeman (2002) list 13 public values. Amongst others, they mention political accountability, equal treatment, Rechtstaat ('rule of law'), regime stability, social cohesion and local self-governance as public values. Further research on the 'public values universe' led them to a list of about 80 public values (Jorgensen & Bozeman, 2007) related to seven themes: (1) the public sector's contribution to society, (2) the transformation of interests to decisions, (3) the relationship between public administrators and politicians, (4) the relationship between public administrators and their environment, (5) the intra-organizational aspects of public administration, (6) the behaviour of public sector employees, and (7) the relationship between public administration and the citizens.

A literature review of the so-called management matters thesis found that 42 per cent of the studies in major PA journals used test scores of Texas school districts as a measure of performance (De Caluwe & Van Dooren, 2012). Another 26 per cent of the articles used scores of the comprehensive performance assessment of Welsh and English local governments. A more solid foundation seems to be warranted to establish the true impact of management on performance. This conceptual gap may be filled by the literature on public sector values.

Hood (1991) distinguishes between three types of public values (see also Voets *et al.*, 2008 for an application on network performance).

■   A first set of values seeks to keep the public sector lean and purposeful – to match resources to defined tasks. Thus, frugality of resource use in relation to given goals is the criterion of success, while failure is counted in terms of instances of avoidable waste and incompetence (Hood, 1991: p. 12). Good value implies the efficient and effective production of high-quality goods and services – hence the label 'product' values.

■ A second set of values intends to keep government fair and honest. Government has to pursue honesty, fairness and mutuality through the prevention of distortion, inequity, bias and abuse of office (Hood, 1991: p. 13). These values are institutionalized in appeal mechanisms, public reporting requirements and ethical codes. Good value implies open and honest processes – hence the label 'process' values.

■ A third set of values is designed to keep the public sector robust and resilient. Government has to keep operating even in adverse 'worst case' conditions and has to adapt rapidly in a crisis (Hood, 1991: p. 14). Reliability is often an argument for choosing public production instead of private production. Good value implies the assurance of strong regimes to fall back on – hence the label 'regime' values.

Two visions on how public values and public performance conceptually relate to each other can be developed. Performance can be seen as one value amongst others in the public values universe. In Hood's framework, performance would roughly be equivalent to the first set of values. This approach builds on the controversy around the performance movement: performance defined as efficiency and effectiveness in this view is at the expense of other, non-mission-based values (Piotrowski & Rosenbloom, 2002). An important author is Beryl Radin whose 2006 book critiques what she calls the performance movement: a loosely coupled group of actors in academia, government and society who promote public values such as efficiency, effectiveness and accountability. Radin (2006) amongst others argues that the performance movement forgets about the context, interferes with professionalism, is not concerned with equity, and is apolitical. She argues that the performance movement stresses too much the product subset of public values and too little the process and regime values.

Alternatively, performance is seen as the realisation of public values. Values and performance are distinct concepts, and all public values can lead to performance. Besides efficiency and effectiveness, successful practices of for instance participation or innovation could also be seen as dimensions of performance. Boyne (2002: p. 19) listed sixteen different possible performance dimensions that resound public values: outputs (quantity and quality), efficiency, service outcomes (formal effectiveness, impact, equity, cost per unit of service outcome), responsiveness (consumer satisfaction, citizen satisfaction, staff satisfaction, cost per unit of responsiveness), and democratic outcome (probity, participation, accountability, cost per unit of democratic outcome).

In analytical terms, values are the frame of reference for the assessment of performance. Values and performance thus ask different questions about the same issue. A *performance assessment* will analyse to what extent public organizations and programmes further influence the general interest. Are public services provided in an efficient and effective way? What are the impacts of a programme on equity?

**29**

Have sufficient measures been taken to guarantee the functioning of the public sector, even in the wake of disastrous events? A *value assessment* will ask questions about the values that prevail, whether they are in conflict or whether they are complementary. In order to make this assessment of dominant values in the public sector, a researcher may need to have a look at behaviour. One can study intentional behaviour that is aimed at the fulfilment of the general interest (performance). A researcher could also look at non-intentional behaviour.

## 1.3 Micro, meso and macro performance

Performance has a potentially broad stretch. It includes micro, meso and macro levels. Bouckaert & Halligan (2008) call this the depth of performance (p. 18), indicating that performance can be discussed at different levels. Three levels of analysis can be distinguished (Figure 2.4). The *macro level* typically includes general discussions on the performance of a country, but it also encompasses performance of supra-national governments (Euro zone, the OECD countries) as well as local and regional governments. The key element of macro performance is its government-wide character, irrespective of the tier of government. *Micro performance* is defined at the level of an individual organization and its interface with citizens and other organizations. In between macro and micro, *meso performance* refers to either the performance of a policy sector (e.g. education) or the performance of governing a chain of events (e.g. the food chain) or networks (e.g. an urban development project).

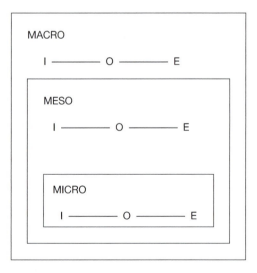

**Figure 2.4** Input (I), output (O) and effect (E) at macro, meso and micro levels

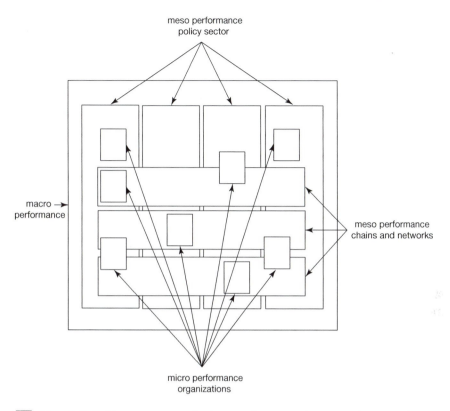

**Figure 2.5** *Macro, meso and micro performance in a complex nested configuration*

In reality, the macro–micro configuration is a complex pattern for different reasons (Figure 2.5). First, policy sectors, chains and networks cut across each other. The food safety chain for instance involves education (policy sector: education) as well as judicial punishments for non-compliance (policy sector: justice). Second, individual organizations are regularly involved in a multitude of policy sectors. A prison for instance primarily belongs to the sector of justice, but also has dealings with other sectors such as mental health, job reintegration and education. Third, organizations may also be involved in governing different chains and networks. An environmental inspectorate intervenes in chains that lead to the conservation of nature as well in economic value creation. Finally, reality is even more complex than Figure 2.5 suggests, because chains and networks are not always entirely contained by the performance of the macro level entity. Immigration for instance is a phenomenon that does not respect national borders. As a result, the performance of a single country is relative to the performance of others.

Complexity is a mixed blessing for performance measurement. The general argument seems to be that complex, networked contexts preclude well-functioning performance management systems (Moynihan *et al.*, 2011). Performance indicators are not able to capture complexity (see below). The dispersed nature of authority in networks, featuring multiple actors with different goals and interests, is expected to run counter to the simple lines of accountability for performance between political principals and agencies. Yet, governments have also relied on performance indicators to keep complex public services aligned. In the United Kingdom and elsewhere, joined-up government rested heavily on a number of key outcome indicators (Pollitt, 2003). Similarly, European economic governance makes use of a limited set of public budgeting indicators to align economic policies of member states. Clearly, the relation of performance management and complexity is far from settled (OECD, 2013).

## 2 PERFORMANCE MEASUREMENT

Performance measurement is the bundle of deliberate activities for quantifying performance. The result of these activities is performance information.

This definition of performance measurement follows quite naturally from the discussion of performance. When we talk about performance information in this book and unless indicated otherwise, we mean quantitative performance information. The definition also emphasizes that performance measurement is a bundle of tangible activities in organizations. We identify five activities: defining a measurement object, the formulation of indicators, data collection, data analysis, and reporting. In chapter 4, we describe those activities in more detail. Finally, the definition highlights that performance measurement is a deliberate, intentional activity. Tacit knowledge is excluded. This is not to say that performance measurement does not have unintended consequences. In chapter 9, we discuss the behavioural consequences of measurement.

Measurability has become an important discussion in the performance measurement literature in particular because performance information has become a central tenet of contemporary accountability schemes. Some activities, outputs and outcomes, it is argued, are easier to measure by nature. Ouchi (1977) for instance argued that output controls are only feasible in organizations that have measurable outputs. If that is not the case, behavioural or clan control are more appropriate. NPM reforms have strongly promoted the use of performance information for accountability purposes. Organizations regularly claim that low measurability makes it impossible for them to account for quantified performance. This complaint is often heard in organizations that play a role in policy advice (see Box 2.4).

Several authors have attempted to define the operational characteristics of measurability (Bouckaert, 1995). We review some key frameworks that help us understand measurability. In the 1960s, Downs (1967) identified eight structural aspects of bureaus, each of which can be used to assess measurability of an

## BOX 2.4 MEASURING THE QUALITY OF POLICY ADVICE

Policy advice comprises many activities, including research, data analysis, proposal development, consultation with stakeholders, formulation of advice for decision-makers, guiding policy through governmental and parliamentary processes, and the subsequent evaluation of the outcomes of the policy (Gregory & Lonti, 2008). According to Nicholson (1996), performance of policy advice can be measured based on whether advice has accurate, comprehensive, up-to-date information and is responsive to client needs. Other criteria are clarity, practicality, appropriateness, fairness, cost-effectiveness and consultation with interested parties.

Gregory & Lonti (2008) assessed the measurement of policy advice in the New Zealand public sector. Their main critique was the inadequacy of performance measures to accurately reflect the political nature of policy advice. A former British cabinet minister, Roy Hattersley, is quoted, saying that 'a disgruntled civil servant noticed that my policy advisor's main task was to give a spurious intellectual justification to my prejudices . . . but you could say that his job was to demonstrate the fundamental wisdom of my beliefs' (quoted on p. 848). They conclude that although policy advice can be genuinely and meaningfully gauged from a number of different perspectives – including those of ministers, parliament, policy stakeholders and the public at large – the performance measures that are being used seem to reflect a narrower managerialist predisposition to count what can most easily be counted (p. 852).

organization. All but the last are matters of degree (Table 2.1). Behind the criteria lay two opposite images of organization: organizations as machines versus organizations as transformation and flux (Morgan, 1997). Measurement is believed to be more straightforward in the former. Similar arguments can be developed from contingency theorists such as Thompson (1967).

Wilson (1989) developed a well-known scheme, which is related to the second structural dimension of Downs. He distinguishes between measurability of output and outcome and combines these two dimensions in order to distinguish four types of organizations: production, procedural, craft and coping (Table 2.2). Both the output and the outcome of *production organizations* are observable. Examples are mail services and routine tax collection. Performance measurement and management is possible. *Craft organizations* have observable outcomes, but their output is not visible. Results can be observed, not the processes. Park rangers are an example of this type of organization. One notices when the number of poachers is reduced, but we do not know precisely which activities the park rangers have performed.

**Table 2.1** *Downs' structural characteristics of bureaus and the implications for measurability*

| | Profile for highly measurable organizations | Profile for hardly measurable organizations |
|---|---|---|
| The clarity with which the functions of the bureaus can be defined | High ⟷ | Low |
| The ease with which the results of bureau actions can be perceived and their effectiveness evaluated | High ⟷ | Low |
| The stability of the bureau's internal technological environment over time | High ⟷ | Low |
| The stability of the bureau's external environment over time | High ⟷ | Low |
| The operational interdependence of its various functions | Low ⟷ | High |
| The complexity of its functions | Low ⟷ | High |
| The scope of its functions, that is, the breadth of the different activities those functions encompass | Low ⟷ | High |
| The power setting of the bureau in its environment; that is, the nature of its institutional surroundings | Nominal variable | |

Many other examples are found in the health profession. We know when people are getting better, but most of us do not have an understanding of what doctors have done in order to attain this result. *Procedural organizations* have outputs that are observable and outcomes that are less well defined. Many counselling services fall under this category. An example is mental health. Generally, discussions with psychiatrists are understandable, but whether mental health actually improves is hard to observe. Finally, *coping organizations* have problems in observing both output and outcome. Diplomatic efforts by embassies are an example. Diplomatic activities and outcomes are diverse and hard to define. Moreover, outcomes are contingent upon many other variables besides the diplomatic intervention.

The use of the typologies risks evoking a rather stereotypical image of the organizations based on a limited number of activities. Organizations however usually capture an extensive bundle of goods and services. Residential care, for example, entails a complex package of services including the provision of meals, infrastructure, nursing and psychological support. Even a typical coping organization such as an embassy will have some routine production activities – for instance issuing passports. The apparent ease of measurement of the aggregate package

**Table 2.2** *Wilson's (1989) typology of organizations*

| | Outcomes observable | |
| --- | --- | --- |
| Outputs observable | Yes | No |
| Yes | Production organizations *Examples*: mail services, tax collection, sanitation, vehicle registration, revenue collection | Procedural organizations *Examples*: mental health, counselling, military (peacetime), youth penitentiary |
| No | Craft organization *Examples*: field inspections, military (wartime), doctors, forest rangers | Coping organizations *Examples*: diplomacy, intelligence, research |

might conceal significant difficulties in measurement within some of the constituent components. Therefore, the typologies are mainly useful to typify activities and not organizations or programmes.

Hackman & Oldham (1980) developed a scheme at a lower analytical level. They distinguish between task routine and task ambiguity. Routine refers to whether a task is repeated while ambiguity refers to whether the course of action is clear or not. Measurement becomes increasingly difficult when routine is lower and ambiguity rises (Figure 2.6).

1   Measurement of activities with high ambiguity and a low routine is most challenging. Typical examples would be interest representation in embassies or creative work in cultural institutions. The measurement base in these cases is progress.
2   Activities with average routine and ambiguity have group and human relations as a measurement base. Typical examples are the many social services where client characteristics introduce a certain level of ambiguity and break the routine.
3   Finally, high routine and low ambiguity is typically found in administrative processes such as registering vehicles, processing standard tax forms and payroll administration. The measurement base is time.

Blankart (1987) also touches upon the measurability of services when he discusses the limits of privatization. He assumes that only those goods and services of which the quality of the output is measurable are liable for privatization (Table 2.3). He distinguishes between three types of consumption technology. *Inspection goods* (raw materials, stationery) can be privatized easily because quality is tangible and measurable. *Experience goods* (e.g. advice, debt collection) can also be privatized. Although quality of discrete service delivery is not as easily measureable as that

**35**

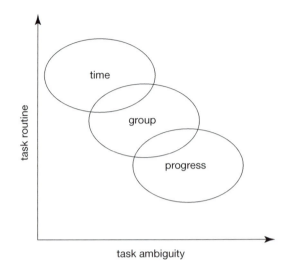

**Figure 2.6** *Hackman & Oldham's (1980) analysis of measurability*

**Table 2.3** *Blankart's (1987) clusters of services*

|  | *Inspection* | *Experience* | *Trust* |
|---|---|---|---|
| Criteria | Quality is tangible | Quality is predictable | Quality is intangible |

of inspection goods, an assessment can be made based on the extrapolation of experiences and the accumulation of goodwill by clients. In this way, quality becomes predictable. Finally, *trust goods* (courts, police, general public administration) are difficult to privatize, because they are hard to evaluate, even through experience. Measurement of quality in the latter cases is very difficult.

However useful these schemes may be, in practice, most people find in particular their own organization and policy sector hard to measure. An outsider may judge the work of a fire patrol to be easy to measure – that is, extinguishing fires as quickly as possible. Firefighters however will see the complexity of a big conflagration, the risk of flashovers and back-draft, and the importance of choosing the right extinguisher. Therefore, they will often oppose counting fires as if they are all alike. Teachers, doctors and road construction workers will voice similar concerns. Just because we know our own situation better, we often believe it is more complex, interconnected and ambiguous and thus less apt for measurement. This observation does not invalidate the empirical search for differences in measurability, but rather serves as a warning sign for not jumping to conclusions when assessing measurability from outside.

# 3 PERFORMANCE MANAGEMENT: WHAT IT IS AND WHAT IT ISN'T

In the previous paragraphs, we suggested three ways to make sense of performance, performance measurement and measurability. The next question then is how this relates to performance management. *The answer is relatively straightforward: performance management is a management style that incorporates and uses performance information for decision-making.* As we will discuss later, incorporation is about integrating performance information into policy and management cycles of amongst others policy-making, budgeting and contract management. The uses are grouped in three clusters of decisions: learning, steering & control, and account giving (see Table 2.4).

**Table 2.4** *Three clusters of performance management*

|  | *To learn* | *To steer and control* | *To give account* |
|---|---|---|---|
| Key question | How to improve policy or management? | How to steer and control activities? | How to communicate performance? |
| Focus | Internal | Internal | External |
| Orientation | Change/future | Control/present | Survival/past |

Notions such as management-by-objective, strategic management, performance budgeting, managing for results, results-based management and entrepreneurial budgeting all share a common logic that public organizations should produce performance information and use this information to inform decision-making (Moynihan, 2008). We follow this relatively down-to-earth approach to performance management, which is broad but precise and analytical rather than normative.

The performance literature sometimes equates performance management and performance measurement. Under the heading performance management, discussions mainly focus on performance measurement without further clarification of its use (Bovaird & Gregory, 1996; De Bruijn, 2002). This text will make a clear distinction between performance measurement and management, which is needed for a better insight into the functioning of performance management systems.

Since the performance discourse sounds so familiar to many, it may be useful to end by asking what the alternative for performance management would be. On what else than performance could management be based? We use Weber's discussion of the bases of authority in bureaucracy for a short thought experiment. Weber identified three types of authority, which can be transposed to three sources of management capacity (Fry & Raadschelders, 2008). None of the three approaches particularly focuses on results, and thus they are distinct from performance management (Table 2.5). The Weberian ideal-typical approaches to public management are still relevant today, although the relative importance may have shifted.

## BOX 2.5 MAX WEBER'S TYPES OF AUTHORITY AS ALTERNATIVES TO PERFORMANCE MANAGEMENT

Weber's authority types translated to management styles.
Why this management style differs from performance management.

### Charismatic authority

The personal qualities of the leader/manager determine legitimacy. Weber speaks of the belief of ordinary man in the exceptional powers and heroism of the leader. The leader demands obedience by virtue of his mission. In keeping with the transient nature of charisma, charismatic administration is loose and unstable. Weber, writing during the second industrial revolution in Germany (1870–1914), saw charismatic authority to be on the wane. The contemporary leadership literature however seems to re-establish some of the virtues of charismatic leadership. According to Van Wart (2003), while reviewing the leadership literature, leaders are nowadays required to be visionary, entrepreneurial and charismatic.

Charismatic management is about building goodwill, creating a sense of mission and developing a cult around managers. The Richard Bransons and Steve Jobses are witnesses of the enduring appeal of this management style. Performance can be instrumental in developing this cult, since it can be assumed that it radiates from charisma. Yet, for charisma, performance indicators remain peripheral.

### Traditional authority

Here, the position of the manager determines legitimacy, which is based on respect for traditions and routines; Weber speaks of the eternal past. In contrast to charismatic authority, traditional authority is stable. People obey persons in positions rather than rules. Normative institutionalists have continued to study the constraints that routines and norms enforce on rational agency (Scott, 2001).

Traditional management is about establishing and institutionalising routines. Although performance may be at play when routines are developed, it typically is no longer taken into consideration when those routines become institutions – in Selznick's words, when they become infused with value (1957). All organizations need routines and a sense of institutional integrity that needs to be guarded, rather than challenged based on performance arguments (Selznik, 1957).

### Legal authority

Legitimacy of managers is based on them acting in accordance with their duties as established by a code of rational rules and regulations. Managers are a 'trustee' of an impersonal, compulsory institution. Weber abstains from suggesting an evolutionary, linear progress towards legal authority. Although he sees a general trend towards legal domination, it is punctuated by bursts of charisma and regressions towards tradition (Fry & Raadschelders, 2008).

### Bureaucratic

Bureaucratic management, finally, is about coordination and directing within and based on the rules that are set out. It is assumed that these rules are rational, which means that they are means to a political end (Weber, 1948). Performance may be a consideration when rules are developed. Good managers, however, operate within this regulatory framework, which is not to be challenged.

The implication is that public management is always a blend of ideal-types. Performance management in its pure form does not exist.

## 4 CONCLUSION

This chapter laid the conceptual groundwork for the book. Performance, performance measurement and performance management were treated as separated and well-defined concepts. Performance is defined as the realization of public values such as efficiency, effectiveness, equity, robustness, openness and transparency. Performance measurement is the process of acquiring performance information. Measurability of activities is a key concern. Performance management is the incorporation and use of performance information in decision-making.

## FURTHER READING

The OECD (2009) published a volume titled *Measuring Government Activity* which discusses some of the conceptual debates in the field. It is based on the technical papers supporting the 'government at a glance' initiative. The production logic of performance is discussed in several contributions: Pollitt & Bouckaert's *Public Management Reform* (2011) and Hatry (1999) are a good starting point. McDavid & Hawthorn are a reference from the evaluation literature (2006). An overview of econometric performance methods is provided by Coelli & Rao (1998). A seminal article outlining the different values underpinning public management is Hood's 'Public Management for All Seasons' (Hood, 1991). Jorgensen & Bozeman (2007) have undertaken more recent research on public values. The distinctiveness of the public sector, including the measurability of activities, is described in a lucid way by Wilson (1989). Finally, Fry & Raadschelders (2008) provide a good overview

**39**

of the work of old masters such as Max Weber. These works are often a good sparring partner for contemporary performance research.

## REFERENCES

Atkinson, A. B. (2005). *Atkinson Review: Final Report: Measurement of Government Output and Productivity for the National Accounts*. London: Palgrave Macmillan.

Blankart, C. B. (1987). 'Limits to Privatization'. *European Economic Review*, 31, 346–51.

Bouckaert, G. (1995). 'The Range of Performance Indicators in the Public Sector: Theory vs. Practice'. In Halachmi, A., & Grant, D. (eds) *Reengineering and Performance Measurement in Criminal Justice and Social Programmes*. Perth: IIAS.

Bouckaert, G., & Halligan, J. (2008). *Managing Performance: International Comparisons*. London: Routledge.

Bovaird, T., & Gregory, D. (1996). *Performance Indicators: The British Experience*. Westport, CT: Quorum Books.

Boyne, G. A. (2002). 'Public and Private Management: What's the Difference?', *Journal of Management Studies*, 39(1), 97–122.

Coelli, T., & Rao, P. (1998). *An Introduction to Efficiency and Productivity Analysis*. Boston: Kluwer.

De Bruijn, H. (2002). *Managing Performance in the Public Sector*. London: Routledge.

De Caluwe, C., & Van Dooren, W. (2012). 'A Review of the Management Matters Thesis'. Paper presented at the European Group of Public Administration Annual Conference, Bergen (Norway).

Downs, A. (1967). *Inside Bureaucracy*. Boston: Little, Brown and Company.

Easton, D. (1965). *A Systems Analysis of Political Life*. New York: Wiley.

Fry, B. R., & Raadschelders, J. C. N. (2008). *Mastering Public Administration: From Max Weber to Dwight Waldo*. Washington, DC: CQpress.

Gregory, R., & Lonti, Z. (2008). 'Chasing Shadows? Performance Measurement of Policy Advice in the New Zealand Government Departments'. *Public Administration*, 86, 837–56.

Hackman, J., & Oldham, G. R. (1980). *Work Redesign*. Reading, MA: Addison-Wesley.

Hatry, H. P. (1999). *Performance Measurement: Getting Results*. Washington, DC: Urban Institute Press.

Hood, C. (1991). 'A Public Management for All Seasons'. *Public Administration*, 69, 3–19.

Jorgensen, T. B., & Bozeman, B. (2002). 'Public Values Lost? Comparing Cases on Contracting Out from Denmark and the United States'. *Public Management Review*, 4, 63–81.

—— (2007). 'Public Values: An Inventory'. *Administration & Society*, 39, 354–81.

Kelly, G., & Muers, S. (2002). 'Creating Public Value'. Strategy Unit, Cabinet Office.

McDavid, J. C., & Hawthorn, L. R. L. (2006). *Program Evaluation and Performance Measurement: An Introduction to Practice*. Thousand Oaks: Sage.

**40**

Moore, M. H. (1995). *Creating Public Value*. Cambridge, MA: Harvard University Press.

—— (2012). *Recognizing Public Value*. Cambridge, MA: Harvard University Press.

Morgan, G. (1997). *Images of Organization*. Thousand Oaks: Sage.

Moynihan, D. P. (2008). *The Dynamics of Performance Management: Constructing Information and Reform*. Washington, DC: Georgetown University Press.

Moynihan, D. P., Fernandez, S., Kim, S., Leroux, K. M., Piotrowski, S. J., Wright, B. E., & Yang, K. (2011). 'Performance Regimes amidst Governance Complexity'. *Journal of Public Administration Research and Theory*, 21 (supplement 1), i141–i155.

Nicholson, J. (1996). 'Measures for Monitoring Policy Advice'. In Uhr, J., & Mackay, K. (eds) *Evaluating Policy Advice: Learning from Commonwealth Experience*. Canberra: Federalism Research Centre.

OECD (2009). *Measuring Government Activity*. Paris: OECD.

—— (2013). *Government at a Glance*. Paris: OECD.

Ouchi, W. G. (1977). 'The Relationship between Organizational Structure and Organizational Control'. *Administrative Science Quarterly*, 22, 95–113.

Piotrowski, S. J., & Rosenbloom, D. H. (2002). 'Nonmission-Based Values in Results-Oriented Public Management: The Case of Freedom of Information'. *Public Administration Review*, 62(6), 643–57.

Poister, T. H. (2003). *Measuring Performance in Public and Nonprofit Organizations*. San Francisco: Jossey-Bass.

Pollitt, C. (2003). 'Joined-Up Government: A Survey'. *Political Studies Review*, 1(1), 34–49.

Pollitt, C., & Bouckaert, G. (2011). *Public Management Reform: A Comparative Analysis* (3rd ed.). Oxford: Oxford University Press.

Radin, B. A. (2006). *Challenging the Performance Movement: Accountability, Complexity, and Democratic Values*. Georgetown: University Press.

Schick, A. (1966). 'The Road to PPB: The Stages of Budget Reform'. *Public Administration Review*, 26, 243–58.

Scott, W. R. (2001). *Institutions and Organizations*. Thousand Oaks: Sage Publications.

Selznik, P. (1957). *Leadership in Administration*. New York: Harper Row.

Thompson, J. D. (1967). *Organizations in Action: Social Science Bases of Administrative Theory*. New York: McGraw-Hill.

Van Wart, M. (2003). 'Public-Sector Leadership Theory: An Assessment'. *Public Administration Review*, 63, 214–28.

VNG (n.d.). *Factsheet | De kortingen op de decentralisatie jeugdzorg in 2015*. Retrieved 10 July 2014 from http://www.vng.nl/onderwerpenindex/decentralisaties-sociaal-domein/decentralisatie-jeugdzorg/factsheet-de-kortingen-op-de-decentralisatie-jeugdzorg-in-2015.

Voets, J., Van Dooren, W., & De Rynck, F. (2008). 'A Framework for Assessing the Performance of Policy Networks'. *Public Management Review*, 10, 773.

Weber, M. (1948). 'Politics as a Vocation'. In Kegan, P., Gerth, H., & Mills, C. (eds) *From Max Weber*. London: Routledge.

Wilson, J. Q. (1989). *Bureaucracy: What Government Agencies Do and Why They Do It*. New York: Basic Books.

**41**

# Chapter 3

# The history of performance management

## LEARNING OBJECTIVES

- To understand the contingency between the political and social environment and the rise and fall of performance movements.
- To develop a historical consciousness with regard to performance management.

## KEY POINTS IN THIS CHAPTER

- Performance has been on the agenda at several points in time; it is not an NPM invention.
- Most performance movements share a stable set of concepts (i.e. the production model).
- What did change was the intensity and pervasiveness of the use of the performance information.

## DISCUSSION QUESTIONS

- Is performance management new wine in old bottles? Is NPM Taylor revisited?
- Why does performance management revive every decade?
- Are we witnessing an end in the growth of performance management?

The antecedents to contemporary performance measurement and management have a long lineage. Performance ideas have been around for a hundred years or more. Nevertheless, historical consciousness on the issue is generally low. It is often forgotten that long-term trends have supported the ascendancy of performance ideas as a central force in public management internationally. The observation that performance measurement and management extends well beyond NPM has been made on several occasions. Williams (2003) for instance analysed management practices in early twentieth-century New York, and found many of the features of contemporary performance measurement (see also Stivers, 2000). These analyses paint a somewhat sobering picture. They seem to suggest that a whole century of study and practice of performance management did not really add anything. Moreover, they run counter to observations on the increasing influence of performance measurement and management (Bouckaert & Halligan, 2008; Radin, 2006).

The question of this chapter is how the face of performance management changed to make an impact that it never had before. In order to answer this question, we need to analyse in what respect performance management has changed or has *not* changed. We will argue that it is mainly changes in use that account for the impact of the contemporary performance movements. The most striking feature of performance management is its expansion within and across public sectors over the last two decades, making this current period its most influential. Before we analyse change and continuity, we briefly discuss the most important performance movements in the twentieth and twenty-first century (Van Dooren, 2008).

## 1 PERFORMANCE MOVEMENTS IN THE TWENTIETH CENTURY

The chapter is organized around a number of performance movements. The concept of 'movement' is analogous to the sociological term 'movement'. Unlike other forms of organization, movements are informally organized around a set of thoughts and practices that form the glue. Members of a performance movement share an agenda of change with a particular vision of performance, its measurement and management.

We discuss eight movements that have propagated performance management. They are clustered into three time segments: (1) pre-World War II, (2) the 1950s to the 1970s, which roughly parallels the development of the welfare state and the related growth of government, and (3) the 1980s onwards, when welfare states came under pressure from a variety of sources.

In the list of movements, a distinction between policy movements and management movements can be made. Policy movements mainly focus on performance in terms of the *outcomes* of organizations and public programmes. Management movements have more of an internal focus on *outputs* and efficiency. Yet, there is a grey zone, with management movements taking into account some elements of outcome and vice versa.

## 1.1 1900–1940s

Three performance movements developed at the end of the nineteenth century and the beginning of the twentieth century: (1) the social survey movement, (2) scientific management and the science of administration, and (3) cost accounting. These movements emanated from different milieus, respectively social reformers, engineers and specialist administrators, and large corporations. Yet, all three movements were a response to the social context of industrialization, poverty and social unrest, and governments plagued by corruption. The performance movements of the day sought to answer these societal issues through rationalization and quantification of policy and administration.

The *social survey movement* was a movement of social reformers who needed facts about social problems (Bulmer *et al.*, 1991). The best-known work of the social survey movement is Charles Booth's study *Life and Labour of the People of London* (1886–1903) (Linsley & Linsley, 1993). Booth believed that the poverty debate was underdeveloped because three questions remained unanswered: how many people were poor, why were they poor and what should be done to alleviate poverty? These questions demonstrate not only the performance dimension of the social survey movement, but also that measurement was an instrument to influence a policy agenda.

While the social survey movement mainly targeted the social inequalities, the driver behind the second movement, *scientific management* and *the science of administration* (see Box 3.1) was the need for infrastructure and resource mobilization that ensued from industrialization (Rose, 1976). Corruption and adhocracy plaguing government stood in the way of the development of large infrastructures such as national railways and sanitation works. Ridley & Simon (1938: p. 1) expressed this concern when claiming that 'a generation ago a municipal government was considered commendable if it was honest. Today we demand a great more of our public service. It must be not only honest but efficient as well'. Government institutions therefore needed a professional workforce and rational, Weberian-style regulation. Administration was now seen as a profession and a science in its own right.

A third evolution in the early twentieth century was the development of *cost accounting*, which was a joint venture of the public and the private sector. Claims of control and openness echoed in both the public and the private sector (Previts & Merino, 1979; Rivenbark, 2005). In addition, stronger information systems were needed in order to manage the increasingly large and complex organizations and corporations. Cost accounting is in essence the process of

**44**

## BOX 3.1 THE SCIENCE OF ADMINISTRATION AND SCIENTIFIC MANAGEMENT

There is some debate about the differences of scientific management and the science of administration. Williams (2004) pointed to some discrepancies. Scientific management for instance supported distributed management, while the science of administration advocated a hierarchical executive branch. Although the concrete practices they developed were sometimes contradictory, the movements share a number of important principles. Mosher (1968: pp. 72–3) summarized this common ground of two sub-movements in six points (see also Sayre, 1958).

1  Rationality: the applicability of the rule of reason;
2  Planning: the forward projection of needs and objectives;
3  Specialization: of materials, tools and machines, products, workers and organizations;
4  Quantitative measurement: applied as far as possible to all elements of operations;
5  'One best way': there is one single best method, tool, material and type of worker;
6  Standards and standardization: the 'one best', once discovered, must be made the standard.

tracking, recording and analysing costs associated with the activity of an organization. Through cost accounting, output indicators are incorporated into the financial system. Cost accounting has become institutionalized in the private sector. In the public sector, it is still considered innovative in most OECD countries (Pollitt & Bouckaert, 2011).

The New York Bureau of Municipal Research (NYBMR) was a synthesis of scientific management, cost accounting and the social survey (Schachter, 1989; Stivers, 2000). The New York Bureau of Municipal Research put in practice many of the performance measurement concepts that are in use today (Williams, 2003). Data collection was embedded in accounting practices. Record keeping efforts such as time sheets and work plans, as well as output and outcome indicators, were developed. Social indicators supplemented these indicators. The fact that this integration of ideas was conceivable in practice points to a common trend in all three movements: the rationalization and de-personification of management and policy.

Gulick & Urwick (1937: pp. 44–5) recorded the accomplishments of the Bureau of Municipal Research in New York state and city:

the development of efficiency surveys and reorganization programs; the organization of other bureaus of government research in the United States, and Canada, and abroad, and the growing attention which has been directed to administrative reforms, the factual study of government and principals of administration are all a vindication of the unique experiment which was set in motion . . . when the Bureau of Municipal Research, was established.

The NYBMR practice spread to other cities that created their own bureaus of efficiency. The initial decades of the twentieth century resulted in many institutions focusing mostly on municipal efficiency. Many ideas were taken national, however, and several institutions emerged: the Institute for Government Research (the predecessor of the Brookings Institution, 1916), a Bureau of Efficiency (1912, abolished in 1933), the Bureau of the Budget (the predecessor of the Office of Management and the Budget, 1921) and the General Accounting Office (1921) (Van Riper, 1983).

## 1.2 1950s–1970s

A second generation of performance measurement activity emerged with post-World War II experiments. The mission statement of the next performance movement, *performance budgeting*, resounded in the fifth finding of the first Hoover Commission (1947–9), officially named the Commission on Organization of the Executive Branch of the Government, stating that 'the budgetary processes of the Government need improvement, in order to express the objectives of the Government in terms of the work to be done rather than in mere classification of expenditure' (Hoover Commission report in Shafritz & Hyde, 2004: p. 162).

Performance budgeting became well established in the 1960s with the introduction of the Planning Programming Budgeting Systems (PPBS). New programme expenditures had to be weighed against the marginal benefits of each programme in a systemic way. PPBS inspired subsequent initiatives such as Management by Objectives (MBO) and Zero-Based Budgeting (ZBB). Performance budgeting was found in other countries as well. Great Britain introduced it in the Ministry of Defence in the late 1960s and then extended it to other departments, particularly in education and science. The French PPBS variant, RCB (rationalization des choix budgétaires), was first applied in 1968 in the Ministry of Defence and then in sectors of energy, town planning, postal services and telegraph. By the early 1970s, PPBS had become an integral tool of national economic planning. PPBS practices were also implemented in, amongst other places, Australia, Austria, Belgium, Canada, Ireland and Japan (Novick, 1973).

The consensus however is that PPBS, MBO and ZBB failed. PPBS is judged to be a success in the British Ministry of Defence, where it is still in use today (McAffery & Jones, 2004). The transfer to other departments however was

**Table 3.1** *US performance budgeting initiatives*

| Acronym | | |
|---|---|---|
| PPBS | Planning Programming Budgeting System | PPBS assumed that different levels and types of performance could be arrayed, quantified and analysed to make the best budgetary decisions. In essence, PPBS introduced a decision-making framework to the executive branch budget formulation process by presenting and analysing choices among long-term policy objectives and alternative ways of achieving them. (Initiated in 1965 by President Johnson.) |
| MBO | Management by Objectives | MBO sought to link agencies' stated objectives to their budget requests. MBO is a process to hold agency managers responsible for achieving agreed-upon outputs and outcomes. Agency heads would be accountable for achieving presidential objectives of national importance; managers within an agency would be held accountable for objectives set jointly by supervisors and subordinates. Performance was primarily defined as agency outputs and processes, but efforts were also made to define performance as the results of federal spending – what would today be called 'outcomes'. (Initiated in 1973 by President Nixon.) |
| ZBB | Zero-Based Budgeting | ZBB proposed to develop budgets from scratch, rather than to build them incrementally. In practice, agencies were expected to set priorities based on the programme results that could be achieved at alternative spending levels, one of which was to be below current funding. In developing budget proposals, these alternatives were to be ranked against each other sequentially from the lowest level organisations up through the department and without reference to a past budgetary base. In concept, ZBB sought a clear and precise link between budgetary resources. (Initiated in 1977 by President Carter.) |

(based on General Accounting Office, 1997)

problematic. The dominance of system thinking, attempting to link everything together in a large scheme, left its mark on the management tools of the day. PPBS overcommitted itself to this systematic dimension, which eventually led to its collapse. Amongst others, Aaron Wildavsky (1969) cogently attacked the system, arguing that in particular the fixation on the programme structure is pernicious. There is not sufficient analytical capacity to provide a meaningful programme structure for all the activities, to explore causality and to develop a sensible weighing scheme. Further, he points to the conflict between analysis by analysts and the value judgements of politicians. The former cannot resolve the problems of the latter. With his criticism, Wildavsky (1969) attacks not only PPBS, but also the holistic system approach to public administration.

Besides performance-based budgeting, a new effort of collecting outcome indicators emerged. In 1966, Bauer branded this work as the social indicators movement, when he published a book on the social side effects of the NASA space investment programmes (Bauer, 1966). After almost two decades of economic growth and prosperity, the limits of growth were felt, and the development of the welfare state triggered the demand for social data (De Neufville, 1975). The social indicator movement sought to construct such standard measures of the state of health, crime, well-being, education and many other social characteristics of a population and living environments. The movement conjured up visions of 'social engineering', which again fitted well into the prominence of system thinking.

The economic crises of the second half of the 1970s and the cutback management of the 1980s explain why the movement ran out of steam (Bulmer, 2001). The social indicator movement, however, did have a manifest impact. The statistical apparatus of governments was expanded to cover more phenomena, and new time series were developed. Moreover, the extended statistics on the social condition of the population allowed performance measurement systems to cover the outcomes of government action better. We still see the impact of this movement in contemporary social indicators on quality of life, happiness and sustainable development (Eckersley, 1998).

## 1.3 1980s–2010s

In the 1980s, fiscal hardship led to considerable pressure on government, which was reinforced by the ascent of New Right ideologies. A number of countries, notably New Zealand, Australia and the UK, responded to this pressure by experimentation with managerial approaches. In the 1980s, savings were the prime focus. Under Reagan, the President's Private Sector Survey on Cost Control, the Grace Commission, estimated potential yearly savings of $US3 billion. Performance management at that time was cutback management. Performance measurement became a growth industry in the UK as well following the launching of the Financial Management Initiative in 1982, which was designed to focus on objectives and to measure outputs and performance. A significant component of the approach was the use of performance indicators (PIs), Prime Minister Thatcher proclaiming in the 'manifesto of the revolution . . . that a thousand PIs should flourish' (Carter *et al.*, 1992: p. 2). By 1987, departments had 1,800 PIs (Pollitt, 1993).

Managerialism in the 1980s resulted in a diffuse set of management reforms that spread globally in the 1990s and became known as the New Public Management (NPM). Under the banner of NPM resides a broad array of management tools, the compatibility of which is often contested (Williams, 2000). Notwithstanding the internal variation, the NPM doctrine has all the characteristics of a performance movement (Hood, 1991). It prescribes that public agencies should be subdivided into small policy oversight boards and larger performance-based managed organizations for service delivery. The latter organizations were to compete with private sector organizations. Performance was to be the criterion to evaluate agencies, and this required measurement in an all-inclusive way. The use of performance information is not restricted to policy advice, as for social indicators, or to budget and planning documents, as for performance budgeting. Performance information is incorporated in almost all management functions. In chapter 5, on incorporation, we will discuss financial management, contract management and some aspects of HRM.

Notwithstanding its apparent failure in previous decades, performance budgeting made a remarkable comeback in NPM, with a clear lineage between preceding and contemporary performance budgeting efforts (Kelly & Rivenbark, 2003; Robinson & Brumby, 2005). In the USA, the Government Performance and Results Act (GPRA) and the Program Assessment Rating Tool have been the main proponents of current performance budgeting (General Accounting Office, 1997; General Accounting Office, 2004). Other countries also undertook performance budgeting initiatives: the output-outcome budgeting systems of New Zealand and Australia, the British Financial Management Initiative Public Service Agreements, and the French Loi organique relative aux lois de finances (LOLF) (see Schick, 1990 for an overview).

From the vantage point of the end of the decade, a range of international observers agreed that something special was happening around the world in the 1990s. A UK specialist noted that 'the 1980s and especially the 1990s saw the rise of "performance" as an issue in public sector theory and practice' (Talbot, 1999). Similarly a US expert reports that 'if there is a single theme that characterizes the public sector in the 1990s, it is the demand for performance. A mantra has emerged in this decade, heard at all levels of government, that calls for documentation of performance and explicit outcomes of government action' (Radin, 2000: p. 168). These trends continue into the 2000s. 'If you can't measure it, you can't manage it' has become a familiar refrain. Pollitt & Bouckaert (2011) demonstrate how measurement gradually becomes more extensive, more intensive and more external.

New Public Management has an interesting place in these developments. Originally derided by many OECD members (generally those who had not accepted its precepts), the take-up of NPM elements that involves performance (much less so market aspects) has spread almost universally across Europe (Curristine & Flynn, 2013). While NPM has been partly superseded in first generation countries, performance management has been further institutionalized in countries such as Australia and the United Kingdom. The language of NPM has become more prevalent now in late reforming countries.

The most recent performance movement is Evidence Based Policy (EBP). If we accept that outcomes of programmes are key in performance and performance management, EBP does fit the description of a performance movement. EBP prescribes that facts and figures on outcomes, rather than ideologies or opinions of the day, should inform policy decisions. EBP has a predominantly British origin (Solesbury, 2001) and was initially mainly pursued in the medical and public health sector (Davies *et al.*, 2000). By the end of the 1990s, EBP had spread to virtually all policy sectors. Solesbury (2001) identifies three conditions that furthered the EBP movement in the UK. First, there has been a utilitarian turn in research funding. Research should not only improve understanding, but also offer guidance. Second, he observes a decline in confidence in the professions: a 'retreat from priesthood', he calls it (p. 6). Third, New Labour propagated the replacement of ideology by pragmatism. As such, EBP seemed to fit well into the Third Way politics of UK PM Tony Blair and US President Clinton, but also of Bob Hawke and Paul Keating in Australia, Jean Chrétien in Canada and Gerhard Schröder's 'Neue Mitte' in Germany. Burnham (2001) typifies this strategy as 'the politics of depoliticisation'.

In a sense, EBP echoes some of the promises of social engineering in the social indicator movement. Critique on EBP reiterates some of the critiques on social indicators as well. The belief that evidence can overcome political conflict is seen as naive at best. Some radical political scientists such as Mouffe (2000) even consider these trends dangerous for democracy. On a more mundane level, the House of Commons warns that the government 'should certainly not seek selectively to pick pieces of evidence which support an already agreed policy, or even commission research in order to produce a justification for policy, the so-called "policy-based evidence making"' (House of Commons Science and Technology Committee, 2006: p. 164).

In the 2010s, a number of countries have been reviewing and revising their performance systems (see also chapter 1). An example is Australia's Commonwealth Financial Accountability Review, which has addressed the need to modernize the financial and performance framework. One focus is a 'clear line of sight' between appropriations, portfolio budget statements and information in annual reports to enable comparison of planned and actual performance (Department of Finance and Deregulation, 2012). The fiscal crises in particular drew attention to public financial management in many other countries (see chapters in the IMF volume of Cangiano, Curristine & Lazare, 2013). The relative emphasis on public financial management's three key objectives – maintaining a sustainable fiscal position, effective allocation of resources, and efficient delivery of public goods and services – has shifted from the effectiveness and efficiency arguments to fiscal sustainability (Cangiano, Curristine & Lazare, 2013: p. 14). A stronger use of input budgeting, spending controls and regulation, and budgetary frameworks is a consequence. Yet, at the same time new information needs on fiscal risks and programme evaluation are formulated. With regard to performance information, the IMF publication noted that 'nearly all OECD countries have developed performance information and many have introduced procedures to integrate it into accountability, budgeting, and management processes. The issue is getting this information used in decision-making'

**Table 3.2** *Performance movements in the twentieth century*

| Performance movement | Timescale | Characterization |
| --- | --- | --- |
| Social survey movement | 1900s<br>–1940 | Social reformers needed facts about social problems |
| Scientific management and the science of administration | | Government needed a scientific approach as opposed to adhocracy |
| Cost accounting | | Large corporations and government needed insight into costs of products and services for management and transparency |
| Bureau of Municipal Research and its offspring | | Synthesis in practice of previous three movements |
| Performance budgeting | 1950s<br>1960s<br>1970s | Shift attention in the budgetary process from inputs to outputs and objectives<br>Coincides often with an agenda of executive control |
| Social indicators | 1960s<br>1970s | Social engineering of the welfare state |
| New Public Management (2nd generation performance budgeting) | 1980s<br>1990s<br>2000s | Public sectors worldwide are under pressure and adopt performance strategies<br>PB is picked up, at least in rhetoric |
| Evidence-Based Policy | 1990s<br>2000s | Research and indicators rather than ideology and opinion have to undergird policy |
| Revisionism | 2010s | Review and revision of performance management frameworks in several countries (e.g. Australia, the Netherlands, the United Kingdom and the United States) |

(p. 11). The strong focus on the *use* of performance information in the following chapters of this book also addresses this concern (see chapters 6, 7 and 8). Table 3.2 provides an overview of the performance movements.

## 2 CHANGE AND CONTINUITY IN THE PERFORMANCE MOVEMENTS

There have been at least eight performance movements in the twentieth century: social surveys, scientific management and the science of administration, cost accounting, performance budgeting, social indicators, NPM and evidence-based policy. Notwithstanding the withering away of some of these performance movements, quantification of government activity has been a recurring tendency. As a consequence, observers may have a been-there-done-that reflex. In what follows, we paint a more nuanced picture of change and continuity in the history of the performance movements.

## 2.1 Continuity

The eight performance movements resemble each other in some remarkable ways. Probably the most striking similarity is the conceptual stability (1). The performance mindset did not change fundamentally throughout time. Other elements of constancy are the coexistence of policy and management movements (2), the political nature of the movements (3), the homogeneity of the sets of carriers for performance ideas (4) and the existence of deliberate strategies to diffuse practices to other administrations and countries (5).

### 1 Conceptual stability

Concepts are the intellectual artefacts we use to comprehend reality. Williams (2003) demonstrated that most of the concepts we use today to make sense of the very broad concept of performance were already used by the New York Bureau of Municipal Research. He argues that by 1912, performance measurement exhibited many of the features associated with the contemporary practice: measuring of input, output and results; attempting to make government more productive; making reports comparable among communities; and focusing on allocation and accountability (Williams, 2003: p. 643). The conceptual framework that sees government intervention as a process of turning inputs into outputs that subsequently should have outcomes in society is a recurrent feature of all performance movements. Although more refined models have been developed since its conception, the performance mindset has not changed fundamentally throughout time.

### 2 Management and policy movements; coexistence, not a pendulum

Each performance movement has either a policy or a management orientation. Some performance movements were mainly concerned with output and efficiency, while others focused on outcomes and effectiveness. The social survey, the social indicator and the evidence-based policy movements were mainly policy movements. Scientific management, cost accounting, PPBS and the New Public Management were predominantly management movements.

But how do policy and management movements relate to each other? Is there a pendulum that swings from management to policy and back, or do policy and management movements coexist? The pendulum hypothesis seems attractive, since the deficiencies of a too strong focus on management might be remedied by a stronger focus on policy, and vice versa. Yet, this does not seem to have been the case: movements coexist. Social surveying, cost accounting and scientific management ran parallel in the early twentieth century. The NY Bureau of Municipal

Research integrated elements from all three movements (Stivers, 2000). A similar pattern of coexistence is found in the 1970s, with the performance budgeting and social indicator movements running parallel, and in the 1990s, with the evidence-based policy movement and NPM.

This is a noteworthy observation. In the twentieth century, new impetuses to performance measurement for policy and management occurred every few decades. The coexistence of performance movements in policy and management may point to a spirit of the times that values quantification as indication of both rational policymaking and rational management. This is in line with Feldman & March's (1981) argument that the use of information symbolizes a commitment to rationality. Adopting performance measurement, being the symbol of rationality, reaffirms the importance of this social value. The mere activity of measurement as such defines managerial performance or successful policymaking. Davies echoes this perspective when he attributes the rise and fall of the English municipalities' Comprehensive Performance Assessments to the (unrealistic) rhetoric of positivism in English government (Davis, 2011). The government dropped the performance management system based on the Public Service Agreements.

## 3 All performance movements are political

All performance movements are political in the sense that they all have a power dimension. Agendas, hidden or not, are always an ingredient of the movement. Performance movements have been the subject of tactical manoeuvres between legislatures, and executives, between politics and administration, between horizontal and vertical departments, and between political parties. The early twentieth-century attempts to separate politics from administration had as a purpose a power shift from political appointees to administrators. The agenda of performance budgeting reforms in the USA and Australia in the 1990s was to reinforce control of the political executive over the departments and the agencies (Sterck, 2007). PPBS was, besides a planning system, an attempt of the executive to get a grip on a fragmented public sector. In the 1930s, the New Deal programmes addressing the Great Depression were mainly executed through new organizational structures such as the Tennessee Value Authority. These organizations and agencies were deliberately located outside of the realm of the traditional Washington bureaucracies. This led to a fragmentation of the executive branch of government. Performance budgeting was expected to re-establish executive control through a clear line of executive authority (Kelly & Rivenbark, 2003). More recently, Lavertu et al. (2013) showed that the nominally neutral Program Assessment Rating Tool (PART) of the Bush presidency was politicized because political reformers treated liberal- and conservative-leaning programmes differently by exercising greater scrutiny over implementation in liberal agencies.

**53**

## 4 Performance movements have a similar set of carriers for performance ideas

We defined movements as informally organized around a set of ideas. Since ideas are the glue holding the movement together, ideas need to be distributed. Performance management ideas need carriers. A common set of carriers can be found in most movements.

(a) Movements need some main proponents that symbolize the movement. Names such as Frederick Taylor (scientific management), Woodrow Wilson (science of administration) and Vice President Al Gore (NPM) are emblematic for their respective movements in the United States. Performance heroes need not however be persons. Often, cases – labelled best practices – serve the same heroic function. The New York Bureau of Municipal Research, PPBS in the American army and NPM in New Zealand and Australia are some examples. These figures and cases make movements identifiable in different places and times.

(b) Movements need to be endorsed by organizations and associations promoting the ideas of the movement. The International City/County Management Association for instance had a long history in disseminating performance measurement in the local public sector in the United States. A more recent example is the Public Management Section (PUMA) of the OECD, which promoted NPM concepts in its member countries. Pal (2012) reviews the OECD story of management reform.

(c) Movements need their 'biblical' texts – academically flavoured and typically written by the main figures of a movement. Such key texts are used for research, training and advocacy. One of the key texts of the NPM movement in the USA for instance has been Osborne and Gaebler's *Reinventing Government* (1993). It is well written and persuasive. Although the book is practice-oriented, it is larded with scientific argumentation. Other movements have had similar key texts. Bauer's (1966) assessment of the side effects of the NASA space programme has had a similar function for the social indicator movement.

(d) Movements need to influence the curricula of the universities. Almost all twentieth-century movements set up courses, academic conferences and their own journals, such as social indicators research and a host of journals for evidence-based practices in healthcare, social work, schools, nursing and mental health, and so on.

## 5 The export of practices has been a deliberate policy

In the twentieth century, the export of performance practices has become a deliberate strategy of actors that confess to a performance movement. The NYBMR intentionally exported its work to other communities through the provision of services and through contacts with agencies and officials. The PPBS system too was intentionally promoted in other countries as well as in the private sector. The same applies to NPM. In the late 1990s, many international delegations visited the NPM champions, such as New Zealand and the United Kingdom. German local officials travelled to the city of Tilburg in the Netherlands – an acknowledged NPM champion. It led a Dutch academic to conclude that everyone seemed to be applying the Tilburg model, apart from Tilburg itself. While the city was hiring an external consultant to organize the reception of delegations, the city itself was already changing its course (Kickert, 2003).

## 2.2 Change

Despite the continuities, there are some remarkable changes too. First, there has been a technological revolution that revitalized old concepts. Second, and most importantly, the intensity of the use of performance information has changed.

## 1 Technological evolution enables the reinvention of old concepts

The technological infrastructure for measuring performance has improved significantly. The most relevant evolutions have been the unparalleled increase in processing power of computers and the development of networks. Information technology enables better generation, display and analysis of the performance information, and performance data can be generated more easily thanks to the automation of administrative record keeping. This is in particular the case for collecting output data and less so for outcome measures. The latter usually are not embedded in the administrative information systems and therefore remain notoriously difficult to collect.

These technological evolutions allow the revival of old concepts. Geographic Information Systems (GIS) are a good illustration (Goodchild & Janelle, 2004). In essence, GIS provides knowledge about *what* is happening *where* and *when*. The modern concept of building a spatial data infrastructure is not conceptually different from Charles Booth's attempts to build a social map of London where social characteristics were attributed to spatial data (the location of the houses). Modern techniques however have expanded the amount of data that can be linked to the reference map. Different layers of data can be combined, for instance linking up crime, unemployment, traffic congestion and air quality in the neighbourhoods of

**55**

a city. The prospect of big data and cloud sourcing applications opens up new avenues for evidence-based management. A high-profile example is Google's flu prediction, which could enable health actors to take pre-emptory measures (Lazer, Kennedy, King & Vespignani, 2014). Despite its benefits, big data also raises new privacy concerns (Tene & Polonetsky, 2012).

## 2 Institutionalization, professionalization and specialization of use

Probably the most important change in the subsequent performance movements is in the use of performance information (Bouckaert, 1990). Performance information use has become (a) more institutionalized and (b) more professional.

(a) The use of performance information has gradually been institutionalized. Early twentieth-century movements such as the social survey and the NYBMR generally operated in the periphery of government. Although these movements were innovative and influential, the impact on the government of the day should not be overrated. Davidson (1991) concluded from a historical analysis that, although senior researchers of the social survey movement were appointed to positions in the British government, there is little evidence of their impact (p. 360). Similarly, it took scientific management and the science of adminis-tration several decades to penetrate the core of government. Arguably, this only happened with the mandatory adoption of PPBS in the federal adminis-tration (Schick, 1966). By that time, the science of administration was included in the curricula of the most important schools (Williams, 2003). Nowadays, performance measurement has become a focal part of management that is often laid down in management scorecards and management information systems. Increasingly, performance management is seen as part of the job of the contemporary manager. We argued before that a commitment to measurement can also be of a symbolic nature – a commitment to rationality. Yet, since contemporary performance movements such as NPM are furthering the performance discourse, it becomes real in its consequences.

(b) Parallel with institutionalization, there has been an increasing profession-alization of measurement. This trend has two dimensions. On the *supply side* of information, professionalization implies that measurement has become a profession with a mounting number of measurement professionals: manage-ment accountants, management consultants, policy advisors in think tanks and analysts in statistical offices. This measurement profession may run counter to traditional professions that experience measurement as an intrusion upon their autonomy (Johnsen, 2008; Brodkin, 2011). On the *demand side* of information, information is handled more professionally. The most important trend seems to be that performance information has gradually become embedded in systems of accountability between the executive and top managers, between tiers of government, between institutions (schools, hospitals) and central departments, and between employees and their supervisors. These systems of accountability were the hallmark of NPM applications of performance management. Increasingly, the accountability approach to performance management is critiqued. We will argue in the following chapters that other uses of performance information may be more fruitful.

## 3 CONCLUSION

Mintzberg's (1994) influential article on strategic planning argued that it is always our own age that is turbulent and that therefore turbulence is normalcy. Does this apply to measurement in and of the public sector too? Is change in performance measurement mainly superficial spin while the bottom line remains untouched? Are recent measurement efforts about normalcy rather than change? We do not think so. Although there are tides of reform, every performance movement leaves some sediment which is acquired for future movements. The mapping of poverty was something novel in the late nineteenth and early twentieth centuries. Nowadays, poverty indicators are an institutionalized means of assessing government performance in the provision and redistribution of prosperity.

One of the most notable evolutions in the twentieth-century performance movements has been the ever-increasing integration of measurement in the core processes of the public sector. The quantification of government started at the periphery of government. The twentieth century has witnessed a growing integration of measurement within and by the public sector itself. Quantitative approaches to policy and management became an inclusive part of government.

NPM was the first movement that introduced performance information in public management on a government-wide scale, on an international scale and in all management functions. However, NPM did not come out of the blue. It was conceptually conceived in the early twentieth century. Only after a long incubation period does the performance mindset seem to have reached the fibres of government, for the better and the worse.

## FURTHER READING

This chapter is based on a book chapter titled 'Nothing New Under the Sun? Change and Continuity in the 20th Century Performance Movements' (Van Dooren, 2008). Another historical overview of performance movements is Bouckaert's 'The History of the Productivity Movement' (1990). Williams (2004, 2003) published several articles about performance measurement in the early twentieth century. Schachter (1989) pointed to the relevance of Taylor for public administration (and for performance management). Bulmer *et al.* (1991) described the social survey movement. Kelly & Rivenbark (2003) documented the historical roots of performance budgeting.

## REFERENCES

Bauer, R. A. (1966). *Social Indicators*. Cambridge: MIT Press.

Bouckaert, G. (1990). 'The History of the Productivity Movement'. *Public Productivity & Management Review*, 14, 53–89.

Bouckaert, G., & Halligan, J. (2008). *Managing Performance: International Comparisons*. London: Routledge.

Brodkin, E. Z. (2011). 'Policy Work: Street-Level Organizations under New Managerialism'. *Journal of Public Administration Research and Theory*, 21 (supplement 2), i253–i277.

Bulmer, M. (2001). 'Social Measurement: What Stands in Its Way?' *Social Research*, 68, 455–80.

Bulmer, M., Bales, K., & Sklar, K. K. (1991). *The Social Survey in Historical Perspective, 1880–1940*. Cambridge: Cambridge University Press.

Burnham, P. (2001). 'New Labour and the Politics of Depoliticisation'. *British Journal of Politics and International Relations*, 3, 127–49.

Cangiano, M., Curristine, T., & Lazare, M. (eds) (2013). *Public Finance Management and Its Emerging Architecture*. New York: International Monetary Fund.

Cangiano, M., Curristine, T. & Lazare, M. (2013) 'The Emerging Architecture of Public Financial Management'. In Cangiano, M., Curristine, T. & Lazare, M. (eds) *Public Financial Management and Its Emerging Architecture* (pp. 1–17). New York: International Monetary Fund.

Carter, N., Klein, R., & Day, P. (1992). *How Organizations Measure Success: The Use of Performance Indicators in Government*. London: Routledge.

Curristine, T., & Flynn, S. (2013). 'In Search of Results: Strengthening Public Sector Performance'. In Cangiano, M., & Curristine, T. (eds) *Public Finance Management and Its Emerging Architecture* (pp. 203–32). New York: International Monetary Fund.

Davidson, R. (1991). 'The Social Survey in Historical Perspective: A Governmental Perspective'. In Bulmer, M., Bales, K., & Sklar, K. K. *The Social Survey in Historical Perspective: 1880–1940*. Cambridge: Cambridge University Press.

Davies, H. T. O., Nutley, S. M., & Smith, P. C. (2000). *What Works? Evidence-Based Policy and Practice in Public Services*. London: The Policy Press.

Davis, P. (2011). 'The English Audit Commission and Its Comprehensive Performance Assessment Framework for Local Government, 2002–8'. *Public Performance & Management Review*, 34(4), 489–514.

De Neufville, J. I. (1975). *Social Indicators and Public Policy: Interactive Processes of Design and Application*. Amsterdam: Elsevier.

Department of Finance and Deregulation (Commonwealth of Australia) (2012). 'Sharpening the Focus: A Framework for Improving Commonwealth Performance'. Canberra: Department of Finance.

Eckersley, R. (1998). *Measuring Progress: Is Life Getting Better?* Collingwood: CSIRO Publishing.

Feldman, M. S., & March, J. G. (1981). 'Information in Organizations as Signal and Symbol'. *Administrative Science Quarterly*, 26, 171.

General Accounting Office (1997). *Performance Budgeting: Past Initiatives Offer Insights for GPRA Implementation (GAO/AIMD-97–46)*. Washington, DC: U.S. General Accounting Office.

—— (2004). *Performance Budgeting: OMB's Program Assessment Rating Tool Presents Opportunities and Challenges for Budget and Performance Integration (GAO-04-439T)*. Washington, DC: General Accounting Office.

Goodchild, M. F., & Janelle, D. G. (2004). *Spatially Integrated Social Science*. Oxford: Oxford University Press.

Gulick, L., & Urwick, L. (1937). 'Notes on the Theory of Organizations. With Special Reference to Government'. In *Papers on the Science of Administration* (pp. 1–45). New York: A. M. Kelley.

Hood, C. (1991). 'A Public Management for All Seasons'. *Public Administration*, 69, 3–19.

House of Commons Science and Technology Committee (2006). *Scientific Advice, Risk, and Evidence Based Policy Making*. London: The Stationery Office.

Johnsen, A. (2008). 'Performance Information and Educational Policy Making'. In Van Dooren, W., & Van De Walle, S. (eds) *Performance Information in the Public Sector: How It Is Used*. Basingstoke: Palgrave Macmillan.

Kelly, J. M., & Rivenbark, W. C. (2003). *Performance Budgeting for State and Local Government*. Armonk, NY: M. E. Sharpe.

Kickert, W. (2003). 'Beyond Public Management'. *Public Management Review*, 5, 377–99.

Lavertu, S., Lewis, D. E., & Moynihan, D. P. (2013). 'Government Reform, Political Ideology, and Administrative Burden: The Case of Performance Management in the Bush Administration'. *Public Administration Review*, 73(6), 845–57.

Lazer, D., Kennedy, R., King, G., & Vespignani, A. (2014). 'The Parable of Google Flu: Traps in Big Data Analysis'. *Science*, 343 (14 March), 1203–5.

Linsley, C. A., & Linsley, C. L. (1993). 'Booth, Rowntree, and Llewelyn Smith: A Reassessment of Interwar Poverty'. *Economic History Review*, 46, 88–104.

McAffery, J. L., & Jones, L. R. (2004). *Budgeting and Financial Management for National Defence*. Greenwich, CT: Information Age Publishers.

Mintzberg, H. (1994). 'The Fall and Rise of Strategic Planning'. *Harvard Business Review*, 72, 107–14.

Mosher, F. C. (1968). *Democracy and the Civil Service*. New York: Oxford University Press.

Mouffe, C. (2000). *The Democratic Paradox*. London: Verso Books.

Novick, D. (1973). *Current Practice in Program Budgeting (PPBS): Analysis and Case Studies Covering Government and Business*. London: Heinneman.

Osborne, D., & Gaebler, T. (1993). *Reinventing Government: How the Entrepreneurial Spirit Is Transforming the Public Sector from Schoolhouse to State House*. Reading, MA: Addison Wesley.

Pal, L. (2012). *Frontiers of Governance: The OECD and Global Public Management Reform*. Basingstoke: Palgrave

Pollitt, C. (1993). *Managerialism and the Public Services: Cuts or Cultural Change in the 1990s?* Oxford: Blackwell.

Pollitt, C., & Bouckaert, G. (2011). *Public Management Reform: A Comparative Analysis* (3rd ed.). Oxford: Oxford University Press.

Premfors, R. (1998). 'Reshaping the Democratic State: Swedish Experiences in International Perspective'. *Public Administration*, 76, 141–59.

Previts, G. J., & Merino, B. D. (1979). *A History of Accounting in America: An Historical Interpretation of the Cultural Significance of Accounting*. New York: Wiley.

Radin, B. A. (2000). 'The Government Performance and Results Act and the Tradition of Federal Management Reform: Square Pegs in Round Holes'. *Journal of Public Administration Research and Theory*, 10, 111–35.

—— (2006). *Challenging the Performance Movement: Accountability, Complexity, and Democratic Values*. Georgetown: University Press.

Ridley, C. E., & Simon, H. (1938). *Measuring Municipal Activities. A Survey of Suggested Criteria and Reporting Forms for Appraising Administration*. Chicago, IL: The International City Managers' Association.

Rivenbark, W. C. (2005). 'A Historical Overview of Cost Accounting in Local Government'. *State & Local Government Review*, 37, 217–27.

Robinson, M., & Brumby, J. (2005). 'Does Performance Budgeting Work? An Analytical Review of the Empirical Literature'. IMF Working Paper. Washington, DC: IMF.

Rose, R. (1976). 'On the Priorities of Government: A Developmental Analysis of Public Policies'. *European Journal of Political Research*, 4, 247–89.

Sayre, W. S. (1958). 'Premises of Public Administration: Past and Emerging'. *Public Administration Review*, 18, 102–5.

Schachter, H. L. (1989). *Frederick Taylor and the Public Administration Community: A Reevaluation*. New York: State University of New York.

Schick, A. (1966). 'The Road to PPB: The Stages of Budget Reform'. *Public Administration Review*, 26, 243–58.

—— (1990). 'Budgeting for Results: Recent Developments in Five Industrialized Countries'. *Public Administration Review*, 50, 26–34.

Shafritz, J. M., & Hyde, A. C. (2004). *Classics of Public Administration*. Harcourt: Brace College Publishers.

Solesbury, W. (2001). *Evidence Based Policy: Whence It Came and Where It's Going*. London: ESRC UK Centre for Evidence Based Policy and Practice.

Sterck, M. (2007). 'The Impact of Performance Budgeting on the Role of the Legislature: A Four-Country Study'. *International Review of Administrative Sciences*, 73, 189–203.

Stivers, C. (2000). *Bureau Men, Settlement Women: Constructing Public Administration in the Progressive Era*. Kansas: University Press of Kansas.

Talbot, C. (1999). 'Public Performance – Towards a New Model?'. *Public Policy and Administration*, 14, 15–34.

Tene, O., & Polonetsky, J. (2012). 'Privacy in the Age of Big Data: A Time for Big Decisions'. *Stanford Law Review Online*, 64, 63.

Van Dooren, W. (2008). 'Nothing New Under the Sun? Change and Continuity in the 20th Century Performance Movement'. In Van Dooren, W., & Van De Walle, S. (eds) *Performance Information in the Public Sector: How It Is Used*. Basingstoke: Palgrave Macmillan.

Van Riper, P. P. (1983). 'The American Administrative State: Wilson and the Founders – An Unorthodox View'. *Public Administration Review*, 43, 477–90.

Wildavsky, A. (1969). 'Rescuing Policy Analysis from PPBS'. *Public Administration Review*, 29, 189–202.

Williams, D. W. (2000). 'Reinventing the Proverbs of Government'. *Public Administration Review*, 60, 522–34.

—— (2003). 'Measuring Government in the Early Twentieth Century'. *Public Administration Review*, 63, 643–59.

—— (2004). 'Evolution of Performance Measurement until 1930'. *Administration Society*, 36, 131–65.

# Chapter 4

# Performance measurement

**LEARNING OBJECTIVES**

■ To identify the main steps and the design parameters in the measurement process.

■ To understand variation in the potential measurement designs.

**KEY POINTS IN THIS CHAPTER**

■ Performance measurement is a process in five steps: prioritizing, indicator selection, data collection, analysis and reporting.

■ Quality is a point of attention in each of these steps.

■ Each step involves a range of choices, which should be made based on the envisaged *use* of performance information.

**DISCUSSION QUESTIONS**

■ Consider a set of indicators (for instance in an annual report or reported in a newspaper).

 – What is the mental map behind the indicators?
 – How relevant are indicators for the framework?
 – What are the motivations behind the prioritizing of the indicators?
 – Are the indicators data driven or not?
 – What are the data sources?
 – What is the level of analysis?
 – What is the quality of the set (validity, reliability, functionality, legitimacy)?

Wordnet, an online dictionary at Princeton, defines measurement in general terms as *the act or process of assigning numbers to phenomena according to a rule* (Miller, 2009). This chapter discusses the process of assigning numbers to the phenomenon of public sector performance. According to the definition, the assignment of numbers should follow a rule. The formulation of the performance indicators can be conceived as the measurement rule for public sector performance.

Performance measurement is conceived as a *process* in five steps (Figure 4.1). The first step is about prioritizing the measurement efforts. The question of what is being measured needs to be answered. Next, indicators need to be selected. Subsequently, data need to be collected and results need to be analysed. Finally, findings need to be reported. Throughout the process, quality of measurement is an important point of attention.

We use the stages as an ideal-typical representation of the measurement process. To depict measurement as an orderly process of distinct and chronological steps may however not necessarily correspond to reality. It is for instance a quite common practice to select only those indicators for which data are available. Data collection in this case precedes and determines indicator selection and, as a result, measurement may be biased towards measureable dimensions. The description of the ideal type however is useful for identifying such deviations from a pure measurement model.

**Figure 4.1** *An ideal-typical model of the performance measurement process*

## STEP 1: PRIORITISING MEASUREMENT EFFORTS

The first phase in the measurement process is about prioritizing measurement efforts. It is impossible to measure everything, and hence, choices have to be made. It is even epistemologically inconceivable to measure everything. Performance measurement possesses the dialectic nature of knowledge creation: the more we know, the more we become aware of what we do not know. Bouckaert (1993) describes a study by mathematician Mandelbrot, who demonstrated that the length of the British coastline approaches infinity when more measurement points are introduced (Figure 4.2). With the introduction of more detail in measurement, more bays, inlets and peninsulas are uncovered and included in its measurement. Similarly, while probing the performance concept, every indicator will generate new questions and uncover new dimensions that are not yet measured. For example, quantification of performance in the academic world through international publications, citation indices and impact factors led to a renewed debate on the quality of research and the failure of many performance indicators to accurately grasp these dimensions (Merton, 1988).

The question is then how to prioritize measurement. To measure 'performance' of the 'organization', 'programme' or 'policy' does not usually give a precise clue. Through interaction however, people develop mental maps that make sense and define these terms (Weick, 1995). Implicit and partially shared definitions are codified on several occasions, for example when an organization draws up a new

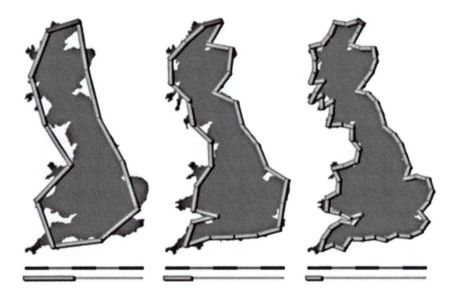

**Figure 4.2** The length of the British coastline (source: Wikipedia)

organization chart, a policy programme sets out its objectives, or a minister drafts a policy brief. In order to target measurement efforts, the implicit mental picture of the organization, programme or sector needs to be exposed. These frameworks *in* which and *through* which we can think about management, policy and performance are of vital importance for measurement efforts. Before developing

---

## BOX 4.1 THE RISK OF CONCEPT REDUCTION

The risk of concept reduction occurs when a solution for the problem of fractional measurement is to define the social concept as only that which is measured by the operational definition. This is according to Etzioni & Lehman (1967) a more apparent than real solution, since concepts have an established content, institutionalized either in common parlance or in technical, theoretical formulations – and occasionally in both. To act as if an operational definition were automatically the same as the underlying concept is a questionable procedure, and it is also likely to have important negative consequences in the realm of policymaking, they argue.

Etzioni & Lehman (1967) discuss the example of intelligence tests, which were initially assumed to measure native intelligence. However, as data have accumulated, it has become apparent that such factors as cultural background, social class, past learning experiences and the like influence performance on these tests. They argue that concept reduction by stating that intellectual capacity is whatever intelligence quotient (IQ) tests measure is harmful for two reasons. First, people told that they have a low IQ will continue to interpret this statement as if they lack intellectual capabilities; and second, by denying the significant residue in the concept, the road towards better IQ tests and more encompassing measurements is blocked.

As a solution, Etzioni & Lehman (1967) point to the importance of mapping the dimensions of concepts. They argue that

> the concept of mental health implies more than the avoidance of psychiatric hospitalisation; the quality of a society's educational system cannot be gauged solely by the number of Ph.D.'s it produces; and a man's satisfaction with his job involves more than satisfaction with his income.
>
> (p. 3)

Similarly, the measurement of performance of a public agency requires a careful analysis of the dimensions of performance as well as the dimensions of the agency.

*(Etzioni & Lehman, 1967: pp. 8–9)*

performance indicators, the mental maps of what we are supposed to measure (in our case, performance) need to be on the table.

When people employ a framework, they are imposing a way of thinking about the world. Too often people do not critically reflect upon the frameworks in use. We are susceptible to confirmation bias and thus tend to see what we are looking for. This may lead to what could be called the implicit prioritizing of measurement efforts – although implicit *attribution* might be a better term since there is no intentionality or deliberation in selecting the indicators. As a result, indicators risk reconfirming and even reinforcing preconceived standpoints, rather than providing an account of performance. Etzioni & Lehman (1967) explain by means of the example of IQ tests how a complex concept such as intelligence is reduced to its operational definition in the test (see Box 4.1).

Three issues are thus of importance when discussing the mental maps that are used for measurement.

1    What is the mental picture or map of the organization, programme or policy?
2    What are the priorities for performance measurement?
3    What is the argumentation for making a priority?

1    In order to decide what to measure, we first need an understanding of what we are measuring. A representation of the organization, programme or policy field is needed. As we argued above, such representations or models are quite common in everyday situations. In everyday life, we need a menu to decide what to eat, a map to decide where to go and a travel guide to decide where to take our vacation. Similarly, we need a representation of the organization, programme or policy field in order to decide what to measure. Such a representation can be conceived in different ways.

One of the most common representations of an organization is the *organizational chart*, which visually depicts the division of tasks and responsibilities. The chart defines the structure of the organization and hence it is a representation of the organization.

*Management models* such as the Balanced Scorecard, the Common Assessment Framework, the EFQM model and the ISO model provide managers with a representation of the dimensions of good management (see Bovaird & Löffler, 2003 for an overview).

*Trees of objectives.* Strategic planning processes prescribe the development of a logically consistent tree of objectives. Starting from a mission statement, organizations have to develop strategic goals from which operational goals are derived. The operational objectives guide the use of resources. It is a representation of the purpose of the organization.

*Stakeholder analysis* can provide a representation of the external relations of the organization (see Mitchell, Agle & Wood, 1997 for an overview of stakeholder theory). Measurement can be targeted to the concerns of those stakeholders that matter most.

A *programme logic* represents the inputs and components of a programme, as well as short-term and long-term outcomes, along with the assumed linkages. Programme logic models help to identify the outputs and outcomes of organizations and programmes. They are seen as a necessary step preceding the selection of indicators for policy programmes (Hatry, 1999).

There is a substantial literature on *programme theory*. A programme logic rarely outlines the underlying mechanisms that are presumed to be responsible for the linkages between outputs and outcomes (Rogers *et al.*, 2000). These underlying mechanisms need to be reconstructed. Leeuw (2003) regroups the methods for reconstruction in a policy-scientific cluster, a strategic assessment cluster and an elicitation cluster.

2    Once we have gained an understanding of the organization, programme or policy, it is possible to prioritize measurement efforts. As previously argued, it is unrealistic to pursue a measurement system that perfectly mirrors every aspect of the organization or programme, its policies and environment. The complexity and multi-dimensionality of public management and policy make it practically impossible to measure everything. If it is assumed that it is impossible to measure everything, a choice has to be made on what to measure and what not to measure. Table 4.1 suggests different cut-outs for which measurement can be developed. The measurement object can be delineated by selecting a part of the organization or programme (internal focus) and/or by selecting a set of policy variables (external focus). The appropriate approach will depend on what the performance information is needed for (see chapter 6 on use).

**Table 4.1** *Definition of the measurement object*

- Which part of the organization or programme will be measured?
- Which part of the organization chart? All the divisions or only a selection?
- Which input? Which entries of the budget? Which staff members?
- Which activities? Which processes?
- Which outputs? Which products of the organizations (goods and services) are being measured?
- Which part of the policy objectives is being measured?
- Which intermediate ends? Which target groups? Which geographical circumscriptions?
- Which outcomes? Only the intended outcomes, or also the side effects and cross-cutting impacts?
- Which contextual factors are taken into account?

**67**

3    Finally, we turn to the arguments that could help in prioritizing measurement. These arguments are often mutually exclusive. Moreover, there are no generally right or wrong argumentations. Measurement prioritization depends, again, on the (planned) use of performance information (see chapter 6).

(a) *Indications of problems.* Measurement can be initiated when there are indications of problems through symptoms such as complaints or waiting lists. It is assumed that measurement is needed to get a better grip on the problems at hand.

(b) *Financial importance.* In many organizations, a small amount of the activities accounts for the majority of the budget. By measuring these activities, the organization has a good coverage of the budget. Similarly, by measuring a limited amount of activities, most of the personnel may be comprised in the measurement system.

(c) *Societal visibility.* Some activities which may not have a high financial impact may still have a high societal visibility. Theories of issue salience and agenda setting have demonstrated that media, politicians and the civil society have a selective interest in particular activities (see for instance Galtung & Ruge, 1965 for media salience and Baumgartner & Jones, 1993 for a model of agenda setting). By measuring these activities, the organization may be able to respond to most of the issues that those actors bring up.

(d) *Feasibility.* Some processes or outcomes are easier to measure than others (see chapter 2). Feasibility of the measurement effort is a valid criterion from a developmental perspective. In order to overcome resistance and to make people accustomed to measurement, some quick wins from measurement may be beneficial.

(e) *Diffusion.* Measurement efforts can be dispersed throughout the organization, programme or policy field. The strategy to have some measurement for many rather than doing an intense measurement for some may for instance be prompted by the desire to introduce a results-oriented culture in the whole organization. The plea of many practitioners' texts for a limited set of key performance indicators (KPIs) fits into this line of reasoning. Kaplan & Norton's book on the Balanced Scorecard is good example (1996).

(f) *Cost of measurement.* Measurement can be a costly activity, and in some cases the potential benefits of measurement do not weigh up against the costs. It should be noted that benefits of measurement are usually much more difficult to observe than the costs of measurement.

(g) *Predetermination.* Often, there is no choice on what to measure. This is for instance the case for international reporting obligations. Within the European Union, the Lisbon criteria are an example of a predetermined indicator set that is imposed upon member states.

## STEP 2: SELECTION OF THE INDICATORS

The second step deals with the selection of the indicators. After deciding *what* to measure, one needs to determine *how* to measure. The selection of indicators largely depends on the specialized expertise in organizations or policy domains. Obviously, performance indicators will differ in a cultural programme, a fiscal administration or an environmental agency. In this section, we do not discuss the substance of developing indicators but focus on indicators in general terms.

The production model of performance, represented in chapter 2, is a widely shared base for defining indicators. This model guides the development of single and ratio indicators that combine the dimensions of the model (Table 4.2). The choice of the indicators depends on how performance information will be used (see chapter 6).

Several criteria for good indicators are in circulation (see for instance Broom, 1998; Hatry, 1999; United Way of America, 1999; Treasury, 2001). The list below provides the main qualities of the indicators.

First, good indicators are *sensitive to change*. For instance, a measure for customer satisfaction that relies on a yes/no question will fail to register the difference between someone being just satisfied and very satisfied. Indicators should also be *precisely defined*. There needs to be an unambiguous understanding of the indicator. Building such understanding amongst experts in an organization is often a lengthy process that results in quite detailed indicator descriptions. Another requirement

**Table 4.2** *Single and ratio indicators*

| Single indicators | |
| --- | --- |
| Indicators on input | What goes into the system? Which resources are used? |
| Indicators on output | Which products and services are delivered? What is the quality of these products and services? |
| Indicators on intermediate outcomes | What are the immediate impacts of the output? |
| Indicators on final outcomes | What are the ultimate outcomes achieved that are significantly attributable to the output? |
| Indicators on the environment | What are the contextual variables that influence intermediate and final outcomes? |

| Ratio indicators | |
| --- | --- |
| Efficiency | Cost/output |
| Productivity | Output/input |
| Effectiveness | Output/outcome (intermediate or final) |
| Cost-effectiveness | Input/outcome (intermediate or final) |

however posits that indicators should be *understandable for users*. To define an indicator that is both easy to understand and precise is a balancing act (Box 4.2). A fourth requirement is that indicators are *documented*. This implies the development of meta-documentation that includes amongst others things the definition of the indicator, the measurement unit, the data sources, the time series, possible breaks in the time series and the responsibilities for administering the indicator. Documentation is important to assure that the measurement processes can be verified, for instance by external auditors. Fifth, indicators need to be *relevant and actionable*. They should reflect important dimensions of the concept that is being measured and guide the users towards actions to improve performance. For indicators to be relevant for decision-making, they also need to be *timely*. Next, data collection needs to be *feasible*. Finally, indicators should *comply with coordinated data processes and definitions*. The dual trend of increasing specialization/fragmentation on the one hand and coordination/interdependence on the other also reflects on performance measurement. Many performance indicators will

---

## BOX 4.2 INDICATORS NEED TO BE PRECISELY DEFINED AND EASY TO UNDERSTAND – A BALANCING ACT

The OECD, in a publication called *Pensions at a Glance*, defines the indicator of the Net Pensions Replacement Rate (2006). It seems a straightforward concept: the percentage of a pre-retirement income that is acquired through a retirement allowance. Nonetheless, several clarifications are needed to attain an acceptable level of precision.

> The net replacement rate is defined as the individual net pension entitlement divided by net pre-retirement earnings, taking account of personal income taxes and social security contributions paid by workers and pensioners. Otherwise, the definition and measurement of the net replacement rates are the same as for the gross replacement rate (see previous indicator). The results again cover full-career workers with median earnings and with 0.5, 0.75, 1, 1.5 and 2 times average (mean) earnings.
>
> (OECD, 2006: p. 34)

In a study of the use of prescription data by Dutch GPs, De Bont & Grit (2012) argue that performance measurement can be done better by general, less accurate measurements than by complex – and possibly more accurate – ones. They further argue that indicators do not have to be complex, as long as they connect with day-to-day practices and vice versa.

only be useful when they can be compared with results of other organizations or when joint analyses can be made. Compliance with definitions is a necessary.

## STEP 3: DATA COLLECTION

Data collection procedures and sources are vital. Each method has different strengths and weaknesses (Hatry, 1999). A first distinction is whether organizations use internal or external data sources. Internal data is produced by the organization itself, while external data is purchased or obtained from outside. Internal data is usually cheaper and more readily available than external information. However, in principal agent relationships, the principal (e.g. a department) may not trust information produced by the agent (e.g. an executive agency). Therefore, third parties may be asked to collect the data, or at least to audit the data provided by the agent.

A further refinement of the data sources is represented in Table 4.3, which also assesses the advantages and disadvantages of different data sources (Weiss, 1998; Hatry, 1999; United Way of America, 1999).

Most organizations have administrative registration systems of their activities: project planning and monitoring, dossier tracking systems, time registration systems, client databases, etcetera. Such *existing registration systems* have several advantages. The data usually are cheap, readily available, uninterrupted and well understood (see also Pollitt's article from 2000 on institutional amnesia for an appreciation of administrative registration systems). The main disadvantage is their path-dependent character. These systems are gradually built throughout time, and past decisions may strongly affect future options for registration. Administrative registration for instance does usually not focus on outcomes and does not have data on drop-out cases or target groups that are not reached by policies.

Nonetheless, it seems useful to look at existing administrative registration systems first as a default data source. Only when administrative registrations cannot provide the data, as will be often the case, other data sources should be considered. We briefly sketch the alternatives.

1   First, *extra registrations* could be added to existing registrations. For instance, in the context of gender programmes, counter clerks could be asked for the gender registration of the applicants for social benefits. The main cost of extra registration is the staff time invested. This cost is less visible compared to the financial costs of outsourced data gathering. Additional registrations will yield data more quickly when the typical dossier of the organization has a short processing cycle. An employment counselling service for instance will have extra data more swiftly compared to a fiscal administration (with typically a one-year cycle) or an organization that deals with foreign investment projects (with a multi-year cycle).

**71**

**Table 4.3** *Advantages and disadvantages of different data sources*

| Data source | Advantages | Disadvantages |
|---|---|---|
| Existing registrations | – continuity (time series)<br>– low cost<br>– in-house, good insight into quality and content<br>– readily available | – path-dependent focus<br>– no drop-out data<br>– less focus on outcome |
| Additional registrations | – continuity<br>– in-house, good insight into quality and content | – 'hidden' costs<br>– medium- to long-term availability |
| Surveys | – suitable for outcome information | – high cost<br>– medium-term availability<br>– response rate issue |
| Self-assessments | – low cost<br>– combination of quantitative and qualitative approaches<br>– linked to operations | – perceptual<br>– risk of gaming |
| Technical measurement | – non-obtrusive | – limited applicability on human services<br>– risk of technocracy |
| External observers | – limited obtrusiveness<br>– observers are not involved | – high costs for specialized observers<br>– medium- to long-term availability |
| Other public organizations | – usually low cost<br>– short-term availability | – confidentiality and privacy issues may interfere with data exchange<br>– less insight into quality and content (definitions) |
| Statistical, international and research institutions | – good quality<br>– authoritativeness<br>– readily available<br>– moderate costs<br>– continuity | – not directly tailored to organization's needs<br>– only outcomes |

2   A second option is to conduct a *survey* of customers or citizens. Often, surveys are the only way of obtaining outcome information, for instance in order to address changes in attitudes or knowledge. The main disadvantages are the costs of a survey and the growing difficulty of obtaining adequate response rates. Polling may yield data in shorter notice compared to a full-fledged survey, albeit often at the expense of validity and/or reliability.

3   Third, *self-assessments* have the advantage of combining measurement with qualitative assessments. A limitation is the perceptual nature of a self-assessment. Self-assessments are also vulnerable to strategic behaviour (gaming), in

particular when an outsider (media, principals) is known to be watching over the shoulder of the self-assessors.

4   Fourth, the main advantage of *technical measurement* is its non-intrusive character. Applications may be found in the environmental sector (e.g. air quality, water quality), in housing (e.g. level of humidity as an element of housing quality) and in public health (e.g. toxic substances in the population). The main disadvantage is its inapplicability to the majority of public service provision (i.e. most human services). Moreover, technical measurement may lead to technocratic measurement that is not understood by policymakers and managers and as such violates the quality criterion of intelligibility mentioned above.

5   Fifth, *external observers* may provide a neutral opinion on performance in a relatively unobtrusive way. US cities for instance used observers to assess the cleanliness of the streets. Disadvantages are the high costs (unless the external observers are volunteers) and the medium-term availability (given the time needed to train the observers).

6   Sixth, *administrative registrations of other organizations* may be useful. Ecological awareness programmes for instance could use the vehicle registration databases to assess their success in promoting environment-friendly cars. Privacy issues and an inadequate understanding of definitions and methods may complicate the use of other organizations' data.

7   Finally, *statistical institutions* (internationally and nationally) may provide good-quality data. This data however is seldom sufficiently specific to fulfil the organization's needs. Moreover, these statistics are mainly covering (often distant) outcomes such as employment, economic welfare and life expectancy. Sometimes it may appear that the authoritativeness of statistical institutions is used as a substitute for data quality – in particular in the international institutions. A review of the European Central Bank data on Public Sector Efficiency, World Bank data on government effectiveness, World Economic Forum data on public institutions and IMD business school data on government efficiency, however, shows serious weaknesses in all four rankings (Van de Walle, 2006; Arndt & Oman, 2006).

## STEP 4: ANALYSIS

Since numbers rarely speak for themselves, data need to be analysed. In essence, the purpose is to transform *data* into *information* that may lead to decisions. We distinguish three interpretative strategies: norm and target setting, breakouts, and causal analysis.

(a)   A first strategy is to confront a result with a norm (Weiss, 1998). When a norm is set in advance, it is called a target. While norms and targets often are plain numbers, more sophisticated variants take into account margins of error (Rubenstein

**73**

*et al.*, 2003). In some cases, there seems to be no conscious deliberation at all about the norm setting. Yet, behind this appearance of arbitrariness, implicit frames of reference may be at play.

There are several frames of reference for norms and targets. First, targets can be based on the *time dimension*. The norm then usually is to do at least as good as

**Table 4.4** *Foundations for targets*

| Fundament | Assessment | Example |
|---|---|---|
| Time | – fit for unique policy initiatives<br>– fit for organizations that have no counterpart<br>– fit for confidential information<br>– contextual variables may cause disturbance<br>– risk of stagnation, no innovative impulses from the outside | – trends in the number of youth in special care |
| Other organizations within the sector | – fit for comparing results of policies<br>– learning effects through confrontation with other practices<br>– controls for contextual variables | – the stress index for personnel of different organizations in the public sector<br>– the crime figures of one big city compared to another big city |
| Other organizations outside the sector | – fit to compare management results<br>– learning effects through confrontation with other practices<br>– comparability is harder to achieve | – sick leave in the private sector versus the public sector |
| Other countries | – fit for monopolists that have no national counterparts<br>– learning effects through confrontation with other practices<br>– difficulty of overcoming cultural and structural differences | – comparison of educational achievement through the OECD's 'education at a glance' reports |
| Scientific standards | – well funded, less debatable<br>– technical, risk of technocracy | – the vaccination level of the population that should be attained in order to eradicate a disease |
| Political and ideological norms | – embedded in the system, higher acceptation of the whole measurement system<br>– not always realistic (but not necessarily unrealistic) | – a zero norm for traffic casualties |

last year. In order to mitigate exceptional variation over time, a moving average may be suitable. Second, norms can be based on *comparisons with other organizations*: within the sector, outside the sector or in other jurisdictions or countries. Within organizations, divisions may be compared. The norm can be the average, the top quartile or the best-performing parts, or any other threshold. Third, *scientists* can calculate the norms. Tolerance levels of harmful substances in food and the living environment are examples. Fourth, norms may have a *political* foundation with mainly a symbolic function. Absolute norms, for instance to have no traffic casualties, are utopian. However, for symbolic reasons, they are maintained. Many countries have followed up on the Swedish Vision Zero campaign to have no traffic casualties. The message is that we should not rest on our laurels when for instance a 95 per cent target is attained.

Benchmarking techniques often support comparison with other organizations or countries. Useful technical approaches are Data Envelopment Analysis (DEA) and Free Disposal Hull (FDH) (Coelli & Rao, 1998). Figure 4.3 displays the two techniques. On the X-axis are the inputs used to produce outputs represented on the Y-axis. Different organizations will have different combinations of inputs and outputs, and thus, a different efficiency. Both DEA and FDH define a best-practice frontier of organizations. Organizations on the frontier are efficient, because there are no other organizations that produce more or the same output with the same or fewer inputs. The frontier can be shaped in different ways. DEA assumes a convex curve with diminishing returns to scale. Free Disposal Hull, the staircase-shaped line, makes no assumption as to the shape of the curve.

Every organization that is not on the frontier is inefficient. Compare for instance organization A with organization B on the FDH curve. B has a slightly higher

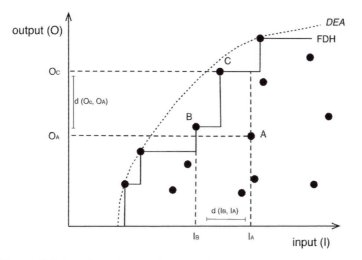

**Figure 4.3** Benchmarking techniques: free disposal hull and data envelopment analysis

**75**

output with substantially fewer inputs. The distance on the X-axis from IA to IB is the input inefficiency for organization A. B will be a good benchmark for A in order to learn about cost cutting and economies. Compared to organization C, A is using somewhat more inputs. Yet, C is producing substantially more outputs. The distance on the Y-axis from OA to OC is the output inefficiency for organization A. If A is mainly interested in improving performance and not so much in reducing inputs, C would be a good organization to benchmark with.

Stroobants & Bouckaert (2014) apply FDH and DEA to libraries. They also reviewed previous studies on libraries. Input measures that have been used include library staff, area of library space, expenditures, holdings and hours of operation. Typical output measures have been the number of reader visits, book circulation, website visits and the number of enquiries. In their study, they use expenditures (I), staff (I), circulation (O) and opening hours (O). From a comparison of the two techniques, they find that FDH (more efficient libraries) is not as strict as DEA (with fewer efficient observations). They also find that FDH is more suitable for learning because FDH can identify concrete libraries to compare with. DEA is more helpful in setting targets.

(b)    A second interpretative strategy is to break out data in order to understand *where*, *when* and for *whom* (e.g. for which target groups) performance is manifesting. This will require the breaking out or aggregation of the data to the appropriate level. For some purposes, more detailed information will be needed (for instance for cost accounting). For other purposes, the information may have to be more general and consolidated (for instance for reporting to parliament). Different purposes will require different aggregation levels. Breaking out and aggregation can be directed at the measurement objects or at the indicators.

1    The breaking out and the consolidation of information may be oriented towards the measurement *object*, such as regions or target groups. The indicator 'traffic casualties' for instance can be broken out for different regions or even different roads, or can be consolidated on a national level. The indicator of educational achievement can be broken out for gender, ethnicity or socio-economic background of the pupils, or can be aggregated.
2    Second, the breaking out and consolidation may be oriented towards different *indicators* that say something about a single measurement object. An example is the composition of a quality of life index for a neighbourhood. Indicators may for instance reflect the average surface of the houses, the number of crimes per capita, population density, amount of traffic, availability of parks, etcetera. Table 4.5 gives an example for water quality. The level of aggregation thus may range from a single indicator to an index of indicators on the one hand and from a single unit to a multitude of observations on the other hand.

**Table 4.5** *An illustration of breakouts and aggregation of data*

| Direction indicator<br><br>Direction subject | Indicator<br>Oxygen | Indicator<br>Fish stock | Indicator<br>Nitrogen | Σ indicators |
|---|---|---|---|---|
| Measurement subject River 1 | Oxygen in river 1 | Fish stock in river 1 | Nitrogen in river 1 | Water quality in river 1 |
| Measurement subject River X | Oxygen in river X | Fish stock in river X | Nitrogen in river X | Water quality in river X |
| Measurement subject River Xn | Oxygen in river Xn | Fish stock in river Xn | Nitrogen in river Xn | Water quality in river Xn |
| Σ measurement subjects | Oxygen in all rivers | Fish stock in all rivers | Nitrogen in all rivers | Water quality in all rivers |

The methodology for breaking out and consolidation should be revealed. Composite indicators are often suspicious, in particular when the methodology is not stated (Best, 2001). On the one hand, positive results can be sought by breaking out for the right categories. For instance, in order to mollify the perception of youth unemployment as being problematic, an employment agency may search for the optimal age brackets for breaking out unemployment statistics. On the other hand, negative data can be presented in a much nicer way by diluting them in a composed measure. Problems with a waiting list for hearing devices for instance can be hidden in an overall index of waiting lists for services for the disabled.

Three conditions need to be met before a meaningful aggregate index of diverse indicators can be compiled (Innes, 1990). First, there needs to be a *conceptual model* that provides meaning to the addition of elements. The index should correspond to an idea we can understand. For instance, the Consumer Price Index or the ecological footprint are comprehensible concepts – respectively the price of a basket of goods and services and the ecological impact of a person. Second, there needs to be a reasonable method to transform unlike things *to a common scale*. Economic indicators have money as a common unit of measurement. Many indices of non-economic phenomena such as quality of life struggle to meet this condition (Rossi & Gilmartin, 1980). How to combine for instance noise nuisance (measured in decibels) with proximity to shops and public services (measured in kilometres) in a single quality of life index? Third, indices often give different *weights* to the composing indicators. Since such weights are usually highly debatable and sometimes even necessarily arbitrary, the opportunities for embellishing performance are substantial. The weighting at least should be made explicit. Box 4.3 represents an extended list of criteria as defined by the OECD.

---

## BOX 4.3 OECD CRITERIA FOR CONSTRUCTING COMPOSITE INDICATORS

The OECD formulated a number of criteria for constructing composite indicators. Many recommendations boil down to the disclosure of methodologies and theories or, in other words, exposing the mental map that underpins the index.

- Clear theoretical framework
- Indicators selected on the basis of their quality and relevance
- The methodological choice in weighting and aggregation exposed
- Different approaches for imputing missing values exposed
- Indicators normalized to make them comparable
- Indicators aggregated and weighted according to the underlying theoretical framework
- Explicit assessments made of the robustness of the composite indicator
- Composite indicator correlated with other data
- Presentation should clarify, not mislead
- Underlying indicators or values should be readily available

*Source: OECD, 2009*

---

(c)  A third interpretative strategy is to search for causes of (under-)performance. This approach is connected to breaking out data. The choice of the breakout categories is often based on (often implicit) hypotheses about the explanatory variables. When for instance absenteeism statistics are broken out for gender, it may be assumed that women are more absent from work because of family affairs. However, when absenteeism data are broken out for commuting distances of staff, it is implicitly assumed that long travel times may be the cause for absenteeism.

The search for causes of performance however is substantially more far reaching than the simple breaking out of data. The relations can also be tested in statistical analyses, applying standard research methodologies. In many cases, however, the statistical analysis will not be sufficient. In order to get a more profound insight into the causes, qualitative research (interviews, focus groups, etc.) may be undertaken.

Attribution is an endemic debate in the performance literature. Often, it is very difficult to ascribe performance to the intervention of a particular programme or organization. The main reason is usually sought in the interference of socio-economic factors such as economic growth, demographics or ecological trends that lie beyond the scope of individual organizations or programmes. Noise in attribution analysis is however not only caused by socio-economic variables. Often it stems from other public programmes and organizations. The failure of a trade agency to attract foreign

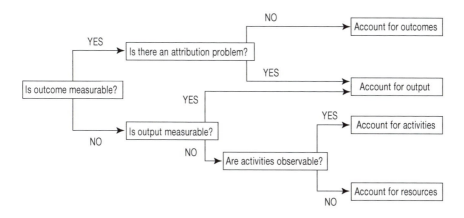

**Figure 4.4** *Outcomes in accountability relations (translated from Bouckaert, Van Dooren & Sterck, 2003)*

investment may be caused by failure of the agency, but also by fiscal policies imposing new taxes or by patent registration becoming more complex. Joined-up government (JUG) programmes, including JUG indicators, have been devised to overcome the negative effects of public programme interference (Bogdanor, 2005).

Attribution is important because indicators are often used to hold organizations accountable for their performance (see chapter 6). It would be unfair to judge organizations on outcome indicators when it is acknowledged that these measures are inadequate. Similarly, it is unreasonable to hold an organization responsible for success or failure when the outcomes can only be partly attributed to the programme or organization. In these cases, it would be better to account for output. Sometimes, when output is not measurable either, accountability can be based on activities/efforts. When even efforts are not observable, for instance in many diplomatic services, the only option will be to account for input. Figure 4.4 represents this accountability scheme based on the measurability of outcome and output, attribution of outcomes to an organization or public programme and the extent to which activities are observable.

## STEP 5: REPORTING

The last step in the process of measuring performance is reporting. The main point here is that the format should be appropriate for the target group (Rossi & Gilmartin, 1980; Hendricks, 1994). Obviously, the reporting of performance information to top management will require other reporting formats than for media or interest groups. Two questions thus should be answered.

*Who is consuming the information?* The most important target groups of performance information are represented in Box 4.4. The first category, the general public, is the proposed target group of many initiatives. In reality, it is hard

## BOX 4.4 TARGET GROUPS OF PERFORMANCE REPORTING

- the general public
- mass media: newspapers, radio, television
- interest groups
- advisory boards
- international institutions
- other governments
- executive politicians
- parliament
- the board of the organization
- top management
- middle management

to reach a significant part of the general public. The most evident way to reach the general public is through the mass media (for instance by buying publicity, releasing press statements). Other target groups may be interest groups, advisory boards, international institutions and other governments, for which performance information will have to be more specialized and detailed. The same detail is usually not expected by politicians – who want snapshot information. Managers usually prefer scorecard reporting, which can be quickly confronted with professional judgement (see chapter 7 for a discussion on the users of performance information).

*What is the right format?* Different formats for reporting performance information exist. Box 4.5 gives the main options. Annual reporting for instance will be a good instrument for reporting to stakeholders and interest groups. It should be noted

## BOX 4.5 FORMATS OF PERFORMANCE REPORTING

- annual reports and annual plans
- financial documents: budget and accounts
- specific publications in hard copy and/or on a website
- interactive information on a website
- oral witnesses
- news flashes
- publicity
- scorecards

that annual reports are for specialists. It is improbable that they have a direct impact on the public in general. Oral communications will be suitable for reporting to the middle and top management, together with scorecards. News flashes and publicity are instruments to reach the general public through the mass media.

# 1 QUALITY OF PERFORMANCE MEASUREMENT

Quality of performance information is important. First, when users of information learn about the weaknesses of performance information, the chances are that they disregard it. Non-use of performance information is a waste of resources. Moreover, it will be hard to regain trust in performance measurement that was discredited before. Second, and even more perniciously, poor quality information may nonetheless be used, which consequently may lead to wrong decisions and actions. Users of information (decision-makers, politicians, media) often lack the time and/or competences to assess the quality of performance information. Chapter 8 includes a more elaborate, theoretical discussion of the non-use of performance information.

The organization of quality assurance ideally parallels the control pyramid of auditors. The first level is the internal control system of the organization itself, which is performing the controls in order to obtain reasonable assurance about the operations of the organization. The second level is the internal audit that controls the control processes and assesses the risks. The internal audit reports to the management of the organization. Third, the external audit reviews the quality independently from the organization. When financial information is concerned, this system is well established. Non-financial information is however seldom included in the audit systems (Wholey, 1999).

Quality should not be confined to statistical quality. Quality should be an issue in the whole production process of performance information, where the quality of a preceding step is a necessary condition for the next step. Indicator development can only be done properly when the subject of measurement is well prioritized within an explicit mental framework of the programme or organization. Focused data collection has to be based on well-defined indicators. Meaningful analyses are only possible with high-quality data and reporting is only feasible based on appropriate analyses.

Bouckaert (1993) identifies three aspects of quality. First, quality implies the *functionality* of the measurement system. Measurement should be fit for use. There are two gradations of non-conformity to the functionality requirement: non-functionality and dysfunctionality. Non-functionality implies that the information is disregarded while dysfunctionality implies that there are negative effects due to measurement. The organization in that case is worse off than before (see chapter 9 for an elaborate discussion on the effects of performance measurement).

**81**

**Table 4.6** *Reliability and validity*

|  | High validity | Low validity |
|---|---|---|
| High reliability | Right | Precisely wrong |
| Low reliability | Roughly right | Wrong |

Second, quality implies indicators that are *valid and reliable*, which are established notions in social scientific research. Measurement is valid when a study is measuring what it is supposed to measure. It is about the accuracy of measurement. In performance measurement, the selection of the indicators defines the validity of measurement. Reliability is the consistency of measurement, or the degree to which an instrument measures the same way each time it is used under the same condition with the same subjects. Reliability is the repeatability of measurement. Indicators can be valid, but not reliable, as well as reliable but not valid. A thermometer put in boiling water should measure 100°C. When it measures 90°C at repeated attempts, measurement is reliable but invalid. When it measures 100°C at first attempt, 110 at the second and 90 at the third, the first measurement is valid, but not reliable. Validity is the more important quality criterion, given that it is better to be roughly right than precisely wrong.

The third quality dimension is legitimacy of a measurement system. In an ideal scenario, all organization members support the measurement system. Manipulation and gaming with performance information are less likely when ownership is high. Only when unobtrusive indicators exist may ownership be less vital for the measurement effort.

## 2 CONCLUSION

This chapter described the design parameters of an ideal-typical measurement process. The five-step model starts with the decision of what to measure, which is followed by the identification of the indicators and the collection of the data. The fourth step is the analysis of data, and finally, performance information needs to be reported, with the right format for the right target group.

There is no one best way to do performance measurement. The design of the measurement system needs to be conditioned by the envisaged use of the performance information. This chapter has described the choices that have to be made. In chapter 6, the contingency with the foreseen uses is further explored. For now, the main lesson is that a simple how-to-do guide is insufficient for successful measurement.

## FURTHER READING

One of the most clearly structured and practical handbooks on how to measure performance was developed by Hatry (1999) at the Urban Institute. A case book from the state level in the USA was published a few years later (Liner *et al.*, 2001). One of the most thoughtful guides on customer satisfaction measurement is provided by the European Institute of Public Administration (EIPA) (2008). A combination of case studies and theoretically grounded practical guidance is de Lancer Julnes *et al.*'s (2007) *International Handbook of Practice-Based Performance Management*. One of best critiques on measurement is Etzioni & Lehman's article on the dangers of social measurement (1967). Innes (1990) analyses the institutionalization of indicators. By far the most thorough critique on the quality of governance indicators is offered by Arndt & Oman (2006). The quality criteria they use to assess governance indicators could easily be transferred to other contexts. Bouckaert (1993) also provides a useful model to assess quality using three criteria: validity, functionality and legitimacy. Finally, it may be worthwhile to critically assess the performance measurement guides provided by oversight agencies such as the UK Audit Commission (Audit Commission, 2000) and the National Audit Office (2001).

## REFERENCES

Arndt, C., & Oman, C. (2006). *Uses and Abuses of Governance Indicators*. Paris: Organisation for Economic Co-operation and Development.

Audit Commission (2000). *On Target: The Practice of Performance Measurement*. London: Audit Commission.

Baumgartner, F. R., & Jones, B. D. (1993). *Agendas and Instability in American Politics*. University of Chicago Press.

Best, J. (2001). *Damned Lies and Statistics: Untangling Numbers from the Media, Politicians, and Activists*. University of California Press.

Bogdanor, V. (2005). *Joined-Up Government*. Oxford: Oxford University Press.

Bouckaert, G. (1993). 'Measurement and Meaningful Management'. *Public Productivity & Management Review*, 17, 31–43.

Bouckaert, G., Van Dooren, W., & Sterck, M. (2003). *Prestaties meten in de Vlaamse overheid; een verkennende studie*. Leuven: Public Management Institute.

Bovaird, T., & Löffler, E. (2003). 'Evaluating the Quality of Public Governance: Indicators, Models and Methodologies'. *International Review of Administrative Sciences*, 69, 313–28.

Broom, C. (1998). *Performance Measurement Concepts and Techniques*. Washington, DC: American Society for Public Administration.

**83**

Coelli, T., & Rao, P. (1998). *An Introduction to Efficiency and Productivity Analysis.* Boston: Kluwer.

De Bont, A., & Grit, K. (2012). 'Unexpected Advantages of Less Accurate Performance Measurements: How Simple Prescription Data Works in a Complex Setting Regarding the Use of Medicine'. *Public Administration,* 90(2), 497–510.

De Lancer Julnes, P., Aristigueta, M., Yang, K., & Berry, F. S. (2007). *International Handbook of Practice-Based Performance Management.* Thousand Oaks: Sage Publications.

Etzioni, A., & Lehman, E. W. (1967). 'Some Dangers in "Valid" Social Measurement'. *The Annals of the American Academy of Political and Social Science,* 373, 1.

European Institute of Public Administration (2008). *European Primer on Customer Satisfaction Management.* Maastricht: EIPA.

Galtung, J., & Ruge, M. H. (1965). 'The Structure of Foreign News: The Presentation of the Congo, Cuba and Cyprus Crises in Four Norwegian Newspapers'. *Journal of Peace Research,* 2, 64–90.

Hatry, H. P. (1999). *Performance Measurement: Getting Results.* Washington, DC: Urban Institute Press.

Hendricks, M. (1994). 'Making a Splash: Reporting Evaluation Results Effectively'. In Hatry, H. P., Wholey, J. S., & Newcomer, K. (eds) *Handbook of Practical Program Evaluation.* San Francisco: Jossey-Bass.

Innes, J. E. (1990). *Knowledge and Public Policy: The Search for Meaningful Indicators.* New Brunswick: Transaction Publishers.

Kaplan, R. S., & Norton, D. P. (1996). *The Balanced Scorecard: Translating Strategy into Action.* Boston, MA: Harvard Business School Press.

Leeuw, F. L. (2003). 'Reconstructing Program Theories: Methods Available and Problems to Be Solved'. *American Journal of Evaluation,* 24, 5–20.

Liner, B., Hatry, H., Vinson, E., Allen, R., Dusenbery, P., Byrant, S., & Snell, R. (2001). *Making Results-Based State Government Work.* Washington, DC: The Urban Institute.

Merton, R. K. (1988). 'The Matthew Effect in Science, II: Cumulative Advantage and the Symbolism of Intellectual Property'. *Isis,* 79, 606–23.

Miller, G. A. (2009). *Wordnet.* Princeton: The Trustees of Princeton University.

Mitchell, R. K., Agle, B. R., & Wood, D. J. (1997). 'Toward a Theory of Stakeholder Identification and Salience: Defining the Principle of Who and What Really Counts'. *Academy of Management Review,* 22, 853–86.

National Audit Office (2001). *Measuring the Performance of Government Departments.* London: NAO.

OECD (2006). *Pensions at a Glance.* Paris: OECD.

—— (2009). *Measuring Government Activity.* Paris: OECD.

Pollitt, C. (2000). 'Institutional Amnesia: A Paradox of the "Information Age"?' *Prometheus,* 18, 5–16.

Rogers, P. J., Hacsi, T. A., Petrosino, A., & Huebner, T. A. (2000). *Program Theory in Evaluation: Challenges and Opportunities*. San Francisco: Jossey-Bass.

Rossi, R. J., & Gilmartin, K. J. (1980). *The Handbook of Social Indicators: Sources, Characteristics, and Analysis*. Garland: STPM Press.

Rubenstein, R., Schwartz, A. E., & Stiefel, L. (2003). 'Better Than Raw: A Guide to Measuring Organizational Performance with Adjusted Performance Measures'. *Public Administration Review*, 63, 607–15.

Stroobants, J., & Bouckaert, G. (2014). 'Benchmarking Local Public Libraries Using Non-parametric Frontier Methods: A Case Study of Flanders'. *Library & Information Science Research*, 3(36). Retrieved from https://lirias.kuleuven.be/handle/123456789/456342.

Treasury, H. M. (2001). *Choosing the Right Fabric: A Framework for Performance Information*. London: HM Treasury.

United Way of America (1999). *Achieving and Measuring Community Outcomes: Challenges, Issues, Some Approaches*. United Way of America.

Van de Walle, S. (2006). 'The State of the World's Bureaucracies'. *Journal of Comparative Policy Analysis: Research and Practice*, 8, 437–48.

Weick, K. E. (1995). *Sensemaking in Organizations*. Thousand Oaks: Sage Publications Inc.

Weiss, C. H. (1998). 'Have We Learned Anything about the Use of Evaluation?' *American Journal of Evaluation*, 19, 13, 21.

Wholey, J. S. (1999). 'Performance Based Management: Responding to Challenges'. *Public Productivity & Management Review*, 19.

# Chapter 5

# Incorporation of performance information

## LEARNING OBJECTIVES

■ To know what incorporation of performance information means.
■ To understand the requirements of good incorporation.
■ To understand why good incorporation fosters using performance information.

## KEY POINTS IN THIS CHAPTER

■ Using performance information assumes not only measurement but also incorporation.
■ Incorporation should be coherent and systematic; policy, financial and contract cycles are coherent systems for incorporation.
■ The better the incorporation, the higher the chances of using performance information.

## DISCUSSION QUESTIONS

1  What does the budget of a public sector organization look like? How does it incorporate information on inputs, activities, outputs, outcomes, objectives or targets (or not)? When you read the budget, are you able to understand what will happen next year?

2  Download a strategic plan and an evaluation/performance audit report of the same organization. Look for the general objectives/targets of

the organization and the related KPIs. Try to assess, through the performance audit or the evaluation, whether the objectives were reached.

Measuring performance (chapter 4) is necessary but not sufficient to manage performance. In order to manage, performance information should be used (chapters 6 and 7). Yet, use does not just happen. Therefore, measured performance needs to be incorporated into the management and policy systems (Bouckaert & Halligan, 2008) (see Box 5.1 for a discussion on related concepts). This chapter focuses on ways to do this. The emphasis will be on incorporation in the policy, financial and contract cycles, and not so much on incorporation in personnel management and HRM. Before we discuss these policy and management cycles, we further dig into the concept of incorporation of (performance) information.

# 1 INCORPORATION AND USE OF PERFORMANCE INFORMATION

The use of performance information will be stronger when it is incorporated in policy and management. Box 5.1 provides an overview of some common performance management tools (Nõmm & Randma-Liiv, 2012) that can be incorporated into management practice.

## BOX 5.1 EXAMPLES OF PERFORMANCE MANAGEMENT TOOLS

- Annual performance reports of ministries
- Performance budgeting methodology
- Macroeconomic indicators
- Societal indicators
- International assessments
- Service quality measures
- Management scorecards based on outcome/output measures
- Client surveys
- Public opinion polls
- Third-party validation such as quality awards
- Individual performance contracts/targets
- Audit reports
- Programme evaluations

The distinction between incorporation and use reflects the difference between *having* and *doing* performance management. Having a performance scorecard does not necessarily imply that leadership is taking performance scores into consideration. Having a performance budget does not automatically feed into budget decisions. This should not come as a surprise. One of the most persisting critiques on performance management has been that performance management rhetoric is disconnected from reality (Pollitt & Bouckaert, 2011; Schmidle, 2011). All too often, formal compliance drives the development of performance management systems with limited impact on practice (Ohemeng, 2011). Even without formal mandates, the symbolic function of being seen to have performance management may trigger incorporation without use. Performance management signals a legitimizing vision of rationality to the outside world (Meyer & Rowan, 1977).

Several recent studies have used a conceptually comparable distinction in order to assess the use of performance information. Instead of talking about incorporation and use, these studies speak of adoption and implementation. The idea that performance information first needs to be integrated into the management systems before it can be used however remains. The distinction was first introduced by Beyer and Trice in a study of knowledge utilization (Beyer & Trice, 1982). De Lancer Julnes & Holzer (2001) applied the framework on performance information. Adoption is the development of a capacity to act based on performance information, while implementation reflects the actual use of this capacity in decision-making. They found that rational-technical factors were important for adoption while political-cultural factors better explain the level of implementation. Yang & Hsieh (2007) made the distinction between adoption and managerial effectiveness of performance information. They pointed to the significance of politics.

Incorporation and use can be high or low. Some organizations score high on incorporation and low on use. They typically have a good number of performance management tools: performance budgets, scorecards, performance contracts, benchmarks, etcetera. Yet, they do not use these instruments for decision-making. Measurement in these organizations is predominantly outward oriented. The main purpose is to satisfy external audiences that either impose mandatory performance schemes such as PART in the USA or demand cutting-edge, modern management

**Table 5.1** *Adoption and implementation: four profiles*

|  | Low incorporation | High incorporation |
|---|---|---|
| Low use | No performance management | Outward-oriented PM |
| High use | Inward-oriented PM | Full performance management |

Source: Van Dooren, 2005

**88**

practices. There are many measurement initiatives on the shelf, most of them rather dusty. Some organizations score low on incorporation and high on use. These organizations do not have many formal performance management tools, but they seem to use the ones that are in place rather intensely for management purposes in house.

There is performance feedback independent from management routines. Kroll (2013) found that German managers value non-routine performance from informal talks and ad hoc inquiries more than routine performance information from formal reporting. He suggests that we should not be worried if managers pay little attention to routine performance reports as long as they are responsive to other kinds of performance feedback (p. 273). The chances for successful performance management will be higher when it is engrained in management systems. An incorporated performance management system should be the infrastructure for the use of performance. In the last chapter, we discuss the role of information brokers in bridging the gap between routine reporting and non-routine decision- and sense-making

## 2  INCORPORATION OF PERFORMANCE INFORMATION IN POLICY AND MANAGEMENT CYCLES

Policy and management can be conceived as a circular system. First, there is an *ex ante question* in which the future performance of a system is reflected upon and ultimately determined: what shall we do next year (or the next years)? The answer to this prospective question needs to be authorized by a legitimate institution. For instance, an executive office should offer an answer to the legislative branch, which discusses, approves or amends. Within the executive office there could also be a range of often-contradictory debates between finance and line departments, between ministries and agencies, between central and local government, etcetera.

In all these cases, the answers to the prospective question need to be documented with data and information. The richness of the information can vary. As discussed in Table 5.2, a minimalistic answer only refers to input and cash. The answer to the question what will happen next year is to say: 'Next year we will expend this amount of money for personnel, operating costs, transfers, and capital'. What actually happens with this input is unknown. On the other hand, a maximalist answer to the prospective question could be: 'Next year we will spend this amount of money (in cash and in cost) to deliver these outputs (quantity and quality) in the context of these outcomes'. Second, once it is known and approved what needs to be done, there is an *ex nunc question* of what is happening during implementation. This requires a monitoring system that allows making corrective actions during implementation. This stage also needs to be documented with data and information. Again, there could be a minimalistic position exposing the amount of money received and expended, or a maximalist position that reveals not only the current

**Table 5.2** Four key questions and the capacity to provide answers

|  | Input and cash driven systems | Output/outcome and accrual driven systems |
| --- | --- | --- |
| Ex ante: prospective perspective: what will be done? | Next year we will expend this amount of money for personnel, operating costs, transfers, and capital | Next year we will spend this amount of money (in cash and in cost) to deliver these outputs (quantity and quality) in the context of these outcomes |
| Ex nunc: real time perspective: what is happening? | Up to this moment we have received so much money, and we have expended so much money | At this moment the cash position (receipts and expenses) is evolving in this direction; at this moment benefits and costs are evolving in this direction |
| Ex post: retrospective perspective: what has happened? | We have been compliant, and all financial figures are correct | We have been compliant, all financial figures are correct, and we performed in an economic, efficient and effective way |
| Feed forward: what will change? | We used the above information to write the next budget | We used the above information to change our strategy, our performance-based budgets and our contracts |

cash position (receipts and expenses), but also benefits and costs. Third, once the implementation stage is over, there is a need to compare realizations with what has been announced, and to assess this result (*ex post*). This is a retrospective question. Goal attainment should be discussed taking other criteria such as economy, efficiency, openness and transparency into account (see chapter 2). The minimalistic version of a controlling system provides information on compliance and correctness of financial figures. A maximalist version yields insights on economy, efficiency and effectiveness in addition to compliance and correctness of financial figures. Fourth, it is necessary to feed this information forward into the next cycle and to use information on the past for improving the future way of managing performance. In the minimalist design, information can be used to write the next budget in an incremental way. The maximalist design may trigger a change in strategy, and inform performance-based budgets and renegotiating contracts, as Table 5.2 summarizes.

The sequence of these four questions is cyclical, with corresponding documents in each stage. There are three cycles which are relevant to managing performance in the public sector:

- the policy cycle: policy preparation, monitoring, policy evaluation and feedback;
- the financial cycle: budgeting, accounting and auditing;
- the contract cycle: negotiation, monitoring, and evaluation.

From an ideal-typical perspective, there is a hierarchy between the cycles. Policies set out the priorities, which are then translated into budgets. Only then will the question of which agency will perform which task arise. This is the subject of contract negotiations. The policy cycle should thus determine the financial cycle, which then should determine the contract cycle.

In reality, the timing as well as the hierarchical relations between the cycles is much more complicated. Literature on incrementalism demonstrates the importance of past budgets and past task allocations in developing new policies (Lindblom, 1959; Wildavsky & Hammond, 1965). Documents often combine content that could belong to different cycles. In some countries, the contracts are fully part of the financial cycle and budgets and contracts become the same document (Pollitt & Bouckaert, 2011).

## 2.1 The policy cycle

Figure 5.1 shows how performance information will be incorporated in the *policy cycle*. There is a (strategic) plan that includes major objectives and targets for resources, activities, outputs and outcomes. These plans need to be implemented and monitored. Monitoring arrangements, such as the Balanced Score Card (BSC), EFQM (European Foundation for Quality Management), the European CAF (Common Assessment Framework) and the Canadian MAF (Management Accountability Framework) are models which can be used as mental maps to guide incorporation of performance strategies in the organization.

Policy sectors in addition develop other more specialized monitoring instruments: crime monitors (for instance the Compstat movement; see O'Connell, 2001), air quality monitors, neighbourhood monitors, quality of life monitors,

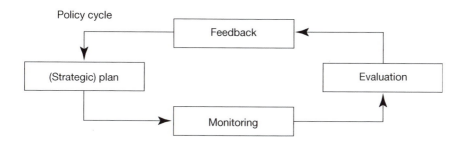

**Figure 5.1** *Incorporating performance information: the policy cycle*

etcetera. The next stage is evaluation, which incorporates performance information for the purpose of assessing past performance. Evaluation reports, which incorporate performance information, feed forward into the next strategic plan. This evaluation stage could also include comparisons and benchmarks, based on surveys of users and citizens. Hence, there are three sets of documents that incorporate performance information: planning, monitoring and evaluation documents.

Many countries and states have set up systems that monitor the effectiveness of nation or state-wide policies (Aristigueta, 1999). The most elaborate schemes can be found in European governance. The Europe 2020 agenda tracks progress on employment, R&D, climate change, education and social exclusion. Indicators are used to monitor policies of member states. The stability and growth pact monitors budgetary performance of member states (mainly deficits and debts). All but three of the Australian States and Territories have whole-of-government strategic plans in place (McMahon & Phillimore, 2013). While these plans are used for joined-up governance and monitoring, a marketing orientation is probably even more prevalent. States use the indicators for political marketing, leading to accusations of political spin, as well as for state branding in competitive federalism. Two US initiatives attracted a lot of attention. The Minnesota Milestones is an indicator set of 60 indicators, organized in four thematic fields – people, community/democracy, economy and environment – and contributing to 19 goals. The initiative started in 1991. Between 2002 and 2010, the Republican governor Tim Pawlenty suspended the initiative. Governor Mark Dayton (Dem) however revived the Minnesota Milestones. The Oregon benchmarks is one of the oldest and most acclaimed initiatives (Kissler *et al.*, 1998). From 1989 onwards, progress towards 90 indicators was tracked. The initiative was defunded in 2009. Other US initiatives include Virginia Performs (established 2003), Hawai'i 2050 (established 2005) and New Jersey Sustainable State (1995–2007).

## 2.2 Financial cycle

The *financial cycle* is composed of budgeting, accounting and audit and is ideally embedded in the policy cycle. This is shown in Figure 5.2.

*Budgets* should be the corresponding documents to strategic plans, or at least their annual slice. Budgets should incorporate the information from the strategic plan in a different way, and for different purposes. The budget authorizes expenditure during the implementation. A limited authorization involves input budgets that allow (and oblige) spending a certain budget on a line item. Output budgets that authorize to spend resources to attain specified output levels have a higher density of incorporation of performance information. One step further would be to budget for outcomes rather than outputs. Some empirical cases of performance budgeting can be found in an OECD publication (Curristine, 2005). Box 5.2 has an example of the National Gallery of Australia.

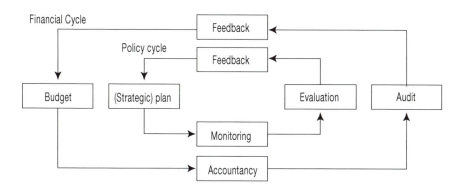

**Figure 5.2** *Incorporating performance information: policy and financial cycle*

---

## BOX 5.2 THE CASE OF THE NATIONAL GALLERY OF AUSTRALIA AT CANBERRA (STRATEGIC PLAN 2013–17 AND PORTFOLIO BUDGET 2014–15)

In the Strategic Plan (2013–17) the following goals, objectives and key strategies are mentioned (excerpt: goal 1).

GOAL 1: Develop, preserve and protect an outstanding national art collection

OBJECTIVE 1.1: Develop and strengthen the national art collection

*Key strategies*

■ Acquire, by purchase, gift and bequest, works of art of outstanding quality in line with our *Acquisitions Policy* and Ten-Year Acquisition Strategy.
■ Encourage, facilitate and acknowledge Government funding, donations, gifts and bequests that enhance the national art collection.

OBJECTIVE 1.2: Preserve, protect and manage the national art collection

*Key strategies*

■ Conserve and maintain the national art collection and provide appropriate storage, security and environmental conditions.
■ Document and manage the national art collection.
■ Continue digitization of the national art collection.

**93**

Our success will be measured by:

- the quality of the national art collection and achievements measured against our *Acquisitions Policy* and Ten-Year Acquisition Strategy
- the level of funding and donations attracted for development of the national art collection
- the number of works of art in the national collection digitized every year
- achievement of other relevant key performance indicators expressed in annual business plans.

In the Portfolio Budget Statement 2014–15, the strategic plan is operationalized.

Government outcomes are the intended results, impacts or consequences of actions by the government on the Australian community. Commonwealth programmes are the primary vehicle by which government agencies achieve the intended results of their outcome statements. Agencies are required to identify the programmes that contribute to government outcomes over the budget and forward years.

The NGA's outcome is described below together with its related programme, specifying the performance indicators and targets used to assess and monitor the performance of the NGA in achieving government outcomes.

*Outcome 1*:
Increased understanding, knowledge and enjoyment of the visual arts by providing access to, and information about, works of art locally, nationally and internationally

*Outcome 1 strategy*:
By improving understanding and enjoyment of the visual arts, the government can provide social benefits for the Australian community and enhance Australia's international reputation. These improvements can be realized through developing and maintaining a quality collection and providing access to information about both the collection and the works of art on loan to the NGA.

The NGA is responsible for developing, maintaining and presenting the national art collection. It develops, researches, preserves, displays, interprets and promotes the collection. In addition, the NGA enhances the understanding and enjoyment of the visual arts through innovative public programmes, dissemination of information and a diverse education programme.

In 2014–15 the NGA will continue to develop and maintain the collection. It will provide access to these works, as well as a range of works from Australian and international collections, through loans, exhibitions, publications, online materials, displays and public programmes.

## Contributions to Outcome 1

*Programme 1.1*:
Collection development, management, access and promotion

*Programme objective*
The NGA aims to build a collection of outstanding quality through purchase, gift and bequest. It will continue to refine the collection through the disposal of works that no longer comply with collection development policies.

The NGA's collection is carefully catalogued to provide information about the collection. The NGA stores, secures and conserves its collection in order to preserve it for the Australian people now and in the future.

The NGA provides access to works of art by displaying, exhibiting and lending its collection, as well as borrowing works from other sources. Access to works from the collection that are not on display is also provided. The NGA enhances the understanding, knowledge and enjoyment of art through publications, visitor services, education, public programmes and multimedia.

*Programme deliverables*
The NGA aims to strengthen the national collection by acquiring, researching and documenting works of art that complement and build on the current strengths of the collection. It will continue to maintain the collection in accordance with endorsed standards.

**Table 5.3** *Estimated deliverables of the National Gallery of Australia, Canberra*

| Estimated deliverables | 2013–14 Actual | 2014–15 Budget | 2015–16 Forward estimate | 2016–17 Forward estimate | 2017–18 Forward estimate |
|---|---|---|---|---|---|
| Works acquired, researched and documented in accordance with endorsed standards | 100% | 100% | 100% | 100% | 100% |
| Works digitized | 15,000 | 10,000 | 10,000 | 10,000 | 10,000 |
| Works subjected to conservation treatment | 3,000 | 3,000 | 3,000 | 3,000 | 3,000 |
| Works of art loaned | 1,200 | 1,200 | 1,200 | 1,200 | 1,200 |

*Programme key performance indicators*

The NGA is committed to building and maintaining an outstanding art collection for the nation and providing access to the collection locally, nationally and internationally. This will be achieved through the ongoing development of the collection and delivery of inspirational exhibitions supported by research, scholarships, education and public programmes.

The performance of this programme will be measured through increased access to the collection and increased levels of visitor satisfaction.

**Table 5.4** *Estimated Key Performance indicators of the National Gallery of Australia, Canberra*

| Estimated key performance indicators | 2013–14 Actual | 2014–15 Budget | 2015–16 Forward estimate | 2016–17 Forward estimate | 2017–18 Forward estimate |
|---|---|---|---|---|---|
| *Visitor interactions* | | | | | |
| Total number of visits to the organization | 995,000 | 1,005,000 | 1,015,000 | 1,025,000 | 1,030,000 |
| Total number of visits to the organization's website | 1,900,000 | 1,920,000 | 1,940,000 | 1,960,000 | 1,980,000 |
| Total number of onsite visits by students as part of an organized educational group | 72,400 | 74,000 | 76,600 | 78,000 | 80,000 |
| *Participation in public and school programmes* | | | | | |
| Number of people participating in public programmes | 32,000 | 33,000 | 34,000 | 35,000 | 36,000 |
| Number of students participating in school programmes | 72,400 | 74,000 | 76,600 | 78,000 | 80,000 |
| *Quantity of school learning programmes delivered* | | | | | |
| Number of organized programmes delivered onsite | 7,088 | 6,000 | 6,000 | 6,000 | 6,000 |
| Number of programme packages available online | 160 | 250 | 310 | 400 | 400 |

**Table 5.4** *continued*

|  | 2013–14 | 2014–15 | 2015–16 | 2016–17 | 2017–18 |
|---|---|---|---|---|---|
| *Estimated key performance indicators* | Actual | Budget | Forward estimate | Forward estimate | Forward estimate |
| Number of educational institutions participating in organized school learning programmes | 1,772 | 1,500 | 1,500 | 1,500 | 1,500 |
| *Visitor satisfaction* | | | | | |
| Percentage of visitors that were satisfied or very satisfied with their visit | 90% | 90% | 90% | 90% | 90% |
| *Programme survey rating (by teachers)* | | | | | |
| Percentage of teachers reporting overall positive experience | 90% | 90% | 90% | 90% | 90% |
| Percentage of teachers reporting relevance to the classroom curriculum | 90% | 90% | 90% | 90% | 90% |
| *Expenditure mix* | | | | | |
| Expenditure on collection development (as a % of total expenditure) | 26% | 26% | 26% | 26% | 26% |
| Expenditure on other capital items (as a % of total expenditure) | 10% | 10% | 10% | 10% | 10% |
| Expenditure on other (i.e. non-collection development) labour costs (as a % of total expenditure) | 33% | 33% | 33% | 33% | 33% |
| Other expenses (as a % of total expenditure) | 31% | 31% | 31% | 31% | 31% |

**97**

**Table 5.4** continued

|  | 2013–14 | 2014–15 | 2015–16 | 2016–17 | 2017–18 |
|---|---|---|---|---|---|
| Estimated key performance indicators | Actual | Budget | Forward estimate | Forward estimate | Forward estimate |
| Collection management and access | | | | | |
| Number of acquisitions (made in the reporting period) | 1,000 | 1,000 | 1,000 | 1,000 | 1,000 |
| Total number of objects accessioned (in the reporting period) | 1,000 | 1,000 | 1,000 | 1,000 | 1,000 |
| % of the total collection available to the public | 63% | 72% | 81% | 89% | 89% |
| % of the total collection available to the public online | 60% | 70% | 80% | 89% | 89% |
| % of the total collection available to the public on display | 3% | 3% | 3% | 3% | 3% |
| % of the total collection available to the public on tour | 1% | 1% | 1% | 1% | 1% |
| % of the total collection digitized | 10% | 10% | 10% | 10% | 10% |

Source: National Gallery of Australia, Canberra, 2012.

Performance budgeting has attracted critiques almost from the beginning. One of the early opponents was Wildavsky (1969), who called performance budgeting a 'shotgun marriage between policy analysis and budgeting' (p. 169). He mainly critiques the feasibility of the endeavour. He amongst others argues that it is hard enough to do a good job of policy analysis without having to meet arbitrary and fixed deadlines imposed by the budget process. Wildavsky (1969) sums up the lack of talent, theory and data to do performance budgeting in a single statement: no one knows how to do programme budgeting (p. 193). This critique persisted, leading Schick (2003) to the conclusion that performance budgeting is an old idea with a disappointing past and an uncertain future. Besides limited feasibility, a second critique on performance budgeting is that it affects the budgetary role of legislators. If legislators have little or no role in setting and evaluating the performance goals, they lose pre-controls on input and gain little or no power in return (Rubin, 1997).

In considering country systems of performance budgeting, it is important to appreciate that no OECD country directly links performance and expenditure, according to a recent survey. There are a number of variants of performance budgeting, many of which use the concept elastically. OECD distinguishes three main systems, ranging from presentational to performance-informed to direct performance budgeting. With the latter, 'budget allocations are based on actual or expected performance' (Schick, 2013; Curristine & Flynn, 2013). The Dutch efforts at performance budgeting are a case in point of these critiques (Box 5.3).

---

## BOX 5.3 THE DUTCH PERFORMANCE BUDGETING SYSTEM: LESS IS MORE?

In Europe, the Netherlands is regarded as a performance management leader (van Hofwegen & de Jong, 2012). In 1999, the country implemented a major, NPM flavoured initiative called Van Beleidsbegroting tot BeleidsVerantwoording (VBTB): from policy-based budgeting to policy-based accountability. The budget format was reorganized to show the link between inputs and results. The Dutch Court of Audit published coverage rates of the share of objectives covered by measurable indicators. Soon, the *availability* of indicators became the focus of attention instead of the indicators themselves. Compliance with reporting obligations was more important than genuine analyses of performance. When line departments did provide indicators, they mainly used them to legitimize policies and expenditures rather than to critically reflect on results. Moreover, the parliament felt that they were losing control over the budget. Parliament insisted that they would be able to oversee input information.

After a decade, VBTB was abolished and replaced with a new budgeting initiative called Verantwoord Begroten: accountable budgeting. This new budgeting scheme is less ambitious. It relates more closely to ministerial responsibility. Rather than general accounts of policy sectors, concrete policy instruments are budgeted. Performance information has to have a clear connection with these measures. One of the indicators for foreign policy in the VBTB reporting was progress towards peace in Afghanistan. While the Netherlands did have troops in Afghanistan, the impact of a small European country on a global conflict is arguably very small. Such indicators are no longer tolerated. Finally, in-depth policy analysis should not be part of the budget. However, a programme of evaluations is included. Overall, it seems that after 50 years, the Netherlands took Wildavsky's critique to heart (1969).

## BOX 5.4  BETTER MANAGEMENT THROUGH ACCRUAL ACCOUNTING?

The UK Public Audit Forum (2002) strongly believes in the benefits of accrual accounting. It argues that accrual accounting means better management. No organization should hesitate, in its view, to incorporate performance information into the accounting system. The benefits of accrual accounting are:

- Completeness – accrual-based accounts are more complete than cash accounts. The need to include transactions in the period in which they occur reduces the potential for manipulation of accounts and improves comparability between periods and organizations.
- Better planning, management and decision-making – accurate and objective financial and management information is essential for good management, decision-making and better resource planning and allocation.
- Ability to change behaviours – better management is possible with accrual accounting, but it is not automatic. Achieving some changes may also require policy changes or financial incentives.
- Performance management – good performance management needs effective performance measures. Performance measures, or indicators, have to be calculated on the basis of comprehensive and consistent financial and operational data. Accrual accounting is therefore an essential component of better performance management.
- Assessing financial resilience – one of the purposes of published financial statements is to enable the user to predict future cash flows and assess resilience or risk. Financial statements cannot foretell the future with complete accuracy, but the aim can at least be to give a fair and balanced picture of the past and some signposts to future performance.

More critical sounds are heard amongst academics studying Australian and New Zealand accrual accounting initiatives (Carlin, 2006). Accrual accounting requires massive amounts of output information. Moreover, the complexity of the system is not always understood by politicians who are supposed to exert control (see also Paulsson, 2006, for the Swedish case).

## BOX 5.5  EXAMPLES OF THE WIDE RANGE OF PERFORMANCE AUDITS

From the ANAO (Australian National Audit Office), Australia (www.anao.gov.au)

*Policing at Australian International Airports (March 2014)*: The objective of the audit was to assess the Australian Federal Police's (AFP's) management of policing services at Australian international airports. In order to form a conclusion against this audit objective, the Australian National Audit Office (ANAO) examined if: (1) the transition to the 'All In' model of policing at airports had been delivered effectively; (2) appropriate processes are in place for managing risk and operational planning; (3) effective stakeholder engagement, relationship management and information sharing arrangements are in place; (4) facilities at the airports are adequate and appropriate; and (5) appropriate mechanisms for measuring the effectiveness of policing at airports have been developed and implemented. Different dimensions of performance (product, process and regime) are assessed.

From the NAO (National Audit Office), UK (www.nao.org.uk)

*The performance of the Department of Health 2012–13 (March 2014):* Performance audits usually cover programmes such as policing at airports, flood protection or social benefits. This audit analyses an organization. It essentially reviews the previous audits of the NAO with a bearing on the department of health. The NAO publishes departmental studies of all departments.

*Tax reliefs (April 2014):* The Audit report found that there are more than 1,000 tax reliefs in the UK. Reliefs can help maintain the competitiveness of tax systems and governments can use tax reliefs as a mechanism to redistribute wealth, support economic growth and influence behaviour. Thirty recommendations are made to HM Revenue & Customs to improve the administration of tax reliefs. Some comments are critical (e.g. HMRC does not evaluate tax reliefs systematically, and has commissioned few evaluations of their impact), while others are supportive (e.g. HMRC responds proactively to the serious challenge of administering the complex system of tax reliefs and addressing the opportunities for abuse it creates).

**101**

From GAO (Government Accountability Office), USA (www.gao.gov)

*NASA, assessment of selected large projects (April 2014):* GAO annually assesses how well NASA is planning and executing its major acquisitions. The findings show modest improvement over time in how well NASA is performing in maintaining costs and schedules.

*Government Efficiency and Effectiveness: Opportunities to Reduce Fragmentation, Overlap, and Duplication and Achieve Other Financial Benefits (April 2014):* This performance audit looks at the gains from better collaboration across government. The audit proposes 64 actions for improvement. For instance, GAO found that individuals are allowed to receive concurrent payments from the Disability Insurance and Unemployment programs. Eliminating the overlap in these payments could save the government about $1.2 billion over the next ten years.

In chapter 10, we will address these issues by suggesting that performance management systems should cut back on rigid incorporation in programme structures and reinforce more flexible ways of using performance data or a performance dialogue (see also Ho, 2011).

Implementation is monitored through the *accounting* system. Again, there are both more limited systems (i.e. cash accounting) to answer the question of what is happening, and more developed systems (i.e. full accrual accounting), which allow for extensive cost calculations and comparisons. This option also shows the varying density of incorporation of performance information, which could vary from simple cash information to sophisticated direct or full cost information. Box 5.4 discusses the pros and cons of accrual accounting and cost accounting in the public sector.

The third stage in the financial cycle is audit. Performance audits gain importance over compliance and financial audits, and consequently they are an important avenue for incorporating performance information (Raaum & Morgan, 2001). Performance audit reports are in most cases publicly available. Ideally, these performance audit reports feed into the policy and budget debates for the next years. Box 5.5 gives examples of some recent performance audits in Australia, the UK and the USA.

## 2.3 Contract cycle

The contract cycle is an integrated system embedded or at least derived from the financial cycle. This is shown in Figure 5.3. Contracts are concrete documents that

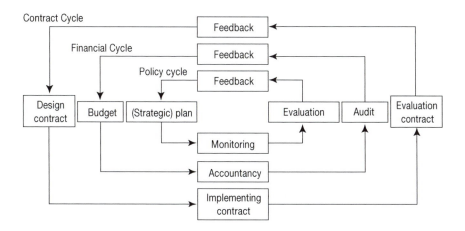

**Figure 5.3** *Incorporating performance information: policy, financial and contract cycle*

define agreements between key actors or organizations in a policy field such as agencies at arm's length. Performance contracts incorporate essential performance information. In return of an envelope of money, a contract states what is expected in terms of activities, outputs or (contributions to) outcomes from outputs provided. There should be a monitoring system for contract implementation, which includes reporting. These reporting and monitoring documents incorporate performance information, which are often called KPIs or key performance indicators. Contract implementation is evaluated to hold agencies accountable. The responsibility defined and granted in the contract is confronted with the results. Finally, the evaluation of the degree of realization (or not, and why) will feed forward into the next contract cycle. In some cases top managers of an autonomous unit may have to go for not having delivered.

The contracting cycle typically produces three sets of documents which incorporate performance information: contracts or agreements, their monitoring, and their evaluation documents. Box 5.6 shows what a resource agreement between a line department and the Australian Treasury looks like. Starting from a general 'government goal', 'desired outcomes' are defined which should be realized by implementing seven 'services' or outputs. There are dollars allocated to these services, as well as FTEs for the personnel side of these services.

Box 5.7 shows how a UK department is funding an agreement with a museum. From the beginning there is a requirement for the museum to contribute to the general objectives of the government. It is also clear from the beginning (ex ante) what indicators will be used, which targets are set, and how this will be monitored. Finally, a delivery plan is provided to demonstrate how these strategic objectives will be realized, through primary activities, deliverables and outcomes. Although

## BOX 5.6 THE CASE OF CULTURE AND ARTS IN WEST AUSTRALIA: RESOURCE AGREEMENT

The following performance information (financial and non-financial) is the subject of a Resource Agreement signed by the Minister, Accountable Authority and the Treasurer under Part 3, Division 5 of the Financial Management Act 2006.

### Government Goal
Enhancing the quality of life and wellbeing of all people throughout Western Australia by providing high quality, accessible services

### Desired Outcomes

*Outcome 1*: A creative, sustainable and accessible culture and arts sector

*Services*
1  Arts Industry Support
2  Screen Production Industry Support
3  Venue Management Services

*Outcome 2*: Western Australia's natural, cultural and documentary collections are preserved, accessible and sustainable

*Services*
4  Art Gallery Services
5  Library and Information Services
6  Museum Services
7  Government Recordkeeping and Archival Services

*Outcome 1*: A creative, sustainable and accessible culture and arts sector:
■ Proportion of funding applicants satisfied with the key elements of the 'creative' funding programs:
   2006–7 Estimated: 82%; Target 2007–8: 82%
■ Perceived values of culture and arts to the Western Australian Community:
   2006–7 Estimated: 80%; 2007–8 Target: 80%
■ Proportion of triennially funded organizations within the culture and arts sector regarded as financially healthy:
   2006–7 Estimated: 27%; 2007–8 Target: 28%

*Service 4*: Art Gallery Services
■ Delivery of the State Art Collection and access to art gallery services and programs through visual arts advocacy, collection development, facilities and services. Services ensure that primary access to art,

heritage and ideas locally, regionally and internationally are preserved and displayed for future generations.

■ This includes indicators such as: total and net cost of services, key efficiency indicators (average cost of art gallery services per Art Gallery access), Full Time Equivalent (FTEs).

*Source:* www.treasury.wa.gov.au

## BOX 5.7 THE CASE OF THE UK BRITISH MUSEUM: FUNDING AGREEMENT

Funding Agreement between the British Museum and the Department for Culture, Media and Sport 2008–11

### THE BRITISH MUSEUM: FUNDING AGREEMENT 2008–11

1   This agreement is between the Department for Culture, Media & Sport (DCMS) and the British Museum.

### British Museum

2   The British Museum was founded as a national institution with an internal frame of reference. Two and a half centuries later it is one of the few and perhaps the only collection in the world where the history of mankind can be told through material culture over a span of two million years; where the nature of objects may be investigated and understood from many different perspectives; and where connections with the past may illuminate the present and show the potential of the future.

3   The British Museum is:
■ The greatest collection representative of the human cultural achievement, ancient and modern, in the world;
■ A space not only for the 'learned and curious' but also 'for the benefit of the general public' – a centre of research and inquiry at all levels;
■ A collection preserved and held for the benefit of all the world, present and future, free of charge;
■ A forum for the expression of many different cultural perspectives;
■ A place to increase understanding of the cultural connections and influences linking Britain and the world;
■ A place where the UK's diverse population can explore its common inheritances.

**105**

4    The British Museum is established under the British Museum Act 1963 and the Museums and Galleries Act 1992. It is also an exempt charity. The constitution of the Body is set out in Section 1 of the British Museum Act 1963. The Body does not carry out its functions on behalf of the Crown. The British Museum receives funding by virtue of Section 9, Schedule 7 of the Museums and Galleries Act 1992.

5    The British Museum has identified four key objectives that it will need to deliver in the next five years to maintain its world-class status:

■ **To manage and research the collection more effectively**
The Museum will improve its documentation of the collections through the Merlin Plan and Collections Online and improve its storage of the collections.

■ **To enhance access to the collection**
The Museum will develop the capacity to accommodate more on-site visits per annum and deliver improvements to the visitor experience; the Museum in Britain programme will develop key partnerships and the international programme will provide opportunities for people in Africa, China, India, and the Middle East to share skills and build capacity.

■ **To invest in its people**
The Museum will deliver an integrated human resource strategy that links Career Review to training and development, to succession planning and talent management.

■ **To increase self-generated income**
The Museum will increase self-generated income through growth from exhibition, retail, hospitality, international touring exhibitions, Membership, and fundraising programmes.

### Financial Allocation

6    The Secretary of State's letter of December 2007 sets out:

■ the British Museum's allocations for 2008–9 to 2010–11, including ring-fenced sums to be spent on particular projects;
■ the Secretary of State's priorities and the Departmental Strategic Objectives (DSOs) for 2008–11 and the British Museum's contribution towards their achievement.

7   The grant in aid allocation is dependent on the British Museum maintaining free admission to the permanent collections. The British Museum's ability to show measureable improvements in service delivery of DCMS's DSOs will be factors in the Secretary of State's decisions on future allocations, in addition to any other performance monitoring processes that may be introduced.

## Compliance

8   In addition, the British Museum has undertaken to:

- comply with all relevant legislation;
- comply with its Management Statement and Financial Memorandum;
- observe the requirements of Managing Public Money.

## Performance and Monitoring

9   The British Museum will supply DCMS each year with the regular financial information set out in the Data collection schedule, as well as returns against 12 performance indicators supplied by DCMS and returns against 5 further measures selected by the British Museum (annexed).

10   This information, together with Annual Reports and any further reports the British Museum prepares in relation to progress against its own corporate priorities, will be used to monitor performance year-on-year. DCMS expects the British Museum to be able to report in its Annual Report progress against the areas that are of greatest priority to Ministers. These include diversity (of both audiences and those employed by the museum or serving on the board) and actions being taken to promote sustainability and mitigate the effects of climate change.

11   In addition, DCMS would like the British Museum to provide updates on the North West Development project and on cultural diplomacy activity at quarterly catch-up meetings.

12   The level of scrutiny that DCMS will adopt in monitoring performance during the period of this funding agreement will be commensurate with the outcome of regular joint risk assessment exercises. The British Museum's risk rating at the start of the funding period is as follows:

| | |
|---|---|
| Delivery of DCMS objectives | Low |
| Systems | Low |
| External environment | Medium |

## Supporting Information

13   The documents relevant to this agreement, and against which the British Museum will be monitored are as follows:

- Allocation letter
- Performance Indicators
- Risk Assessment
- VFM delivery plan
- Data collection schedule
- MS/FM
- Statement of Internal Control
- Managing Public Money
- Annual Reports and Accounts
- Corporate Plan and reports

Department for Culture, Media & Sport

Date   6 June 2008

British Museum

Date   2/6/08

## PERFORMANCE INDICATORS

### Access

1 Number of visits to the museum/gallery (excluding virtual visitors)

2 Number of unique website visits

### Audience Profile

3 Number of visits by children under 16

4 Number of visits by UK adult visitors aged 16 or over from NS-SEC groups 5–8

5 Number of visits by UK adult visitors aged 16 and over from an ethnic minority background

6 Number of visits by UK adult visitors aged 16 and over who consider themselves to have a limiting long-term illness, disability or infirmity

7 Number of overseas visits

### Learning/Outreach

8 Children

- Number of facilitated and self-directed visits to the museum/gallery by children under 16 in formal education
- Number of instances of children under 16 participating in on-site organised activities
- Number of instances of children under 16 participating in outreach activity outside the museum/gallery

9 Adults

- Number of instances of adults aged 16 and over participating in organised activities at the museum/gallery

- Number of instances of adults aged 16 and over participating in outreach activities outside the museum/gallery

### Visitor Satisfaction

10 % of visitors who would recommend a visit

### Income Generation

11  Self generated income

- Admissions
- Trading
- Fundraising

### Regional Engagement

12  Number of UK loan venues

### British Museum measures

13  Number of object records and images available online

14  Fundraising for research programmes

15  % of collection storage space type A, B and C

16  Staff Diversity

17  Fundraising for the North West Development Project

*Source: British Museum, 2007*

the terminology of Box 5.6 is a little different from Box 5.7, there is a similarity in the way of incorporating and connecting performance information.

The UK coalition government of PM Cameron claims a retreat from target setting. We discussed the abolishment of the Audit Commission in chapter 1. The quasi-contractual agreements between the Treasury and the departments that New Labour installed (Public Service Agreements and Departmental Strategic Objectives) made way for business plans. Table 5.5 provides the example of the UK National Offender Management Service. However, it is not clear whether the business plans are really cutting back on the target regime. Talbot (2012, 2013) argues that they are mainly old wine in new bottles. In the business plans, substantially more performance indicators are included. In addition to the business plans, the Permanent Secretaries' 'Individual Performance Objectives' have performance targets. It leads Talbot to conclude that the rhetoric of change in the target regimes between the last government and the current one is not matching the continuity in practice.

## 2.4 Integrating policy and management cycles

Figure 5.4 shows that all stages of the cycles are present simultaneously, but refer to different years. The dynamics of incorporating performance information implies

**Table 5.5** *Business plan of the UK National Offender Management Service*

| Delivering the punishment and orders of courts | Outcome 2012/13 |
|---|---|
| − The percentage of orders and licences that are successfully completed | 77% |
| − Reductions in violence as measured by the violence management report | No single measure |
| − The percentage of prisoners held in crowded accommodation across the prison system | 24.1% |
| − The rate of self-inflicted deaths per 100,000 prisoners (three-year rolling average) | 66 |
| − The rate of drug misuse in prisons as reflected by those testing positive in mandatory drug tests | 7% |
| *Public protection* | |
| − The number of escapes from prison and prison escorts | 2 |
| − The rate of escapes from prison and prison escorts as a proportion of the average prison population | 0.002% |
| − The number of escapes from contractor escorts | 9 |
| − The rate of escapes from contractor escorts as a proportion of the throughput of prisoners | 1 in 96,867 prisoner movements |
| *Reducing reoffending (supplementing the overarching impact indicators)* | |
| − The percentage of offenders in employment at termination of their sentence, order or licence | 37.7% |
| − The percentage of offenders in settled and suitable accommodation at termination of their sentence, order or licence | 86.9% |
| *Reducing costs* | |
| Cost per prisoner | |
| ■ Direct cost per prisoner | £26,139 |
| ■ Overall cost per prisoner | £34,766 |
| Cost per prison place | |
| ■ Direct cost per place | £27,675 |
| ■ Overall cost per place | £36,808 |
| Cost per pre-sentence report to courts | £210 |
| Cost per community order / suspended sentence order | £4,305 |
| Cost per offender supervised on licence post-custody | £2,620 |

**111**

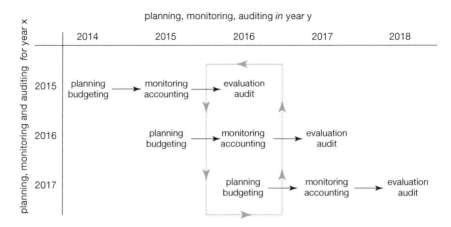

**Figure 5.4** *The dynamics of incorporating performance information*

that in 2016 we are evaluating and auditing the reality of 2015, which was planned, budgeted and contracted in 2014. In 2016 we are monitoring and accounting for plans, budgets and contracts generated in 2014. Finally, in 2016 we are planning, budgeting and contracting for the year 2017. Figure 5.4 shows that incorporation implies that in each year there are three simultaneous exercises, which refer to three different years of activity. Incorporation is therefore linked to the three stages of each cycle, which are connected.

The whole incorporation exercise of performance information requires automatically a time series of at least three years to be useful, coherent and systematic. Hence, stability over time of incorporation efforts becomes more important. Changing performance information over time complicates the way it will be incorporated. This will have a serious negative impact on the use. For that reason it is crucial to consider measurement in the perspective of incorporation and potential use.

## 3 ORGANIZATIONAL READINESS

Finally, we briefly shift our focus from the policy and management cycles towards the implementation of measurement in the organization. The implementation of performance measurement is not fundamentally different from other management practices. The literature on change management provides ample guidance on how to approach change in an organization (Fernandez & Rainey, 2006). There are several 'organizational readiness for performance' checklists that apply change management to performance (see for instance Broom, 1998). Organizational readiness checklists should not be used as a 0/1 total index. Rather, they reflect degrees of readiness that allow for levels of less or more complex systems to manage performance. According to Niven (2003) there are ten criteria to evaluate an organization's readiness to deploy and sustain a performance management system (based on Niven, 2003):

1   A clearly defined strategy
2   Strong, committed sponsorship
3   A clear and urgent need
4   The support of mid-level managers
5   The appropriate scale and scope
6   A strong team and available resources
7   A culture of measurement
8   Alignment between business and IT
9   Trustworthy and available data
10  A solid technical infrastructure

## 4 CONCLUSION

This chapter has discussed the incorporation of performance information into policy and management cycles: the policy cycle, the financial cycle and the contracting cycle. By incorporating performance information, the capacity of organizations to control their goal attainment should be enhanced. In this sense, incorporation is a bridge between measurement and use.

## FURTHER READING

Bouckaert & Halligan (2008) further elaborate on incorporation in their book *Managing Performance: International Comparisons*. De Lancer Julnes & Holzer (2001) published one of the most cited articles on the related concepts of implementation and use (see also Beyer & Trice, 1982; Van Dooren, 2005). For a critical account of performance management incorporation in general, and performance budgeting in particular, the work of Wildavsky (1969) on PPBS and Schick on performance budgeting is a good starting point. The work of Irene Rubin provides lessons on the political impact of performance budgets (Rubin, 1997).

Many cases of incorporation can be found on websites of supreme audit institutions and oversight agencies. Performance contracts are often available through the websites of the contracted agencies. Parliaments usually publish the budget online, which allows for assessing incorporation into the financial cycle.

## REFERENCES

Aristigueta, M. P. (1999). *Managing for Results in State Government*. Westport, CT: Quorum.

Beyer, J. M., & Trice, H. M. (1982). 'The Utilization Process: A Conceptual Framework and Synthesis of Empirical Findings'. *Administrative Science Quarterly, 27*, 591–622.

Bouckaert, G., & Halligan, J. (2008). *Managing Performance: International Comparisons*. London: Routledge.

British Museum (2007). 'Funding Agreement'. London: British Museum.

Broom, C. (1998). *Performance Measurement Concepts and Techniques*. Washington, DC: American Society for Public Administration.

Carlin, T. M. (2006). 'Victoria's Accrual Output Based Budgeting System – Delivering as Promised? Some Empirical Evidence'. *Financial Accountability & Management, 22*, 1–19.

Curristine, T. (2005). 'Performance Information in the Budget Process: Results of OECD 2005 Questionnaire'. *OECD Journal on Budgeting, 5*, 87.

Curristine, T., & Flynn, S. (2013). 'In Search of Results: Strengthening Public Sector Performance'. In Cangiano, M., Curristine, T., & Lazare, M. (eds) *Public Finance Management and Its Emerging Architecture* (pp. 203–32). New York: International Monetary Fund.

De Lancer Julnes, P., & Holzer, M. (2001). 'Promoting the Utilization of Performance Measures in Public Organizations: An Empirical Study of Factors Affecting Adoption and Implementation'. *Public Administration Review, 61*, 693–708.

Fernandez, S., & Rainey, H. G. (2006). 'Managing Successful Organizational Change in the Public Sector'. *Public Administration Review, 66*(2), 168–76.

Ho, A. T.-K. (2011). 'PBB in American Local Governments: It's More Than a Management Tool'. *Public Administration Review, 71*(3), 391–401.

Kissler, G. R., Fore, K. N., Jacobson, W. S., Kittredge, W. P., & Stewart, S. L. (1998). 'State Strategic Planning: Suggestions from the Oregon Experience'. *Public Administration Review, 58*(4), 353–59. doi:10.2307/977565

Kroll, A. (2013). 'The Other Type of Performance Information: Nonroutine Feedback, Its Relevance and Use'. *Public Administration Review, 73*(2), 265–76.

Lindblom, C. E. (1959). 'The Science of "Muddling Through"'. *Public Administration Review, 19*, 79–88.

McMahon, L., & Phillimore, J. (2013). 'State and Territory Government Strategic Plans: Exercises in Managing, Monitoring and Marketing'. *Australian Journal of Public Administration, 72*(4), 404–18.

Meyer, J. W., & Rowan, B. (1977). 'Institutionalized Organizations: Formal Structure as Myth and Ceremony'. *American Journal of Sociology, 83*, 341–62.

National Gallery of Australia, Canberra (2012) 'Strategic Plan and Budget Priorities'. Canberra: National Gallery of Australia, Canberra.

Niven, P. (2003). *Balanced Scorecard Step by Step for Government and Nonprofit Agencies*. Hoboken, NJ: John Wiley & Sons.

Nõmm, K., & Randma-Liiv, T. (2012). 'Performance Measurement and Performance Information in New Democracies'. *Public Management Review*, 14(7), 1–21.

O'Connell, P. E. (2001). 'Using Performance Data for Accountability: The New York City Police Department's CompStat Model of Police Management'. *The PricewaterhouseCoopers Endowment for the Business of Government*. Washington, DC: PricewaterhouseCoopers.

Ohemeng, F. L. K. (2011). 'Institutionalizing the Performance Management System in Public Organizations in Ghana'. *Public Performance & Management Review*, 34(4), 467–88.

Paulsson, G. (2006). 'Accrual Accounting in the Public Sector: Experiences from the Central Government in Sweden'. *Financial Accountability & Management*, 22, 47–62.

Pollitt, C., & Bouckaert, G. (2011). *Public Management Reform: A Comparative Analysis* (3rd ed.). Oxford: Oxford University Press.

Public Audit Forum (2002). *The Whole Truth; Or Why Accruals Accounting Means Better Management*. London: National Audit Office.

Raaum, R. B., & Morgan, S. L. (2001). *Performance Auditing: A Measurement Approach*. Altamonte Springs, FL: Institute of Internal Auditors.

Rubin, I. S. (1997). *The Politics of Public Budgeting: Getting and Spending, Borrowing and Balancing*. Chatham, NJ: Chatham House Publishers.

Schick, A. (2003). 'The Performing State: Reflection on an Idea Whose Time Has Come but Whose Implementation Has Not'. *OECD Journal on Budgeting*, 3(2), 71–103.

—— (2013). *The Metamorphoses of Performance Budgeting*. Presentation at the Annual OECD Meeting of Senior Budget Officials, Paris: OECD, 3–4 June.

Schmidle, T. (2011). 'Performance Management: Laudable Objectives, Limited Usage, Lowered Expectations'. *Public Performance & Management Review*, 35(2), 370–389. doi:10.2753/PMR1530–9576350206

Talbot, C. (2012). 'Targets? What Targets? Change and Continuity in the Performance Regime in Whitehall'. Manchester Policy Blogs. Retrieved from http://blog.policy.manchester.ac.uk/whitehallwatch/2012/08/targets-what-targets-change-and-continuity-in-the-performance-regime-in-whitehall/.

—— (2013). 'Targets, What Targets? Now Perm Secs Targets Are "Published"'. Manchester Policy Blogs. Retrieved from http://blog.policy.manchester.ac.uk/whitehallwatch/2013/01/targets-what-targets-now-perm-secs-targets-are-published/.

Van Dooren, W. (2005). 'What Makes Organisations Measure? Hypotheses on the Causes and Conditions for Performance Measurement'. *Financial Accountability & Management*, 21, 363–83.

Van Hofwegen, J., & de Jong, M. (2012). 'Naar een verantwoorde begrotingspresentatie Over verantwoord omgaan met (on)zekerheden'. (Towards a Responsive Budget Account: On Responsible Dealings with Uncertainties.) In Ministerie van Financiën (ed.), *De toekomst van de financiële functie van het Rijk: een beeld voor 2020* (pp. 75–90). Den Haag: Ministerie van Financiën.

Wildavsky, A. (1969). 'Rescuing Policy Analysis from PPBS'. *Public Administration Review*, 29(2), 189–202.

Wildavsky, A., & Hammond, A. (1965). 'Comprehensive versus Incremental Budgeting in the Department of Agriculture'. *Administrative Science Quarterly*, 10, 321–46.

Yang, K., & Hsieh, J. Y. (2007). 'Managerial Effectiveness of Government Performance Measurement: Testing a Middle-Range Model'. *Public Administration Review*, 67, 861–79.

# Chapter 6

# The use of performance information

## LEARNING OBJECTIVES

■ To distinguish the three categories of uses of performance information and their defining characteristics.

■ To understand the implications of use on the design of a performance measurement system.

## KEY POINTS IN THIS CHAPTER

■ The use of performance information ranges from soft to hard. Learning is generally softer than steering & control, which is in turn softer than use for accountability.

■ The use determines the design of the measurement system.

■ Building a sound data infrastructure may overcome the difficulties of multi-purpose measurement systems.

## DISCUSSION QUESTIONS

■ Consider the use of indicators in a particular context: a police force, the university, hospitals, and so on. How is the information used?

■ Which use (soft or hard) is more appropriate?

■ Evaluate the measurement system of an organization based on the use and the design parameters.

The use of information is often conceived in a bipolar way: either it is used or not. This view assumes a direct 1:1 relation between performance information and managerial or policy decisions. Bipolar thinking is fed by a somewhat technocratic hope that performance information will tell univocally how to allocate resources, how to hold organizations and managers to account, and which employees to reward for excellent performance. Performance measurement systems almost never can do that. Often, these unfulfilled expectations provoke a categorical rejection by users of performance information. In order to reach a middle ground, a more nuanced perspective on use is needed.

We need a more precise understanding of how performance information is used (Hatry, 2008). This book allots a lot of attention to the use of performance information. This chapter discusses *the uses* of performance information. In the next chapter, the perspective of the potential *users* of performance information is explored. The reasons for *non-use* are discussed in chapter 8.

The analysis of the uses of performance information starts with a practical perspective in section 1. The uses in practice are manifold, and not surprisingly, scholars have attempted to make categorizations. The most fundamental categorization however is how performance information will be used, which can range from soft to hard (section 2). The decision on how to use performance information will have ramifications for the design of the whole measurement process. Section 3 reiterates the steps in the measurement process and indicates for each step the variation that follows from the distinction between soft and hard use. It is thus assumed that intended use should determine the design of the measurement system and not vice versa. The form of the measurement system should follow the function. While this may seem self-evident, the practice of performance management shows that many measurement systems are not fit for purpose. The chapter ends with a brief comment on measurement systems that serve the needs of different uses.

## 1 USE IN PRACTICE

Over 40 potential uses of performance information can be identified (Van Dooren, 2006). The practices mentioned in Table 6.1 are traditional management practices that are redefined by incorporating performance information. Allocation of resources for instance allegedly can be more focused if based on performance information instead of on last year's budget. For grantor reporting, it is assumed that grantors will be more interested in results than in whether the grantee has spent the budget. Similarly, the use of performance information in auditing may enrich the findings of the auditors. Note that this list of potential uses does not say anything about the breadth and the intensity of use in organizations.

Although the list of uses demonstrates the variation in practice, the distinction between the 42 uses is not always clear-cut. Performance budgeting, output

**Table 6.1** *The uses of performance information in policy and management practice*

*Potential uses of performance information*

| | | | |
|---|---|---|---|
| 1 | allocation of resources | 22 | capital management |
| 2 | enable consumers to make informed choices | 23 | evaluation of outcomes and effectiveness |
| 3 | changing work processes/more efficiency | 24 | managerial incentive schemes |
| 4 | improving responsiveness to customers | 25 | reducing duplicative services/delivery alternatives (incl. privatization) |
| 5 | formulation and monitoring of licensed or contracted privatized services | 26 | management by objectives |
| | | 27 | adopting new programme approaches/changing strategies |
| 6 | creditor reporting | 28 | staff motivation/non-monetary incentives |
| 7 | rewarding staff/monetary incentives/performance pay | 29 | setting programme priorities |
| 8 | grantor reporting | 30 | strategic HRM |
| 9 | strategic planning | 31 | communication with the legislature and the legislative staff |
| 10 | output budgeting: pay per output ($p \times q$) | 32 | clarifying objectives |
| 11 | communication with the public to build trust | 33 | cost saving |
| 12 | outcome budgeting: pay per outcome | 34 | Quality Models (TQM) |
| | | 35 | setting individual job expectations/ staff performance plans |
| 13 | reporting and monitoring | 36 | sanctioning prolonged low performance |
| 14 | changing appropriation levels | | |
| 15 | accountability to elected officials | 37 | cost–benefit analysis |
| 16 | performance budgeting: alongside budget figures | 38 | allocating discretionary funds to high-performance agencies or programmes |
| 17 | accountability to the public | 39 | trigger for further investigation and action |
| 18 | cost accounting | | |
| 19 | results-based budgeting: justify budget requests | 40 | communication between managers |
| 20 | performance auditing | 41 | coordination of activities internally or externally |
| 21 | motivation rewards for groups, organizations | 42 | organizational development |

budgeting and outcome budgeting are for instance closely related. In order to study use in organizations, scholars have developed classifications of uses into broader categories with similar features. Behn (2003) for instance proposes a categorization of eight managerial uses from evaluation to celebration and learning. He argues that all the purposes are subordinate to one ultimate purpose. He writes, 'for the measurement of performance, the public manager's real purpose – indeed, the only real purpose – is to improve performance. The other seven purposes are simply means for achieving this ultimate purpose' (Behn, 2003: p. 588).

Although many managers indeed use performance information for improvement, research evidence suggests some other, somewhat less decorous purposes. Performance information is also used for *enhancing power positions*. Francis Bacon wrote in 1597 that knowledge in itself is power. This also applies here. An organization that has to provide performance information to outsiders is more vulnerable. The Labour government in England for instance used performance indicators in the early 2000s to strengthen control over the hospital sector (Bevan & Hood, 2006). Besides a power dimension, performance information can also be *symbolic*. Measurement is modern and performance indicators thus can also be used for symbolic reasons – to be seen as modern. The purpose of measurement is not improvement, or learning of any kind. Rather, measurement becomes a goal in itself (Vakkuri & Meklin, 2006; Torres, Pina & Yetano, 2011).

In our text, we will further use a sparser classification of three purposes: *to learn*, *to steer & control* and *to give account* (Table 6.2).

**Table 6.2** Three uses of performance information

|  | To learn | To steer & control | To give account |
|---|---|---|---|
| Key question | How to improve policy or management? | How to be in command of activities? | How to communicate performance? |
| Orientation | Change/future | Control/present | Survival/past |

1   First, performance information may be collected in order to find out what works (and what does not) and why (not). The main function here is *learning*. The key question is how policy or management can be improved. Performance information can be used for process evaluation and outcome evaluation, which envisages, respectively, service improvement and policy improvement. Typical applications are learning circles and peer reviews that make use of performance data. The focus is mainly on the future policy and management (see Box 6.1 for Moynihan's dialogue theory of learning from performance information).

**120**

## BOX 6.1 DIALOGUE THEORY AND LEARNING FORUMS

Donald Moynihan (2005) found that the highest value of performance management lies in its ability to inform dialogue on performance. Managers need to create learning forums to organize dialogue. Moynihan lists the following characteristics of learning forums:

- routine events;
- facilitation and ground rules structure the dialogue;
- non-confrontational approach to avoid defensive reactions;
- collegiality and equality among participants;
- diverse set of organizational actors responsible for producing the outcomes under review;
- dialogue centred, with dialogue focused on organizational goals;
- basic assumptions are identified, examined and suspended (especially for double-loop learning);
- quantitative knowledge that identifies successes and failures, including goals, targets, outcomes and points of comparison;
- experiential knowledge of process and work conditions that explains successes, failures and possibility of innovation.

2   Second, the use for the *steering & control* function of performance information is about keeping track. The key question is whether policies and programmes are on target. Typical applications are management scorecards that monitor the performance of the organization and policy monitors that track changes in a policy field. These systems mainly have a control orientation and are occupied with the present rather than future or past performance.

3   The third purpose is *to give account*. The key question is how to justify performance. The account holder can impose sanctions (positive or negative). In the last decades, accountability mechanisms have shifted from a focus on legality (spend resources lawfully) to a focus on results (demonstrate what is coming out) (Kettl, 2002). It was assumed that accountability for results would put external pressure on public organizations. In this sense, the orientation is not so much change or control, but survival. Performance measurement in this case is mainly about explaining past performance. Account giving is taking place at different scales: between employees and senior management, between organizations and (political) principals, between executives and parliament, and so on.

Different underlying mechanisms explain why accountability for performance exerts pressure on people in organizations. The publication of performance charts can create *reputational pressure*. The potential criticism of the public (and the media) is expected to wield enough pressure for change. Typical examples are citizen's charters and upgraded annual reporting (Bowerman, 1995). In case of (quasi-) markets, for instance in public schools and hospitals, *market pressures* are also at play (Gormley & Weimer, 1999). Rankings of for instance schools are expected to influence the user's choice of public services. Third, accountability for performance stems from *political pressure*. Performance contracts with agencies are a good example. These contracts give autonomy to agencies within a pre-set budgetary framework, provided that the agency commits itself to output or outcome targets (see for instance Greve *et al.*, 1999, for a discussion on the Danish, UK and Dutch practice, Verhoest, 2005, for a Belgian perspective, Laegreid *et al.*, 2008, on Norway, and Radin, 2002, on the USA).

## 2 HARD AND SOFT USE

From the discussion above, we should recall that use of performance exerts pressure on behaviour. A crucial decision is whether performance information will be used in a hard or a soft way. The distinction refers to two dimensions: (1) tight or loose coupling between measurement and the performance judgement, and (2) the consequences of good or bad performance.

1    First, how tightly coupled are performance information and judgement? Is there room for scrutiny before a final assessment on the performance is set? Hard use presupposes a tight coupling between performance information and judgement, while soft use leaves more room. Loose coupling allows that dialogue and interpretation mediate final decision-making (Moynihan, 2008). It is the difference between formula-based use and interpretative use, or between summative and formative use (Charbonneau, 2011). A performance contract that stipulates sanctions for an agency that does not reach its performance targets, regardless of context, is an example of hard use. A benchmarking exercise that requires some performance information to feed into discussions on how to do things differently is an example of soft use.

Other authors also have touched upon this distinction. Carter, Klein & Day (1992) used the metaphors of *dials* and *tin openers*. Performance indicators can be used in a 1:1 relation between the results observed through measurement and the subsequent actions. Alternatively, performance indicators are used to open the tin, without revealing its contents. This is soft use, because the real interpretative work only starts and actions will only follow after interpretation.

The Public Administration Select Committee of the UK House of Commons made a similar distinction when they proposed to make a distinction between a measurement culture (hard use, formula-based) and a performance culture (soft use, interpretation-based). The conclusion of the report was that in the UK

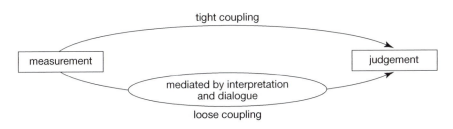

**Figure 6.1** *Loose and tight coupling of performance information and judgement*

organizations were more concerned with measurement than with performance improvement. They recommended moving towards a performance culture. The proposal was not to abandon measurement, but to use performance indicators in a more sensible way (House of Commons Public Administration Select Committee, 2003).

2   The second dimension of hard and soft refers to the consequences of the judgements that are based on the performance information. Some uses have a higher impact on organizations than others. Compare for instance major budget cuts with the publication of performance measures in an internal memo. Table 6.3 provides a non-exhaustive list of parameters that determine the impact of performance information on an organization. When performance information touches upon the core business of the organization it may have a higher impact than when it deals with peripheral issues. In particular when the core identity of the organization is touched, employees will perceive the impact of performance information. Indicators that are closely followed by the media may have a reputational impact on the organization. In some instances, performance targets lead to budget allocation. Other systems reward the reaching of a target with more autonomy for the organization. An organizational context mediates the perceived impact of performance measurement. Arguably, an organization that mainly employs engineers will be more susceptible to measurement than an organization of social workers.

**Table 6.3** *Assessing the impact of performance judgements*

| Low impact | High impact |
| --- | --- |
| Peripheral issues | Core business/identity |
| Not reputational | Reputation at stake |
| No budgetary consequences | Budgetary impact |
| No impact on autonomy | Infringes on autonomy |
| Congruent with organizational culture | Incongruent with organizational culture |

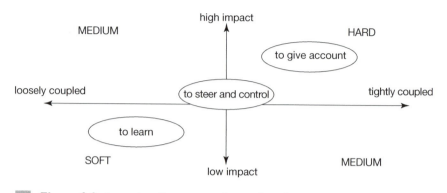

**Figure 6.2** *Assessing the nature of use of performance information*

It is important to have an idea of how hard a performance measurement system is (below, we explain why). Some uses have a soft inclination while others will tend to be hard and formula-based with high impact. Performance contracts have a propensity to be hard while benchmarking tends to be soft. Figure 6.2 plots the three categories of use on a grid. Yet, reality is contingent on the local context of the uses. It is definitely not the case that a specific use or a specific performance management tool is *per definition* soft or hard. Formally, league tables of schools look quite similar across countries. Yet, it seems that use is perceived much harder in some countries than in others. The reason is that in some countries parents use the league tables as one of the most important sources of information for school choice, while in other countries other factors are taken into account. Another example is performance-related pay, which is generally considered a hard use of performance information. People receive monetary incentives, and reaching a target automatically gives a right on a bonus (tight coupling). Yet, when the monetary incentive is small or granted to a team, the pressure may be less.

## 3 HARD OR SOFT USE: IMPLICATIONS FOR THE DESIGN OF THE MEASUREMENT SYSTEM

Hard uses have a higher propensity to engender dysfunctional behavioural effects (see chapter 9). When there is a 1:1 relation between measurement and decision-making, the only way to influence the decision-making is to manipulate measurement. In the same way, soft use only loosely couples measurement and decisions, and therefore is less threatening. In case of hard use, there are three strategies in response to the indicators.

Strategy 1: *functional compliance*. In this case, the expression 'what gets measured, gets done' applies. Organizational and individual behaviour are aligned with the indicators. Management theory that stipulates the formulation of key performance indicators assumes that measurement will lead functional behaviour, that is, a focus on what really matters. Yet, it is often forgotten that compliance is not the only behavioural option.

Strategy 2: *dysfunctional compliance*. A second strategy is to change behaviour in the organization in a way that violates the purposes of the performance indicators. Service or product quality for instance may suffer from an overly strong focus on production and service volumes. What gets measured gets done, but in a substandard way and at the expense of other valuable activities that are not measured.

Strategy 3: *misrepresentation*. Organizational and/or individual behaviour does not change, but is represented in a more flattering way. Because of the manipulation of the measurement system, decisions are based on flawed information.

In case of soft use, a fourth strategy can be added to this list: justification. The organization trusts that after measurement, there will be sufficient opportunity to influence decision-making through performance-based dialogue. As a result, there will be less pressure for dysfunctional compliance or misrepresentation, but also less pressure for direct, functional compliance.

Since the propensity for organizations to resort to dysfunctional compliance and misrepresentation is higher in the case of hard use, the choice for hard uses has implications for the design of the measurement system. Measurement systems need to be more robust. Measurement error, whatever the cause, cannot be corrected through interpretation and dialogue. We now return to the different steps in performance measurement discussed in chapter 4, and make a differentiation for use.

## Step 1: prioritizing the measurement effort

Since it is virtually impossible to measure everything, a reasoned decision on what to measure and what not to measure needs to be taken. The measurement effort should be focused on the foreseen use. This decision can be based on several criteria, such as intuitive indications of problems, added value of measurement, financial coverage and visibility of a service (see chapter 4). Table 6.4 differentiates the criteria for the uses of performance information.

*To learn.* Learning is about finding weaknesses and developing solutions. Intuitive indications of problems that need more evidence may therefore be the basis for measurement. A complaint on waiting lists may for instance trigger a systematic registration of waiting times for a service. Clearly, the added value to the information that is already available and the feasibility of measurement will be additional concerns when targeting the measurement effort.

**Table 6.4** *Criteria for targeting measurement efforts on their foreseen uses*

| To learn | To steer & control | To give account |
|---|---|---|
| – indications of problems | – distribution over divisions | – societal visibility |
| – added value | – financial coverage | – predetermined |
| – feasibility | – staff coverage | |

*To steer & control.* A fair distribution of the indicators in the organization is a relevant criterion for this purpose. Management scorecards usually prescribe this approach (Kaplan & Norton, 1996). Each division of the organization should provide some key performance indicators for management to monitor the operations. Managers are seen as pilots in a cockpit who take corrective action when an indicator signals a problem. Additional arguments could be to require more measurement from divisions with a higher financial importance (financial coverage) or divisions that employ a larger portion of the staff (staff coverage).

*To give account.* Accountability requirements often are imposed on organizations. In this case, the decision of what to measure is predetermined. If however the organization is taking the initiative to improve account giving, social visibility may be the first criterion for selecting the measurement object. An employment agency for instance may want to target measurement efforts on those target groups that are at the forefront of the policy debate. Usually, accountability initiatives are neither completely voluntary nor entirely predetermined. Accountability is negotiated and the performance indicators are negotiated alongside. Negotiation is clearly part of performance contracts between agencies and departments, but the content of league tables or imposed reporting formats are also subject to negotiation and lobbying.

## Step 2: selection of the indicators

The second phase is the selection of the indicators (Table 6.5). Indicators may be single indicators that refer to inputs, outputs, outcomes or the environment in which the organization operates. Indicators may also be ratio indicators that combine single indicators. Efficiency is input over output. Effectiveness is output over effect. Cost-effectiveness is input over effect.

*To learn.* The indicator set has to cover the whole production chain of the organization. Underperformance could result from insufficient inputs, inadequate processes or unrealistic expectations of outputs and outcomes. Measurement will seldom univocally dictate answers. Interpretation through professional judgement and experience is needed to fill the gaps in the measurement system. An incomplete measurement system hence can still be used in dialogue.

**Table 6.5** *Which indicators for which use?*

| To learn | To steer & control | To give account |
|---|---|---|
| – the whole 'production chain of the organization': from input to outcome | – mainly output and efficiency | – optimally outcome, with output as a second best |

*To steer & control.* The indicators will principally have to be a combination of input and output indicators. Following the traditional politics/administration dichotomy, the main responsibility of public managers is to convert resources into products and services that politicians, policymakers and ultimately citizens prescribe. Although scholars have demonstrated that the line between politics and management is never that clear (see for instance Svara, 1985, and Peters, 2001), the distinction remains one of the leading principles in the design of administrative systems.

*To give account.* Outcomes are what matters for society, and therefore the optimal indicators for accountability should be outcome indicators (Hatry, 1999). However, because of the potentially severe consequences of accountability on the organization, room for interpretation is generally not accepted. In addition, outcomes have to be attributable to the organization's activities. These are qualities that outcome indicators seldom have. Therefore, output indicators are often used instead whereas the relation with outcomes is assumed.

## Step 3: data collection

After the selection of the indicators, data need to be collected. Organizations may use internal or external data sources. Internal data are produced by the organization itself while external data are purchased or obtained from other organizations. A broad array of data sources can be used (Table 6.6).

*To learn.* Learning will require a wide range of data in order to cover the span, from input to outcome, of the performance measurement system. *Existing and additional administrative registrations* are useful to measure inputs, outputs and inter-mediate outcomes. *Self-assessments* can be used to measure internal processes. *Technical measurement* and *surveys* can provide insight into the outcome of the organization. Data from other organizations and *statistical institutions* will primarily be useful to establish causality and the influence of contextual factors on the outcome. *External observers* are the only data source that may be less useful. Learning postulates an intrinsic motivation, and therefore the benefit of impartiality is less pressing than the need for ownership of the findings by those who will have to learn from it.

*To steer & control.* Measurement will mainly depend on *existing* and *additional registrations* and *record keeping* within the organization. This is consistent with the internal focus of management. If applicable, *technical measurement* is useful as a

**Table 6.6** *Differentiation of the data sources according to the purpose of performance information*

| To learn | To steer & control | To give account |
|---|---|---|
| *More useful* | | |
| – Existing registrations | – Existing registrations | – Existing registrations |
| – Additional registrations | – Additional registrations | – Additional registrations |
| – Surveys | – Technical measurement | – Surveys |
| – Self-assessments | – External observers | – Technical measurement |
| – Technical measurement | | – External observers |
| – Other organizations | | |
| – Statistical, inter- national and research institutions | | |
| *Less useful* | | |
| – External observers | – Surveys | – Other organizations |
| | – Self-assessments | – Statistical, inter- national and research institutions |
| | – Other organizations | |
| | – Statistical, international and research institutions | – Self-assessments |

control device because of its unobtrusive character. When technical measurement is not feasible, *external observers* can take over the role of neutral bystander. Reliance on other organizations' data, *statistical data* and *survey data* is less useful for internal management since they rather comprehend outcome and contextual information. *Self-assessments* will also be less functional for steering & control because they are mostly project-based and with a learning purpose.

*To give account.* *Administrative registrations* are useful for accountability when organizations have to show which outputs they produced and which target groups and regions they have served. Additionally, *technical measurement*, *external observers* and *surveys* (for instance on client satisfaction) may be used. The subjective elements in surveys is however a problem for reliable accountability. Other organizations' data and data from *statistical institutions* will usually only play a peripheral role in contextualizing success and failure. Finally, *self-assessments* are not useful for the same reason as for the steering & control function.

## Step 4: analysis

The purpose of analysing data is to transform data into information on which decisions can be based. Regularly, interpretation and analytical processing are not formalized. Performance is for instance often compared with past performance in an inexplicit way. In order to fully explore the potential of the information, analysis should be an integral part of the measurement system. Chapter 4 referred to three approaches to analysis: norm setting, aggregation and statistical analysis. Table 6.7 below differentiates the analytical approaches for different uses.

*To learn.* Learning will benefit from a broad range of assessments. Comparisons with *past performance* and confrontations with *scientific standards* can be a starting point for diagnosis of performance. Comparison with *other organizations* may set the organization on track for better practices elsewhere. In addition, *causal analysis* research can answer the question why a result is showing, and *disaggregation* can help to trace results back to divisions of the organization, target groups or geographical circumscriptions, which is key for remedying insufficient performance. Less useful for learning are *symbolic norms* and *highly aggregated* indices. The latter usually are not actionable.

*To steer & control. Past performance* is also of importance here. *Other organizations within the sector* can be a reference for output levels, while *organizations outside the sector* are mainly relevant for comparing the management functions of the organization. In particular cases, *scientific standards* are the point of reference. *International comparison* seems less useful. Foreign organizations mostly operate in an institutional and political context that is too different to be useful for daily steering & control. In order to fulfil the internal management function, *disaggregated* information will be needed. For instance, the allocation of resources based on performance data requires a detailed cost-accounting system that is capable of providing unit costs. *Causal analysis* of performance results is not the prime focus of this category of use. Usually, the causal assumptions will be working hypotheses.

*To give account.* Comparisons of current with *past performance* are also useful for account giving. Doing better is a common expectation for public organizations. Comparisons with *organizations within the sector* are a second important norm for accountability purposes. Organizational report cards (league tables) compare amongst others schools, hospitals, universities, police units and local communities. When the service provider is a monopolist in a country, *international comparisons* can be used. Furthermore, *scientific norms* can be used for accountability. For instance, a health agency may be expected to attain the vaccination grade that is required to avoid epidemics (which is not necessarily 100 per cent). Since *symbolic norms* may be used to keep an issue on the agenda, there is also an accountability aspect to it. Comparison with organizations from *different sectors* appears less appealing for accountability, given the fact that management should not be the core business of service delivery. Mol (2001) for instance pointed to the negative effect of pinpointing accountability on a limited number of secondary processes in the Dutch military. Finally, the causes of performance usually are rather an implicit assumption than an explicit subject of *causal analysis*. In contrast to the learning and management use, accountability often requires *aggregated* information that allows for judgement at a glance by decision-makers.

**129**

**Table 6.7** *Differentiation of the choice of analysis technique according to the purpose of performance information*

| Use | Category | More useful | Less useful |
|---|---|---|---|
| To learn | Norm setting | – Time<br>– Other organizations within the sector<br>– Other organizations outside the sector<br>– Foreign organizations<br>– Scientific standards | – Symbolic norms<br>– Aggregated |
| | Aggregation and breakouts | – Disaggregated | |
| | Causal analysis | – Causal analysis | |
| To steer & control | Norm setting | – Time<br>– Other organizations within the sector<br>– Other organizations outside the sector<br>– Scientific standards | – Foreign organizations<br>– Symbolic norms |
| | Aggregation and breakouts | – Disaggregated | – Aggregated |
| | Causal analysis | | – Causal analysis |
| To give account | Norm setting | – Time<br>– Other organizations within the sector<br>– Foreign organizations<br>– Scientific standards<br>– Symbolic norms | – Other organizations outside the sector |
| | Aggregation and breakouts | – Aggregated | – Disaggregated |
| | Causal analysis | | – Causal analysis |

## Step 5: reporting

The last step in the performance measurement process is the reporting of the information. With regard to reporting, a simple, almost common-sense rule applies. The format should be suitable for the target group (Rossi & Gilmartin, 1980; Hendricks, 1994) (Table 6.8). Yet, performance measurement systems often violate this rule. Reporting of performance information to top management for instance will require other reporting formats compared to reporting to media or interest groups. Different reporting formats can make the same bit of performance

**130**

information suitable for different target groups. Two questions thus should be answered: who is using the information, and what is the right format for that target group? Differentiating for purposes implies answering the first question first: who should be the users of performance information if learning, steering & control, or account-giving is the purpose? The next issue then is to find the right format.

*To learn.* Although different target groups can learn from performance information, the main audience for learning purposes usually will be the *staff*. Contemporary implementation literature has reconfirmed the importance of professionals, street-level bureaucrats and front-line workers (Hupe & Hill, 2007; Noordegraaf & Abma, 2003). The combination of performance information and professional judgement that is accumulated through daily practice is the core of the learning perspective. If we assume, together with implementation scholars, that most of this professional knowledge on how things work is owned at the street level, it seems logical to target learning efforts primarily there. A good flow of information will assure that higher levels are kept informed and can act upon these learning efforts.

Outside of the organization, there may be interest from mainly *executive politicians* in learning from performance information for developing their policies. The evidence-based policy agenda (see chapter 3) supports this perspective. Policy is however not developed in a vacuum. Advisory bodies and interest groups will attempt to put their spin on the performance information. This is not necessarily wrong and can be part of the learning dialogue. Similarly, political opposition may use performance information to build an argument against policies. Finally, there may be some function for performance information in 'educating' *the public* about their behaviour. An environmental agency for instance may mediatize the number of interventions for illegal dumping in rivers and its detrimental effect on fauna in order to sensitize the public and render dumping socially inacceptable.

The reporting format is less important for learning compared to the other uses. As Moynihan (2008) argues in his dialogue theory, the process of measurement is as important as the outcomes. The main format will often be *oral witnesses*. In addition, in order to strengthen organizational memory, a case can be made to document learning outcomes in *specialized reports*. Such reports will also be needed when the findings need to be disseminated beyond the learning group to the whole organization or policy sector.

*To steer & control.* Since steering & control is the main responsibility of management, higher *management* levels should be the prime target group. Management scorecards with key performance indicators such as the Balanced Scorecard are one of the most common reporting formats in this context. *Reports* can also be used, but in contrast to the specialized and irregular reporting of measurement for learning, steering & control will require recurrent reporting that follows a more standardized layout. *Oral witnesses* can supplement these sources and will particularly be required when management scorecards show unexpected results.

**131**

*To give account.* Since relations of accountability can be manifold, performance information may be relevant for a potentially broad set of actors. Accountability is a relationship in which an individual or agency is held to answer for performance that is expected by some significant 'other' (Romzek & Dubnick, 1987). The ultimate significant other in a democracy is the general public, which can be reached through the *mass media*. Journalists are usually best reached through personal contact or press releases. Interest groups in essence have the same function of bridging the gap between the organization and the citizen, albeit usually for a particular concern. Since interest groups typically have fewer deadlines and are more specialized than journalists, *reports* and *interactive websites* can supplement oral witnesses.

Significant others in accountability relations however are also located inside the political system, in both the executive and the legislative branch. *Annual reporting* and planning as well as budgets and accounts are typical accountability formats in this case. In addition, *supranational institutions* may hold governments accountable. The Maastricht criteria and the Lisbon indicators are examples of the European Union holding the member states accountable for their performance on a limited set of criteria. The aim is to align national policies to the European agenda without having to resort to regulation. The EU counts on the reputational damage of a bad score on the performance indicators for member states to react. In EU jargon, this approach to governance is known as OMC, the Open Method of Cooperation (Borras & Jacobsson, 2004).

**Table 6.8** *Differentiation of the reporting format according to the purpose of performance information*

| To learn | To steer & control | To give account |
|---|---|---|
| *To whom* | | |
| − staff<br>− executive politicians<br>− advisory boards<br>− interest groups<br>− general public | − the board of the organization<br>− top management | − the general public<br>− mass media<br>− interest groups<br>− executive politicians<br>− supranational institutions<br>− parliament |
| *Format* | | |
| − specialized reports<br>− oral witnesses | − scorecards<br>− recurrent reports<br>− oral witnesses | − annual reports and planning<br>− budget and accounts<br>− specialized reports<br>− interactive website<br>− oral witnesses<br>− press releases and publicity<br>− scorecards |

**132**

## 3.1 Quality assurance

Quality has three dimensions (Bouckaert, 1993) (Figure 6.3). First, quality implies the functionality of the measurement system. Measurement should be fit for use. Second, quality implies indicators that are valid and reliable. A reliable indicator yields the same values for repeated measurements of the same object. A valid indicator measures what is intended. A thermometer that repeatedly measures 95°C for boiling water is reliable but invalid. A thermometer that yields different values (say 95°C, 105°C and 100°C) but averages 100°C is valid, but unreliable. The third quality dimension is legitimacy of a measurement system, which means that those who are supposed to use the information should support measurement.

The criterion of functionality should be assessed first. Performance measurement systems that are dysfunctional should be abolished or redesigned. The other two criteria may be applied more variably accordingly to the purposes (Table 6.9).

Before discussing the table, two remarks are needed. First, we use the categories *moderately important*, *important* and *critical*, which does not look like a balanced scale. The reason is that a certain level of quality is required in all cases. It would be wrong to state that a particular quality characteristic is not at all important for a particular use. Yet, there is still variation in importance. The marginal costs and

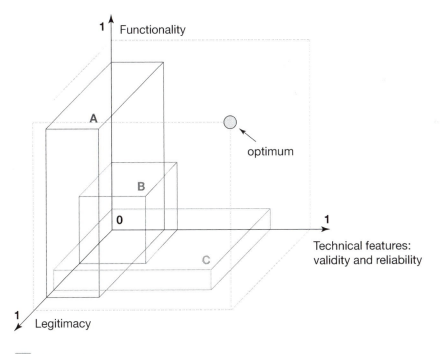

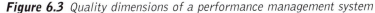
**Figure 6.3** *Quality dimensions of a performance management system*

**133**

**Table 6.9** *Differentiation of the quality dimensions according to the purpose*

|  | To learn | To steer & control | To give account |
|---|---|---|---|
| Validity | moderately important | critical | critical |
| Reliability | moderately important | important | critical |
| Internal legitimacy | critical | important | moderately important |
| External legitimacy | critical | moderately important | critical |

benefits of more quality need to be taken into account. Hatry (2002) for instance argues that pressures from the professional community have overstressed the need for high levels of precision and response rates in customer surveys, which has driven costs up and discouraged practitioners. According to Hatry (2002), the operational principle should be that it is better to be roughly right than to be precisely ignorant.

A second remark regarding Table 6.9 is that the quality dimensions may influence each other as independent and dependent variables. For instance, a high legitimacy within an organization may lead to high reliability because employees are mindful not to make mistakes in registration. Likewise, high validity may lead to high legitimacy because people feel the right things are measured. Untangling the dynamics between quality criteria is an empirical issue that would go beyond the scope of a textbook.

*To learn.* Learning poses the least strict conditions on validity and reliability. Performance information will be complemented by other information sources such as individual experiences of employees. This dialogue on the performance information can also be seen as an ex post validity and reliability check. Crucial however is legitimacy of the measurement effort. Without the conviction of staff that measurement may allow for evaluation and improvement, learning will not occur.

*To steer & control.* Validity and reliability are important for steering & control because sanctions and rewards as well as budget and staff are distributed based on measurement. We assessed validity to be critical and reliability only to be important. The reason is that steering & control usually requires the reiteration of measurement efforts in relatively short cycles (maximal one year, more often quarters). Reliability issues will thus emerge quite naturally and can be corrected in the short term. Validity problems on the other hand will be repeated with every measurement and can only be detected and corrected when the indicators are scrutinized. Legitimacy seems of lesser importance, since it is mainly the responsibility of the manager to control and to allocate resources, and not of the staff or external actors. It can be argued that given the organizational focus of the measurement system, internal legitimacy is somewhat more important than external.

*To give account.* External accountability requires high validity and reliability, because of the high stakes of bad or good results for the organization. Given the behavioural effects that high-pressure systems may trigger (see chapter 9), bias and noise on measurement will distort the activities of the organization. While obviously external legitimacy is critical, internal legitimacy may be of second-order importance. When the information will for instance be used for performance contracts with the organization, legitimacy for measurement in the whole organization may be less important. The main point is that the two sides of the contract, that is, top management and the political level, support the indicators in the contract.

## 4 MULTIFUNCTIONAL MEASUREMENT SYSTEMS

The main argument until now has been that there is no 'one size fits all' measurement process. The design of the measurement system needs to be founded on the foreseen uses of measurement. When use is neglected while measuring, the performance information that comes out of the process has a high chance of being not used or used inappropriately. The differentiation of the design parameters however also introduces incongruence between the designs. The question then arises whether organizations can allocate different uses to one measurement process. Hence, a discussion on such multifunctional measurement systems is warranted.

At first, multifunction measurement systems appear not viable. The reason is that hard use drives out soft use. Once a measurement system is used for the harder purposes such as account giving, it can no longer be used for softer approaches such as learning. Learning requires room for dialogue in which those participating have to take risks. In account giving, room for interpretation should be as much as possible absent. Once performance information is used for accountability, participants in a measurement effort will anticipate the potential consequences by either trying to obtain favourable results (gaming) or covering up unfavourable outcomes.

The solution may be to disconnect measurement processes, which results in a separate measurement process for different uses. In large organizations, different organizational units could run these processes. For instance, measurement for accountability could be the responsibility of the staff of the top managers, steering & control could be in the HRM or finance department, while measurement for learning might be the responsibility of the quality manager or front-line supervisors. An additional advantage of parallel measurement processes is that performance information from one process can corroborate other results.

Although such a set-up may seem best, there are two risks attached to it. First, measurement may fall victim of what has been described in the literature as mushrooming (De Bruijn, 2007). The number of indicators may become unmanageable. Second, the costs of measurement may accrue beyond reason. Measurement costs are overhead for most organizations (an exception being statistical offices), and as such they may divert resources from the front-line work.

A sensible solution seems to be an integration of the measurement processes in some steps and a separation in other steps. The main cost driver for measurement is data collection (step 3). In order to keep costs for measurement under control, without incurring the negative consequences of having a multifunctional measurement process, an integration of data collection could be considered. In fact, the building of electronic data warehouses with an integrated data management strategy is a step in this direction.

## 5 CONCLUSION

This chapter identified three uses of performance information – learning, steering & control, and accountability. The uses put different levels of pressure on the organizations that are measuring performance. Learning generally implies soft use and accountability hard use. Steering & control lies somewhere in between. The performance measurement process will differ according to the envisaged use of performance information.

## FURTHER READING

Carter, Klein & Day (1992) made a distinction between the use of performance information as dials or tin openers. Hatry (1999), Behn (2003) and Hatry (2008) are good texts that discuss the uses of performance information. Moynihan suggests an alternative use of performance information, based on dialogue theory (2008). OECD's *Measuring Government Activity* (2009) provides an overview of some pending issues in comparative performance measurement and the use of performance data.

## REFERENCES

Behn, R. D. (2003). 'Why Measure Performance? Different Purposes Require Different Measures'. *Public Administration Review*, 63, 586–606.

Bevan, G., & Hood, C. (2006). 'What's Measured Is What Matters: Targets and Gaming in the British Health Care Sector'. *Public Administration*, 84, 517–38.

Borras, S., & Jacobsson, K. (2004). 'The Open Method of Co-ordination and New Governance Patterns in the EU'. *Journal of European Public Policy*, 11, 185–208.

Bouckaert, G. (1993). 'Measurement and Meaningful Management'. *Public Productivity and Management Review*, 17, 31–43.

Bowerman, M. (1995). 'Auditing Performance Indicators: The Role of the Audit Commission in the Citizen's Charter Initiative'. *Financial Accountability and Management*, 11, 171–83.

Carter, N., Klein, R., & Day, P. (1992). *How Organizations Measure Success: The Use of Performance Indicators in Government*. London: Routledge.

Charbonneau, É. (2011). 'Assessing the Effects of an Intelligence Performance Regime: Quebec's Municipal Management Indicators, 1999–2010'. *International Review of Administrative Sciences*, 77(4), 733–55.

De Bruijn, H. (2007). *Managing Performance in the Public Sector*. London: Routledge.

Gormley, W. T., & Weimer, D. L. (1999). *Organizational Report Cards*. Cambridge, MA: Harvard University Press.

Greve, C., Flinders, M., & Van Thiel, S. (1999). 'Quangos – What's in a Name? Defining Quangos from a Comparative Perspective'. *Governance: An International Journal of Policy and Administration*, 12, 129–46.

Hatry, H. P. (1999). *Performance Measurement: Getting Results*. Washington, DC: Urban Institute Press.

—— (2002). 'Performance Measurement: Fashions and Fallacies'. *Public Performance & Management Review*, 25, 352–58.

—— (2008). 'The Many Faces of Use'. In Van Dooren, W., & Van de Walle, S. (eds) *Performance Information in the Public Sector: How It Is Used*. Basingstoke: Palgrave Macmillan.

Hendricks, M. (1994). 'Making a Splash: Reporting Evaluation Results Effectively'. In Hatry, H. P., Wholey, J. S., & Newcomer, K. (eds) *Handbook of Practical Program Evaluation*. San Francisco: Jossey-Bass.

House of Commons Public Administration Select Committee (2003). *On Target? Government by Measurement*. London: House of Commons.

Hupe, P., & Hill, M. (2007). 'Street Level Bureaucracy and Public Accountability'. *Public Administration*, 85, 279–99.

Kaplan, R. S., & Norton, D. P. (1996). *The Balanced Scorecard: Translating Strategy into Action*. Boston, MA: Harvard Business School Press.

Kettl, F. D. (2002). *The Transformation of Governance*. Baltimore: Johns Hopkins University Press.

Laegreid, P., Roness, P. G., & Rubecksen, K. (2008). 'Performance Information and Performance Steering: Integrated System or Loose Coupling?'. In Van Dooren, W., & Van de Walle, S. (eds) *Performance Information in the Public Sector: How It Is Used*. Basingstoke: Palgrave Macmillan.

Mol, N. (2001). 'Performance Indicators in the Dutch Department of Defence'. *Financial Accountability and Management*, 12, 71–81.

Moynihan, D. P. (2005). 'Goal-Based Learning and the Future of Performance Management'. *Public Administration Review*, 65(2), 203–16.

—— (2008). *The Dynamics of Performance Management: Constructing Information and Reform*. Washington, DC: Georgetown University Press.

Noordegraaf, M., & Abma, T. (2003). 'Management by Measurement? Public Management Practices amidst Ambiguity'. *Public Administration*, 81, 853–71.

OECD (2009). *Measuring Government Activity*. OECD: Paris.

Peters, B. G. (2001). *The Politics of Bureaucracy*. London: Routledge.

Radin, A. (2002). *The Accountable Juggler: The Art of Leadership in a Federal Agency*. Washington, DC: CQ Press.

Romzek, B. S., & Dubnick, M. J. (1987). 'Accountability in the Public Sector: Lessons from the Challenger Tragedy'. *Public Administration Review*, 47, 227–38.

Rossi, R. J., & Gilmartin, K. J. (1980). *The Handbook of Social Indicators: Sources, Characteristics, and Analysis*. New York: Garland STPM Press.

Svara, J. H. (1985). 'Dichotomy and Duality: Reconceptualizing the Relationship between Policy and Administration in Council-Manager Cities'. *Public Administration Review*, 45, 221–32.

Torres, L., Pina, V., & Yetano, A. (2011). 'Performance Measurement in Spanish Local Governments: A Cross-Case Comparison Study'. *Public Administration*, 89(3), 1081–109.

Vakkuri, J., & Meklin, P. (2006). 'Ambiguity in Performance Measurement: A Theoretical Approach to Organisational Uses of Performance Measurement'. *Financial Accountability & Management*, 22, 235–50.

Van Dooren, W. (2006). 'Performance Measurement in the Flemish Public Sector: A Supply and Demand Approach'. Doctoral dissertation. Leuven, Belgium: Faculty of Social Sciences, Leuven University.

Verhoest, K. (2005). 'Effects of Autonomy, Performance Contracting and Competition on the Performance of a Public Agency'. *Policy Studies Journal*, 33, 235–58.

# Chapter 7

# Users

## LEARNING OBJECTIVES

- To be able to identify the different users and their expectations.
- To appreciate that performance information is used in a range of different ways internally and externally.
- To understand the user-specific conditions needed to ensure the use of performance information.

## KEY POINTS IN THIS CHAPTER

- Users have specific needs and expectations with regard to performance information.
- Use depends on the specific context users work and live in.
- A good understanding of this context is needed to make performance information useful for users.

## DISCUSSION QUESTIONS

- Assume the role of a business consultant who has to promote the use of performance information amongst middle managers and front-line supervisors in a large agency; how would you go about it?
- Should politicians be an important target group for performance information?
- What performance information is picked up by the newspapers of the day? What are the qualities of the information that probably led to use by the media?

Performance measurement efforts are not always specific to the target audiences they envisage. Yet, a clear understanding of the costs and benefits of performance information for the intended users is for two reasons vital for performance management. First, user profiles are connected to ways of use (learning, steering & control, and accountability). Second, different users will require different choices in the design of the measurement process. The most visible manifestation is the reporting format of performance information, which needs to be carefully tailored towards the needs of users.

In this chapter, we put ourselves in the position of the main users and ask whether much use is made of a type of performance information, why use is made of it and under what circumstances or conditions use is likely to occur. On the one hand there is an explosion of the availability of performance information, whereas on the other the take-up from different potential users is often weak. Therefore, it is useful to look at performance information from the users' end.

## 1 DIFFERENT USERS AND PERFORMANCE INFORMATION

Many uses of performance information have been identified earlier, but lists do not always specify users (e.g. Hatry, 1999, proposes ten uses, only two of which — elected officials and citizens — have explicit users. See also Van Dooren's (2006) list of 42 uses in chapter 6). The stage of incorporation has earlier been distinguished, and is internal to public institutions. In the stage of the use of performance information, there is a broadening of the user audiences as it becomes more widely and publicly available and the interest is in the actual use of performance measures and indicators. In matters of use, it makes sense to talk about initial, intermediate and ultimate use. A basic distinction is between 'middlemen' (programme managers, senior officials in central agencies and ministries, and stakeholders who are the users and suppliers of specific services) and 'end users' (ministers, MPs and citizens) (Pollitt, 2006).

In principle, performance information is indispensable to ministers for guidance, control and evaluation; to MPs to authorize expenses and follow-up by guaranteeing oversight on implementation and performance; to civil servants to take responsibility and be accountable; and to citizens to the extent that they have an interest in economic, efficient and effective service delivery and policies. However, this obvious win/win/win/win for ministers, MPs, civil servants and citizens does not always materialize in practice (Pollitt, 2006). A range of studies report communication disconnects and 'missing links' (Bouckaert & Halligan, 2008). North American research on implementation and use indicates a gap between what is intended and what actually occurs (McDavid & Hawthorn, 2006).

The main users of performance information divide into three basic groups: the civil servants who generate the material for use within their agency or reporting within the executive branch (e.g. to central agencies such as a ministry of finance), the elected officials who are often depicted as the main audience, and various public actors – citizens, media and advocacy groups that consume information (Van Dooren & Van de Walle, 2008). The various users want different types of information for their respective tasks, and reflecting the several purposes of performance information: learning, steering & control, and reporting.

## 1.1 Public managers

Decision-makers use performance information, but the influence of outcomes and outputs information on decision-making is variable (see Box 7.1 for a tentative list). There are indications that the success of performance reporting is related to the information used for decision-making and improving programmes: departments with good performance reports scored high on the use of performance information for learning and for decision-making (Bouckaert & Halligan, 2008). In the US, a majority of surveyed officials reported that performance measures were used for guiding management decisions, but the proportion using this data ranged from 25 to 65 per cent (Newcomer, 2007).

Public managers will want to use performance for learning purposes, and for steering & control. Senior managers in large organizations will tend towards the latter use, while more middle managers and front-line supervisors may have more interest in learning purposes. Front-line supervisors are less dependent on performance information for steering & control. Both the physical and the social distance between managers and workers is shorter and therefore other management styles are feasible – think of the notorious management by walking around. For the same reason, front-line supervisors may be better at facilitating learning efforts. They have more situational knowledge that can be combined with measurement.

---

### BOX 7.1  USE OF PERFORMANCE INFORMATION IN MANAGEMENT ACTIVITIES

- Setting programme priorities
- Allocating resources
- Adopting new programme approaches or changing work processes
- Coordinating programme efforts with other internal or external organizations
- Setting individual job expectations
- Refining programme performance measures
- Setting new or revising existing performance goals
- Rewarding staff
- Developing and managing contracts

---

The use of performance information by managers is conditioned by several external factors. A study of middle managers of a regional administration tested a number of explanations of why middle managers incorporate and/or use performance information (Van Dooren, 2005).

- Measurability of the services of the organizations is a key factor for implementation. Organizations that have more routine-based services have a higher incorporation and use of performance measurement.
- Political support for the measurement effort was unimportant for incorporation and for use. The absence of political interference was seized by middle managers as an opportunity to develop and use performance information. This finding may be context specific. In top-down measurement systems, support of political principals may be needed so as to set performance measurement in motion.
- Scale is important. Large organizations measure more. This observation leads to questions about whether a minimal capacity is needed for organizations to measure. Or maybe, performance measurement is mainly functional in large organizations.
- The lack of resources did not explain either incorporation or use. Those who measured and those who did not measure both perceived the lack of resources as a potential barrier to performance measurement. The provision of adequate resources always seems to be a problem; some cope while others do not.
- The linkage between goals and indicators seems to be of particular importance for the use by middle managers. Decoupling did however not seem to impede incorporation. Once performance information is being used in practice, incoherence between indicators and objectives seems to become more problematic.

## 1.2 Politicians

Politicians use performance information for reasons often to do with advancing a cause or critiquing their opponents (Askim, 2007). These uses should not be disposed of *because* they support a political agenda. On the contrary, political debate amongst opposition and majority on the (in)adequacy of public performance is a vital component of a well-functioning democracy. Provided that performance indicators are valid and the performance argumentation is not deceptive, the use of performance information by politicians in political controversy is definitely purposeful. Although the main users of performance information were expected to be elected officials, relatively little is known about the patterns of their use (McDavid & Hawthorn, 2006).

The claim that politics interacts with administrative reform may not be controversial. Yet, since performance management is often staged as a technical tool, the political dimension of performance management often remains uncovered. In order to understand the use of performance information, we should look beyond the technical front and dig into the use by politicians. Hood & Dixon (2010) analyse the *electoral benefits* of the UK target regimes in health and education. They find that the direct electoral benefits, but also the symbolic benefits of being seen as a results-oriented politician, are marginal. One of the explanations they discuss is the negativity bias in the press and the electorate. James & John (2006) also found a reduction in the aggregate vote for incumbents where there has been poor performance (James & John, 2006). Good performance on the contrary was not rewarded.

If electoral benefits are not the main payoff of implementing performance management systems, what else could be the political uses? Lavertu & Moynihan (2012) seek the political benefit of performance management mainly in the political control over bureaucracy. They studied the PART reform of the Bush adminis-tration, and found that the overall positive impact of managers' involvement with PART reviews on information use appears to be largely contingent on an agency being associated with a moderate or conservative ideology (p. 541). Other studies of the PART initiative found that PART reviews were more critical of strategic goals in liberal agencies and that lower PART scores influenced OMB's budget recommendations only in the case of liberal programmes and agencies (Gallo & Lewis, 2012; Gilmour & Lewis, 2006; Lavertu & Moynihan, 2012).

For executive politicians, accountability seems key. Performance indicators are used to align the work of agencies with the policies of ministers. Executive politicians on the one hand and agencies on the other are in a principal–agent relationship. Performance indicators are often codified in performance contracts with the minister. In second order, ministers may also use performance indicators to evaluate and to develop new policy programmes. There is however a policymaking bottleneck in the electoral cycle in the months after the elections when new ministers have to write their policy documents. Time pressure often inhibits a careful use of perform-ance information in outlining policy choices. The policy bottleneck is probably even more pressing for coalition governments that have to negotiate a policy agreement between parties within a time frame of some months.

Although performance contracts are found in many systems, the actual functioning of the indicators is conditioned by contextual factors. Goddard, Mannion & Smith (1999) for instance discuss how the use of soft, qualitative information conditions the use of hard, quantitative performance information. They distinguish between three models, (1) the use of 'soft' information as a complement to 'hard' information; (2) the use of 'soft' information as a substitute for 'hard' information; and (3) the use of 'hard' information as a safety net in the assessment of performance. They argue that one of the main functions of 'hard' information in performance assessment is the latter: to act as a safety net to identify the laggards by highlighting poor performance. They also argue that performance information is rarely used as a means to encourage good performance or to identify best practice.

**143**

## 1.3 Members of Parliament

In this section, we focus more specifically on parliament. Curristine (2005) found from an OECD survey of 27 out of 30 of its member countries that 24 countries provide outcome information to the parliament but MPs use it for decision-making in only five countries and budget committees use the information for allocation in only two countries. Hou *et al.* (2011) surveyed the use of performance-based budgeting in US state legislatures and concluded that performance-based budgeting functions more effectively for executive management. Sterck (2007) found based on a comparative study of Australia, Sweden, the Netherlands and Canada that performance budgeting initiatives seldom lead to the promised improvements in accountability to the legislature. Parliaments are clearly struggling with output and outcome information. The focus of performance budgeting initiatives is mainly on changing the budget structure, but does not seem successful in altering the budget functions. The early critique on performance budgeting that was formulated by Wildavsky (1969) is still relevant today.

An important issue with parliaments internationally is how increased information is used. Despite the growth of vigorous committee systems in Australia since 1970 – with over 3,000 parliamentary reports presented – neither the institution nor the agencies in its environment have been able to make effective use of the vast amount of information now available. There is then a question about information overload confronting parliaments and how they can make effective use of their own reports as well as those of public organizations (Halligan, Miller & Power 2007). US congressional committees' attention to and interest in performance information varies substantially from committee to committee. Some make considerable use of hearings and GAO studies to evaluate the effectiveness of programmes. Other committees are less likely to focus on the performance of programmes and are more likely to focus on oversight episodically or in an effort to promote a political agenda (Joyce, 2005).

A problem with performance budgeting and management in the United States is that they do not engage the decision-making processes in national and state legislatures in large part because the executive branch undertakes reforms without the active involvement of the legislature. Performance information is typically introduced to legislative processes through reporting in the executive budget and is unlikely to be influential, because agencies of executive staff are not trusted as an information source. Legislators rely on 'heuristics and cues', trusting their own experience and that of their staff (Bourdeaux, 2008). Similar evidence comes from the local level where Dutch aldermen place little value and rarely use performance information in municipal reports. Instead they rely on informal and verbal communications and formal meetings with senior staff (Ter Bogt, 2004).

It seems safe to conclude that overall the use of performance information by MPs did not fulfil the expectations of the performance measurement community.

A better understanding of the factors that affect MPs' use of performance information may avoid further disillusionment (Bouckaert & Halligan, 2008; Bourdeaux, 2008; CCAF-FCVI, 2006).

Performance reports do not reflect politicians' interests and world view: politicians often seek confirmation of their ideologically inspired beliefs rather than a rational cost–benefit analysis. Even if they were to engage in cost–benefit assessments, the weighing of costs and benefits is ideologically inspired. Hence, if a performance report does not align with political interests, it will not be used. Hopefully, other politicians pick up the numbers and introduce them in debates.

- Public performance reports lack credibility. Politicians may distrust performance information when it is produced by bureaucracies that they are supposed to scrutinize. Anecdotic evidence of gaming may seriously undermine the credibility of government-wide performance reporting. The level of trust in the system varies across countries. If credibility of performance reports is affected, some mechanisms will be needed to reinstall trust. Investing in external audits to assure quality of information is a possibility.
- Few rewards or incentives to scrutinize government performance. Hardworking MPs that read performance reports, understand the technicalities and challenge ministers and agencies usually do not get a lot of attention in the media. Reading performance reports usually does not win votes.
- Information overloads and time constraints. MPs usually get information from many sources and in many formats: hearings with trade unions, a note from the party, a complaint by a citizen, newspapers, the lobbying of an advocacy group, some small talk on the local market . . . and finally a performance report.
- Public performance reports are not written from their perspective. Performance reports follow the agency or department logic and not the logic of an MP. Performance reports for instance tend to cover all the activities of the organization, while MPs may benefit more from a limited set of performance indicators that allow them to set the agenda or to assess the spearheads of a policy.
- Reports focus on outcomes rather than inputs and outputs. Performance reports for parliaments often assume that MPs are mainly interested in outcomes. This assumption is based on the classic politics/administration dichotomy: politicians determine policies and mandate the administration to implement. It has been demonstrated however that the dichotomy is not followed in practice (see for instance Svara, 1985). Politicians want to have at least something to say about inputs and outputs. MPs may interpret a performance report that focuses only on outcomes as an attrition of their capacity to control the executive (Sterck, 2007).

**145**

Finally, policy-sector dynamics are insufficiently understood, which may explain variation of the use of performance information across parliamentary commissions. Evidence from Belgium for instance shows that performance information is more intensely used in the housing committee and the welfare and public health committee and less in the cultural affairs committee and the internal affairs committee (Van Dooren, 2004). Four explanations are suggested. The first is the level of fragmentation in a particular policy sector. A sector with dominant organizations may be better able to develop a standardized measurement system, whilst a sector with a high level of fragmentation may experience more consolidation problems. Second, different sectors may be confronted with different issues. Issues typologies can be useful here. Less performance information might for instance be expected in principle issues, for example moral, religious and constitutional matters. Third, the measurability of the dominant output in a policy sector may explain differences. Finally, some other factors related to the culture and established practices in a policy field may be of relevance. In this respect, it is important to identify the dominant profession in a field. Economists are probably more open to performance information than art historians.

## 1.4 Citizens/customers

One of the big questions for governments today is how to better connect with citizens. Akram et al. (2014) speak of a crisis of citizen participation. In response to this crisis, public officials have provided performance information to the public. The assumption is that more information will lead to better knowledge, higher trust and more involvement. The use of performance information by citizens also fits in with renewed efforts to foster co-production (see Bovaird, 2007, for an overview and a number of international co-production cases). Under this approach the public agency is decentred as the principal creator of public services, and clients contribute effort and time to producing services. The remixing of client and organizational motivations makes for a different type of engagement than when they are passive recipients of services (Alford, 2002). Until now co-production has mainly been about the stage of implementation. A further step is to take citizens actively on board at all stages of the policy cycle, and in the service delivery cycle, up to even giving them a say in the budget process. This results in a co-design, co-decision, co-production and co-evaluation (Van Dooren et al., 2004; Bouckaert & Halligan, 2008). The co-production of performance information fits into this trend. Box 7.2 suggests four models of citizen engagement in performance measurement.

Without any doubt, citizens in western societies highly value numbers of any kind. Porter (1995) speaks of a pursuit of objectivity. Quantification has a certain appeal. Yet, when it comes to the actual use of performance reports, less enthusiasm is observed. It is not that governments do not try. A British attempt to make

## BOX 7.2 MODELS OF PUBLIC ENGAGEMENT IN PERFORMANCE MEASUREMENT

- *Performance management model*: public managers are dominant, public role is minimal
- *Partnership model*: citizens and officials are in charge, public role is that of co-decision-maker
- *Community indicators model*: community leaders, multiple public roles in initiating, setting agenda and decision-making
- *Co-production model*: a more limited form of public engagement confined to contributions to service production, but with broader implications

*(Ho, 2007)*

## BOX 7.3 CITIZEN-DRIVEN PERFORMANCE MEASUREMENT

One of the largest projects in this area is the Citizen-Driven Performance Measurement project at Rutgers University, NJ, financed by the Sloan Foundation. The programme's approach emphasizes citizen involvement to ensure that what is measured is what matters to citizens and that the data are not corrupted by the natural desire of officeholders to report favourable outcomes. The project has been running for some years now, and the first evaluations of its success have been made (Ho, 2008). The main recommendations are:

- A certain level of trust and mutual respect between government officials and citizen representatives is necessary before any engagement can be launched. If government officials believe that citizens are only there to complain, or if citizens believe that government officials will not sincerely listen to their concerns and report performance honestly, the collaboration will be likely to fail.
- Citizens often have a different perspective on performance measurement than managers do. Generally, they are less interested in input and output measures, and are more interested in outcomes and in citizen perception of service quality, responsiveness, customer services, intra-jurisdictional equity, transparency and effectiveness in public communication.

**147**

- Despite the value of citizen participation, managers still need to manage and citizens cannot replace professional managers. Citizen input may contribute fresh ideas and new perspectives to management problems, but citizens ultimately will have to rely on or collaborate with government officials to implement the ideas.
- Citizen participation in performance measurement does not necessarily guarantee better services and more satisfactory performance. Citizen-initiated performance measures may highlight the concerns and critical issues of a programme from the citizens' perspective, but the measures by themselves are insufficient to guarantee good management and greater public investment to improve services.
- A citizen–official partnership in performance measurement can also be highly fragile. It not only requires government leaders to take risk and make government performance issues more transparent to the public, but also requires community leaders to commit time and resources to support the project, participate in meetings and work closely with government officials to learn about performance issues that can sometimes be highly technical and managerial in nature.

results-based annual reports accessible amongst others in supermarkets attracted scant interest (Pollitt, 2006). The administrative reporting formats do not seem very helpful in connecting with citizens. Researchers and practitioners have sought other ways of making performance information relevant for citizens.

The combination of managerial approaches in the bureaucracy with citizen expectations seems to be the main challenge facing these initiatives (Woolum, 2011). The ownership of performance management initiatives usually lies within the administration. However, administrators repeatedly complain about the lack of public interest in performance information – until things go wrong. This leads to frustration because there is a supply of performance information but no demand. An appealing approach to alleviate the problem is to make performance measurement more demand oriented. This implies the stronger involvement of citizens in the definition of performance (see Box 7.3).

Performance information addresses the citizen in his or her capacity not only of citizen, but also of customer of public services. This is for instance the case when governments create yardstick competition in public institutions such as schools and hospitals (Gormley & Weimer, 1999). Competition will only occur when citizens behave as customers and shop around for the best school or hospital. Citizens are thus expected to find, read and use performance information. For important decisions such as choosing a college, use by citizens/customers seems to be occurring. League tables are used, notwithstanding the often-dubious quality of

---

## BOX 7.4 POSING FOR THE SWIMSUIT ISSUE

Best (2004: p. 120) demonstrates how applicants for colleges in the USA use performance information. There are thousands of colleges in the USA. The more elite schools will refuse access to most applicants, and therefore prospective students send applications to several colleges. But how do candidates make a choice amongst these colleges? Best argues that quality of education is not the prime criterion, since quality is hard to assess. Rather, students use a ranking published by the newsmagazine *US News & World Report*. Amongst college admission officers, the issue with the rankings is known as 'the swimsuit issue', since the indicators are highly cosmetic and do not necessarily reflect academic quality. Different indicators are included in a complicated formula. An important indicator is for instance the qualifications of the admitted students. Colleges that admit students with higher test scores are expected to be better colleges. Educators know that a school with smart students is not necessarily a smart school. Yet, since most prospective students want to study with strong peers, that does not really matter in how the quasi-market of colleges works. Another indicator focuses on the admission process: the number of admissions, the number admitted and the number who accept admission (students usually apply to different colleges). Low admission rates and a high acceptance rate leads to a higher score. Even Google systematically mentions acceptance rates in its search results nowadays. The reputational effect is substantial: reputed schools attract strong students that make better careers and reconfirm the reputation of the school. Yet, the indicator does not necessarily measure what the school adds to this.

---

measurement (see the discussion on target regimes and the effects of measurement in chapter 9).

## 1.5 Media

The media is a significant user of performance information in several forms, including league tables and trends on service levels. While a number of observers have commented upon the disconnect between improved performance based on statistics and public perceptions of the quality of services – attributing the gap substantially to the media's role in shaping public perceptions – Flynn (2007) has examined the position of the media more systematically. He concluded that the UK government's biggest disappointment was the disconnection between improvements in performance and the level of public satisfaction. When polled,

---

**BOX 7.5 MEDIA RESPONSES TO RANKINGS: THE CASE OF THE OECD'S EDUCATIONAL PERFORMANCE RANKINGS**

Most national media pick up on the release of the educational performance rankings of the OECD's PISA tests. Dixon *et al.* (2013) studied media responses in Germany, Finland, France and Britain. They found that media indeed tended to select negative bits of information in the ranking. The share of negative articles in Finland was considerable, notwithstanding the excellent scores of Finland. In Britain, personal blame was directed towards politicians. In Germany, the results fuelled a debate on educational reform. France did not politically respond even though results were worse than in Germany and Britain. Although at the top end of the table, Finland did not respond politically either. Clearly, there is no simple relationship between results and responses.

---

members of the public base their opinions on the standards of public service on factors other than the measurable performance targets carefully crafted by government.

Media do pick up bits of performance information, but it is very difficult to predict which pieces of performance information will be taken out of the performance report (see Box 7.5 on PISA rankings). There is a substantial literature however on news values of events (Galtung & Ruge, 1965). Timely, unexpected, sudden, negative, unambiguous, personal, conflict-prone events are more likely to be picked up in the media, to name a few criteria. If performance information has to figure in the media, it needs to be adapted to increase the news value. Performance information can for instance be personalized by also showing a case or a witness. The release of performance information should fit the media cycle. There has to be a consistent storyline behind the numbers, and focus should be on the unexpected results.

## 2 CONCLUSION

Similarly to chapter 6, this chapter dealt with the use of performance information. The perspective shifted however from the organizational perspective to the perspective of the users. It is important to be very specific about the users that are envisaged by the measurement system. Use of performance information is conditioned by the specific context and incentive structures in which users operate. In order to avoid non-use, a good understanding of the conditional nature of use by users is vital. The next chapter focuses on non-use.

## FURTHER READING

An overview of several user perspectives is found in the edited volume *Performance information in the Public Sector: How It Is Used* (Van Dooren & Van de Walle, 2008). For a perspective on politicians, there are empirical studies by Ter Bogt (2004), Van Dooren (2004), Askim (2007), Sterck (2007), Johnson & Talbot (2008) and Bourdeaux (2008). Pollitt (2006) provides a more reflective perspective on the link between performance and democracy. Citizen involvement in performance management has been developed by the National Centre for Public Productivity at Rutgers University. A good study of report cards and league tables is published by Gormley & Weimer (1999).

## REFERENCES

Akram, S., Marsh, D., & Mccaffrie, B. (2014). 'A Crisis of Participation'. In Richards, D., Smith, M., & Hay, C. (eds) *Institutional Crisis in 21st-Century Britain*, Houndmills: Palgrave Macmillan, 39–59.

Alford, J. (2002). 'Why Do Public-Sector Clients Coproduce? Toward a Contingency Theory'. *Administration & Society*, 34, 32–56.

Askim, J. (2007). 'How Do Politicians Use Performance Information? An Analysis of the Norwegian Local Government Experience'. *International Review of Administrative Sciences*, 73, 453–72.

Best, J. (2004). *More Damned Lies and Statistics*. Berkeley: University of California Press.

Bouckaert, G., & Halligan, J. (2008). *Managing Performance: International Comparisons*. London: Routledge.

Bourdeaux, J. (2008). 'Integrating Performance Information into Legislative Budget Processes'. *Public Performance & Management Review*, 31, 22.

Bovaird, T. (2007). 'Beyond Engagement and Participation: User and Community Coproduction of Public Services'. *Public Administration Review*, 67, 846–60.

CCAF-FCVI (2006). *Users and Uses: Towards Producing and Using Better Public Performance Reporting: Perspectives and Solutions*. Ottawa: CCAF-FCVI.

Curristine, T. (2005). 'Performance Information in the Budget Process: Results of OECD 2005 Questionnaire'. *OECD Journal on Budgeting*, 5(2), 54.

Dixon, R., Arndt, C., Mullers, M., Vakkuri, J., Engblom-Pelkkala, K., & Hood, C. (2013). 'A Lever for Improvement or a Magnet for Blame? Press and Political Responses to International Educational Rankings in Four EU Countries'. *Public Administration*, 91(2), 484–505.

Flynn, N. (2007). *Public Sector Management*. Thousand Oaks: Sage.

Gallo, N., & Lewis, D. E. (2012). 'The Consequences of Presidential Patronage for Federal Agency Performance'. *Journal of Public Administration Research and Theory*, 22(2), 219–43.

Galtung, J., & Ruge, M. H. (1965). 'The Structure of Foreign News: The Presentation of the Congo, Cuba and Cyprus Crises in Four Norwegian Newspapers'. *Journal of Peace Research*, 2, 64–90.

Gilmour, J. B., & Lewis, D. E. (2006). 'Assessing Performance Budgeting at OMB: The Influence of Politics, Performance, and Program Size'. *Journal of Public Administration Research and Theory*, 16(2), 169–86.

Goddard, M., Mannion, R., & Smith, P. C. (1999). 'Assessing the performance of NHS Hospital Trusts: The Role of 'Hard' and 'Soft' Information'. *Health Policy*, 48, 119–34.

Gormley, W. T., & Weimer, D. L. (1999). *Organizational Report Cards*. Cambridge, MA: Harvard University Press.

Halligan, J., Miller, R., & Power, J. (2007). *Parliament in the 21st Century: Institutional Reform and Emerging Roles*. Melbourne: Melbourne University Press.

Hatry, H. P. (1999). *Performance Measurement: Getting Results*. Washington, DC: Urban Institute Press.

Ho, A. (2007). *Engaging Citizens in Measuring and Reporting Community Conditions: A Manager's Guide*. Washington, DC: IBM.

—— (2008). 'Citizen Involvement in Reporting PI'. In Van Dooren, W., & Van de Walle, S. (eds) *Performance Information in the Public Sector: How It Is Used*. Basingstoke: Palgrave Macmillan.

Hood, C., & Dixon, R. (2010). 'The Political Payoff from Performance Target Systems: No-Brainer or No-Gainer?' *Journal of Public Administration Research and Theory*, 20, I281–I298.

Hou, Y., Lunsford, R. S., Sides, K. C., & Jones, K. A. (2011). 'State Performance-Based Budgeting in Boom and Bust Years: An Analytical Framework and Survey of the States'. *Public Administration Review*, 71(3), 370–88.

James, O., & John, P. (2006). 'Public Management at the Ballot Box: Performance Information and Electoral Support for Incumbent English Local Governments'. *Journal of Public Administration Research and Theory*, 17(4), 567–580. doi:10.1093/jopart/mul020

Johnson, C., & Talbot, C. (2008). 'UK Parliamentary Scrutiny of Public Service Agreements: A Challenge Too Far?' In Van Dooren, W., & Van de Walle, S. (eds) *Performance Information in the Public Sector: How It Is Used*. Basingstoke: Palgrave Macmillan.

Joyce, P. G. (2005). 'Linking Performance and Budgeting: Opportunities in the Federal Budget Process'. In Kamensky, J. M., & Morales, A. (eds) *Managing for Results*. Washington, DC: IBM.

Lavertu, S., & Moynihan, D. P. (2012). 'Agency Political Ideology and Reform Implementation: Performance Management in the Bush Administration'. *Journal of Public Administration Research and Theory*. doi:10.1093/jopart/mus026

McDavid, J. C., & Hawthorn, L. R. L. (2006). *Program Evaluation and Performance Measurement: An Introduction to Practice*. Thousand Oaks: Sage.

Newcomer, K. (2007). 'How Does Program Performance Assessment Affect Program Management in the Federal Government?' *Public Performance and Management Review*, 30, 332–50.

Pollitt, C. (2006). 'Performance Information for Democracy: The Missing Link?'. *Evaluation: The International Journal of Theory, Research and Practice*, 12, 39–56.

Porter, T. M. (1995). *Trust in Numbers: The Pursuit of Objectivity in Science and Public Life*. Princeton University Press.

Sterck, M. (2007). 'The Impact of Performance Budgeting on the Role of the Legislature: A Four-Country Study'. *International Review of Administrative Sciences*, 73, 189–203.

Svara, J. H. (1985). 'Dichotomy and Duality: Reconceptualising the Relationship between Policy and Administration in Council-Manager Cities'. *Public Administration Review*, 45, 221–32.

Ter Bogt, H. J. (2004). 'Politicians in Search of Performance Information? Survey Research on Dutch Aldermen's Use of Performance Information'. *Financial Accountability & Management*, 20, 221–52.

Van Dooren, W. (2004). 'Supply and Demand of Policy Indicators'. *Public Management Review*, 6, 511–30.

—— (2005). 'What Makes Organisations Measure? Hypotheses on the Causes and Conditions for Performance Measurement'. *Financial Accountability & Management*, 21, 363–83.

—— (2006). *Performance Measurement in the Flemish Public Sector: A Supply and Demand Approach*. Leuven, Belgium: Faculty of Social Sciences, Leuven University.

Van Dooren, W., & Van de Walle, S. (2008). *Performance Information in the Public Sector: How It Is Used*. Basingstoke: Palgrave Mcmillan.

Van Dooren, W., Thijs, N., & Bouckaert, G. (2004). 'Quality Management and the Management of Quality in European Public Administrations'. In Loeffler, E., & Vintar, M. (eds). *Improving the Quality of East and West European Public Services*. Aldershot: Ashgate, 91–106.

Wildavsky, A. (1969). 'Rescuing Policy Analysis from PPBS'. *Public Administration Review*, 29(2), 189–202.

Woolum, J. (2011). 'Citizen Involvement in Performance Measurement and Reporting'. *Public Performance & Management Review*, 35(1), 79–102.

# Chapter 8

# Non-use

## LEARNING OBJECTIVES

■ To understand the phenomenon of non-use-despite-availability and to appreciate its consequences.

■ To be able to reflect on causes of non-use in practice, based on theoretical explanations.

## KEY POINTS IN THIS CHAPTER

■ Organizations regularly are not using performance information, although information is available.

■ Insufficient quality of performance information is only one amongst several explanations.

■ Psychological, cultural and institutional barriers may also have an impact.

■ Non-use has negative side effects.

## DISCUSSION QUESTIONS

■ Is non-use problematic and why (not)?

■ Consider a well-known performance indicator (for example viewing figures for a public broadcasting company, traffic casualties, educational performance (e.g. in the OECD's *Education at a Glance*)). Why are these indicators used in some circumstances and not used in others? Use theoretical explanations.

The conclusion of the (all in all, scarce) research on how politicians use performance information is that performance reports are often not read or valued (Pollitt, 2006; Ter Bogt, 2004). Chapter 6 argued that organizations can use performance information for three reasons: learning, steering & control, and accountability. This chapter asks why organizations do *not* use performance information. It seems unlikely that they do not want to learn, steer & control, or be accountable. Yet, performance information is often not picked up despite its potential benefits. The discussion of non-use touches upon some fundamental theoretical insights into how information is processed. Such insights may be particularly useful for providers of performance information, who have to develop performance information that is fit for use.

The chapter first portrays empirical evidence on the issue of non-use, after which the causes of non-use are explored: insufficient quality of performance information and psychological, cultural or institutional barriers. Finally, some of the consequences of non-use of performance information are discussed.

## 1 NON-USE

Performance information may not be used simply because it is not available. The reasons why there is no performance measurement can be manifold. Previously, chapter 2 pointed to limited measurability as a potential explanation. Chapter 6 discussed the envisaged uses for measuring performance. If organizations do not see the benefits, they are very unlikely to engage in a measurement effort.

In this section, however, the focus is on those instances where performance information is available and is even incorporated in management systems, but is not or not significantly used. Moynihan argues that performance management is a 'good government reform' that is hard to oppose. Implementation however is much more difficult, and support for performance is therefore often 'a mile wide but an inch deep' (Moynihan, 2008: p. 192). Examples would be performance budgets that are not used in budget negotiations and performance-based annual reports that are not at all read or taken into account by funders of an agency.

Some US survey studies have documented the non-use of performance information. Research conducted by the Governmental Accounting Standards Board (Government Accounting Standards Board, n.d.) found that few government entities used performance measures for planning, resource allocation and programme management. Berman & Wang (2000) surveyed county managers in the US about the breadth and depth of their performance measurement practices (Box 8.2). Only counties that at least did some performance measurement were included in the analysis. Some items on what Berman & Wang call programme outcomes, but what in our terminology are indications of the use of performance information, are included in their survey. The percentages below thus reflect the number of counties that agree with a number of statements. The last item for instance

---

## BOX 8.1  SOME SURVEY EVIDENCE ON USE AND NON-USE

Agreement

| | |
|---|---|
| Increased awareness about the need for accountability | 48.0% |
| Increased ability to determine service efficiency | 45.0 |
| Increased ability to determine service effectiveness | 43.0 |
| Increased ability to determine service timeliness | 40.0 |
| Established performance target levels for programmes/ services | 40.0 |
| Clarified agency or programme goals and objectives | 37.2 |
| Improved accountability of programme performance | 35.6 |
| Ability to achieve improvements despite resource constraints | 32.5 |
| Increased commitment to excellence | 31.5 |
| Improving group decision-making capabilities | 26.6 |
| Determined long-term budget needs | 23.6 |
| Eliminated services that are no longer needed | 16.1 |
| Improve timeliness of management decisions | 15.5 |

*Source: findings from Berman & Wang, 2000*

---

states that 15.5 per cent of the counties that are measuring performance see a value in improving timeliness (see Box 8.1).

It is remarkable that not even the highest score reaches 50 per cent, which implies that in more than half of the counties, performance measurement is not used for creating awareness for accountability. Only 35 per cent acknowledge that performance measurement leads to improved accountability, and 26.6 per cent see a potential for improved decision-making. No more than 16 per cent use performance information to eliminate services and to improve timeliness of decisions.

In judging these numbers, the glass can be half full or half empty. It can be argued that the use of performance information is a gradual learning process. Melkers & Willoughby (2005) report somewhat higher use in a 2005 study, which may confirm the existence of some learning effects. Moreover, it can be debated whether it is realistic and even desirable to expect organizations to use performance information for all the items listed by Berman & Wang (2000). It may suffice that an organization strongly supports a small number of uses rather than doing something on everything. Under this assumption, low numbers are not as problematic as they may appear to be. On the other hand, it seems at least worrying that some of the more far-reaching uses of performance information, such as

■ **156**

## BOX 8.2 NON-USE OR USE UNDER THE RADAR? DECOUPLING OF INDICATORS AND GOALS

In some cases, it is probably too easily concluded that performance information is not used. Researchers typically look for the ideal typical use in performance management systems. This ideal type propagates the formulation of strategic and operational goals that have to guide the formulation of indicators. Such a system, it is argued, has to be integrated. It typically consists of a hierarchical cascade of goals and indicators. Hence, when there are no indications of use in formulating and monitoring objectives, it is concluded that information is not used.

The theoretical perspective of loose coupling may however cast another light on the use of performance information. Orton & Weick (1990) conclude from a literature review that from a Weberian bureaucratic perspective, the recurring surprise is that organizations routinely exhibit looseness. From a decoupling perspective, the recurring surprise is that organizations routinely exhibit coupling (p. 218). We therefore should not be surprised that performance information is not used in an integrated command and control structure. Nevertheless, it may well be that information is used in other locations in the organization.

Some empirical evidence with regard to performance measurement exists. Brignall & Modell (2000) suggest that decoupling of (as opposed to integration between) performance indicators and goals is a viable strategy for seeking simultaneous legitimacy of multiple constituencies. Johnsen (1999) concluded from a case study of four Norwegian municipalities that in complex settings a decoupled implementation mode may be more successful than a coupled one. Laegreid, Roness & Rubecksen (2008) document a case of decoupling in the Norwegian national performance management scheme (Management By Objectives and Results).

improving group decision-making capacity, long-term budgeting and critically assessing the relevance of programmes, are not accepted.

Ter Bogt (2004), who studied the use of performance information by politicians, provides additional evidence of non-use. He concluded that

> sources of performance information which the aldermen made by far the most use of were informal, verbal consultations and formal meetings with top managers, i.e. civil servants. They much less frequently used formal, written information in budgets, annual reports, and interim reports, and other sources of formal and informal information.

(Ter Bogt, 2004, p. 241)

This study reminds us that performance measurement is one source of information amongst many. The non-use of formal knowledge such as performance information does not imply that decisions are not informed. These findings however probe the relation of formal, written information with other more informal sources. Taylor (2011) also found that the use of performance information is limited especially on higher levels. Middle managers were found to use PIs for making decisions significantly more than their senior counterparts. Maybe performance management schemes are not the kind of information that top managers request (in chapter 10 we make a plea for decentralizing performance management).

## 2 WHY IS PERFORMANCE INFORMATION NOT USED?

Why do Americans (until now) not buy small cars? Is it because the cars are not good enough, not safe enough? Is it a manifestation of bounded rationality, where the environmental costs are not taken into account? Or is it a matter of culture? Is a (large) car an expression of success in an individualistic society? Or finally, is it a matter of formal and informal rules? Is the tax regulation more generous for large cars compared with for instance the tax regulation in Europe? A simple question triggers different answers about the quality of the product, the psychological limitations, cultural aspects and institutional variation.

Let us now turn to the question of why information is not used. We use some middle-range theories to suggest four potential answers, being aware that several other theories may yield additional insights. The first explanation of non-use is about the information itself, the second about the user of the information, the third about the cultural setting and the fourth about the institutional context of information and information use.

### 2.1 Insufficient quality

More than three decades ago, Mintzberg (1975) observed that many managerial tasks involve judgement rather than formal analysis. Managers therefore prefer rapid, informal and speculative information to entirely accurate information. Current leadership studies do not seem to suggest a more analytical profile for the contemporary manager. According to Van Wart (2003), contemporary leadership is about the need for vision, entrepreneurialism and charisma. Such labels usually do not embrace an understanding of the technical quality of performance data as a key competence. On the contrary, for substantial knowledge of their business, public managers are expected to rely on professional staff. For managers, it seems, quality of information is not a prime concern for use.

We should however not entirely dismiss the idea that non-use is somehow influenced by the quality of the performance information. Weiss & Bucuvalas (1980) provide a useful scheme to understand the role of technical quality in the

**Table 8.1** Truth and utility tests of new information

|  | Truth test | Utility test |
|---|---|---|
| Conventional wisdom | I Does the process of measurement evidence high quality? | III Does the performance information help to solve problems? |
| Alternative explanation | II Are the findings of performance measurement in line with previous evidence? | IV Does it enlighten in the long term? |

Source: based on Weiss & Bucuvalas, 1980

decision of managers to use performance information. They suggest that decision-makers when confronted with new information are performing two tests: a *truth test* and a *utility test*. For each test, there is the more conventional understanding of how managers use performance information as well as a more counterintuitive claim (see Table 8.1) (Van de Walle & Van Dooren, 2010).

1    Decision-makers appraise the truth of information in terms of its technical merit as evidenced by the professional standards of the measurement process. This is the conventional wisdom held by the measurement profession. Many government or consulting reports treat the non-use of information as something that can be fixed through a number of practical and technical changes (Van de Walle & Bovaird, 2007). The spontaneous reaction to non-use is a plea for more technical training of those who have to use the data. Wholey (2002) however asserts that technical know-how is not enough. Extensive training in strategic planning, programme evaluation and the use of performance information are also required. The impact of technical quality on use should thus not be taken for granted.

2    Decision-makers also test the truth of information by checking the conformity of the findings of performance measurement with their prior understanding and experience. Decision-makers are exposed to a variety of evidence such as direct observation, descriptive accounts, programme data, routine statistics and colleagues' reports, as well as a body of previous research, and they use their stock of knowledge to judge the truth of the findings (Weiss & Bucuvalas, 1980: p. 308). Confronted with a performance statistic, say for instance high dissatisfaction of users of public transport, a manager of a transportation agency will typically react off the cuff, saying things like 'I don't believe that', or else 'I am not surprised'. At that moment, he or she is performing a first truth test. Note that the quality of the measurement process is less relevant here.

Three scenarios of alignment between measurement findings and prior knowledge can be distinguished. In case of *non-alignment*, performance information contradicts prior knowledge. In case of *semi-alignment*, some performance results are counterintuitive while others are not. The case of *full alignment* reflects

**159**

**Table 8.2** Alignment scenarios and the use of performance information

| Scenarios of alignment with prior knowledge | Performance information is used because . . . | Performance information is not used because . . . |
|---|---|---|
| In case of non-alignment | Performance information allows challenging the status quo. Unexpected findings at least attract attention and may be instrumental in 'rocking the boat' and changing power distribution between actors. | Performance information is deemed unrealistic. |
| In case of semi-alignment | Performance information can support a compromise in policymaking or substantiate incremental steps in policy change. | Performance information is not providing direction. |
| In case of full alignment | Performance information reinforces standpoints and beliefs already held. | Performance information is not seen as having an added value. |

performance information that endorses previously held beliefs about performance. Each scenario can lead to use or non-use, depending on the context (see Table 8.2).

3  The utility test also consists of two judgements. Information is assessed on the extent to which it provides explicit and practical direction on matters decision-makers can do something about. Information has to be actionable and has to increase the problem-solving capacity of decision-makers. It also is expected to reduce uncertainty. As a result, the utility test tends to disfavour statistical analysis. The application of statistical standards to performance information is precisely showing the limits of the information (expressed by probabilities and confidence intervals), and this is not what decision-makers in search of certainty and evidence may want to hear.

4  Utility can also be seen as the capacity of performance information to challenge current practices and suggest new perspectives and orientations. This is what Weiss (1979) calls the *enlightenment* function of information. The latter concept points to performance information that slowly and unnoticeably alters the definition of policy and management problems and solutions. Unlike the other three boxes of the quadrant, enlightenment cannot easily be traced back to an individual decision-maker. The metaphor of a 'test' performed by a user is less applicable here.

## 2.2 Psychological barriers

A second set of explanations can be found in the psychological barriers that limit human information processing capabilities. Herbert Simon provided some key insights such as bounded rationality. His theory provides a perspective on why performance information may not be used. The general argument is that performance measurement systems assume a naive model of the rational decision-maker. Simon speaks of the model of the *Economic Man*, which he opposes to the more realistic model of the *Satisficing Man*. Performance measurement processes that take the satisficing model into account have more chances of their information being used.

The Economic Man model is represented in Table 8.3. Based on complete information on the environment, the courses of action and the consequences, a decision-maker will maximize value by processing all information in the light of a stable set of preferences. This view assumes almost superhuman capabilities of the human brain. In actual decision-making, the environment is ambiguous, courses of action are unstable and consequences and risks are unknown. Moreover, preferences are usually not even temporarily stable and cannot be rank-ordered.

These observations led Simon to define the model of Satisficing Man (Simon, 1997). The term 'satisficing' is a combination of 'satisfy' and 'suffice'. A decision-maker will search alternatives for a solution that is acceptable, instead of searching for the optimal decision. The failure of omniscient rationality is largely a failure of knowing all the alternatives, uncertainty about relevant exogenous events, and inability to calculate consequences (Simon, 1979). Hence, rationality is bounded by incomplete information, insufficient processing capacities and the pervasive impact of uncertainty. Simon does not portray the model of Economic Man as undesirable. He in fact considers it an appropriate normative model of decision-making with a precise definition of rationality. However, since the economic model inadequately describes *actual* decision-making processes, it cannot be taken

**Table 8.3** *Rational decision-making according to Simon*

*The model of the Economic Man (Simon, 1997)*

- The decision-maker knows all the relevant aspects of the decision environment
- The decision-maker knows all the courses of action
- The decision-maker knows all the consequences of those alternatives with certainty, or knows the probability distribution of risks
- The decision-maker has a known and temporarily stable preference function for all sets of consequences
- The decision-maker has the computational skills
- The decision-maker maximizes the satisfaction of his or her values by choosing the alternative that is followed by the most preferred set of consequences

for granted. The model of Economic Man is the ideal, while the model of Satisficing Man is a realistic starting point.

What does this imply for the design of a performance measurement system? The main lesson from Simon's work is that bounded rationality rather than full rationality should be the point of departure. Measurement systems need to be designed based on the assumption that users have limited processing capacities and limited computational skills and objectives. This implies for instance that efforts to present performance information in a relevant format should be firmly ingrained in the measurement system. The observation of unstable preferences leads to questions about the flexibility and adaptability of the measurement system. The combination of stringent coupling between indicators and objectives on the one hand and a volatile environment on the other may yield performance information that is quickly superseded.

Although Simon's work can be read as a critique of performance measurement, it also provides it with a rationale. Since pure rational decision-making is preferred over satisficing search-behaviour, performance measurement may be seen as a step towards more rationality. Although measurement always deals with past performance, it may to some degree reduce uncertainty over future performance. Performance measurement is able to provide decision-makers with more information on the decision environment, courses of action, consequences and risks. Moreover, the dialogue around the indicators may lead to a crystallization and stabilization of preferences (Moynihan, 2008).

To conclude, Simon's psychological perspective suggests that performance measurement does have the potential to improve decision-making. However, this potential will only materialize when performance measurement professionals explicitly acknowledge the existence of bounded rationality, and do not take rationality for granted.

## 2.3 Cultural barriers

A third set of explanations for non-use is rooted in cultural theory (Schedler & Proeller, 2007). The causes of non-use are sought in the mismatch between the use of performance information and the cultural traditions of a society, administration or organization. When performance measurement is a culturally extraneous matter, the chances for use are minimal.

The general definition of culture includes three elements that are shared amongst people: cognitions, values and affects (Hofstede, 2005). *Cognitions* are the empirical perceptions of reality: of how the world works. For instance, some cultures stress individual choice and responsibility as the cause of criminal behaviour, while other cultures put an emphasis on the social conditions surrounding the individual. *Values* are the convictions of how it *should* work. For instance, some cultures seem more tolerant towards repression in order to fight crime than others. *Affects* reflect the emotional involvement in cognitions and values. Cultural symbols such as the flag and the national hymn represent a set of cognitions of what a country is, and values about what it should be. Yet, they do not evoke the same affective reactions in all cultures.

Cultural theory yielded numerous analytical schemes that allow describing the potential mismatch between the use of performance information and cultural elements. The cultural theories of Bendix (1974), Sartori (1969), Hofstede (2005) and Douglas (1996) and their relevance for the use of performance information are selected from this theoretical affluence.

Bendix (1974) differentiated between *entrepreneurial cultures* that emphasize personal bargaining and negotiation (e.g. Great Britain) and *bureaucratic cultures* that are based on the acceptance of impersonal rules (e.g. continental Europe). Performance-based accountability (see chapter 6) may better fit entrepreneurial cultures. Personal achievement of top managers is the basis of accountability and can, or better should, be exposed. In bureaucratic cultures, on the contrary, accountability is mainly about following rules and authority. Performance-based accountability may be at cross-purposes with this tradition of rule-based accountability. Or, performance-based accountability regimes take on a quasi-bureaucratic, quasi-regulatory character. This is actually an often-heard complaint amongst practitioners.

Sartori (1969) describes the distinction between *rationalist, deductive cultures* and *pragmatic, empirical cultures*. The former tend to approach problems with coherent argumentation derived from theory, while the latter rely on evidence and testing. In empirical cultures, precedent prevails over theory. Learning from performance information may be easier in pragmatic, empirical cultures than in rationalist, deductive ones. The openness to considering performance information with an open view and to challenging dominant frameworks based on empirical observation is better embodied in empirical cultures.

Hofstede (2005) distinguishes five components of culture: (1) *power distance* reflects the extent to which the less powerful members of organizations accept and expect that power is distributed unequally, (2) *collectivism*, as opposed to *individualism*, is the degree to which individuals are integrated into groups, (3) *masculinity*, as opposed to *femininity*, is the level of competitiveness and assertiveness, (4) *uncertainty avoidance* reflects the tolerance of uncertainty and ambiguity, and (5) *long term orientation* as opposed to *short term orientation* is the degree to which cultures value thrift and perseverance and denounce respect for tradition, fulfilling social obligations and protecting one's 'face'.

Some of Hofstede's dimensions are relevant for understanding the use of performance information. For instance, performance-based pay has a strong competitive element and therefore is more aligned with a masculine culture.

On the contrary, performance dialogues for learning purposes require consensual and emphatic attitudes typical of feminine cultures. Another example is the impact that a long-term orientation may have on the target-setting and performance evaluation. The occurrence of the dysfunction of myopia (see chapter 9) may be less likely in a long-term culture. Finally, the culture of risk avoidance may prohibit learning from performance information, which almost inevitably requires a degree of experimentation.

Douglas (1996) developed the widely applied group-grid theory of culture (see for instance Hood, 2000, for an application in public administration). The first dimension, *group*, is similar to the distinction between individualism and collectivism that Hofstede proposes. It is intended to show the role of group pressure upon individuals stemming mainly from moral compulsion and the degree of group integration. Compare for instance group pressure in a small rural town with the anonymity of a metropolis. The German saying *Stadtluft macht frei* ('Urban air makes you free') perfectly expresses the sense of freedom some experience in anonymous city life opposed to the oppressive informal rules of country life. *Grid*, the second axis, refers to the constraints created by the formal and informal rules that are imposed upon the group members. Compare for instance dense rules of dining in a three star Michelin restaurant with a picnic in a public park.

The combination of the two dimensions yields four ideal-typical cultures (Hood, 2000) (see Figure 8.1).

1    An *individualist culture* scores low on both group and grid. The financial sector in Wall Street may serve as an example. The stress is on individuals as self-interested rational choosers. Organizational problems are defined in terms of faulty incentive structures and lack of price signals, and remedies are sought in market-like mechanisms, competitions and league tables. It is assumed that individuals need more information to support choice. The organizational image therefore is entrepreneurial.

2    A *fatalist culture* scores high on grid but low on group and reflects a situation where people follow rules in a group or society, but without a sense of belonging. The North Korean mass manifestations to honour the leaders of the country may serve as an example of ritualistic adherence to rules without group loyalty. Fatalists define organizational problems in terms of unpredictability and unintended effects. The strong emphasis on fate leads to a minimal anticipation of problems. At most, there is an *ad hoc* response after the event. The organizational image is ritualistic.

3    *Egalitarian cultures* have a high sense of belonging to a group but do not have a low grid of rules. There is a relatively clear idea on who is in or out, but within the group, members are equal and free. A classic example is the hippie movement of the 1960s, but many voluntary organizations also fall into this category. Problems are defined in terms of inadequate group and power structures. Egalitarians will

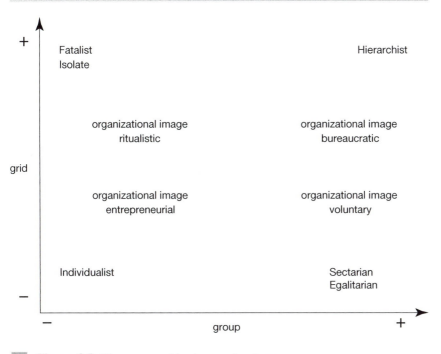

**Figure 8.1** *The group-grid scheme of culture*

more than others blame the system and the abuse of power by top-level government leaders. Participation and communitarianism are typical safeguards against system failure. The organizational image is voluntary.

4    Finally, *hierarchists* have both high group and high grid. A common example is a combat unit in an army that combines camaraderie with strict formal and informal rules. The traditional Weberian bureaucracies would also largely fit this description. Hierarchists put the accent on expertise, planning and forecasting, and management. Failure should be addressed by developing more expertise, tighter procedures and greater managerial grip.

Performance measurement systems will operate in a fundamentally different way according to the culture.

(1) *Individualist cultures* are more likely to adopt performance incentives and performance pay. Many NPM reforms assumed an individualist culture and proposed better (read: performance-based) incentive structures. Osborne and Gaebler's *Reinventing Government* (1993) for instance has a subtitle about the entrepreneurial spirit that is transforming the public sector. (2) *Fatalist cultures* will in all probability adopt ritualistic performance measurement exercises. Window dressing tactics are likely. (3) *Egalitarian cultures* may more easily adopt performance dialogue. Obviously, performance pay and individualized incentives are out of the

**165**

question. (4) A *Hierarchist* culture would require that performance information be integrated in the routines and values of the organization. Performance information that runs counter to the accepted professional norms will meet resistance from professionals.

## 2.4 Institutions

Finally, performance measurement systems also operate in different institutional contexts (Van Dooren, 2008). March & Olsen (1989) distinguish between two logics of action that are shaped by two kinds of institutions: normative and regulatory.

(1) Regulatory institutions reflect the power distribution in a politico-administrative arena. Institutions constrain and regulate behaviour through rule setting, monitoring and sanctioning (Scott, 2001). Rules can be informal (with reputational sanctions) or formal (police and courts). Compliance follows from the calculation of costs and benefits of each alternative. March & Olsen (1989) speak of the logic of the consequences: decision-making is in essence preference based.

Performance reforms often redefine the power distribution. NPM for instance argued for a combination of managerial freedom and performance agreements. This notion was reflected in the catchphrases 'Let managers manage' and 'Make managers manage' (Kettl, 2002). New Public Management somewhat courageously assumed a balance between intrinsic motivation and managerial craftsmanship on the one hand and extrinsic incentives and accountability on the other. It remains unclear how this balance between managers and political principals comes about.

The managerial quest for autonomy does not only concern management issues, as NPM literature suggests. Regularly, managers also seek strategic autonomy on policy matters (Maggetti & Verhoest, 2014). In some contexts, managers may use performance indicators to chalk out their territory, to set the boundaries of political interference. Politicians, who disagree with the limitation of their scope of action, will not use the performance information – not because the information is not good or useful, but because it infringes on political interests. Politicians on the other hand want as much supervision over the bureaucracy as possible. They are afraid that the discretion of managers might enable them to obstruct policies. Political principals therefore search for means to control the bureaucracy and to make them manage. Performance indicators sometimes are mainly a tool for political control over the bureaucracy (see chapter 7 discussing politicians as users). Managers that are subjected to this pressure may attempt not to use the performance information – not because the information is not good or useful, but because it infringes on managerial interests.

**166**

## BOX 8.3 PERFORMANCE INFORMATION AND INSTITUTIONAL READINESS

Institutions can strongly affect the proper use of performance information and hence the success of performance management. Schick (1998) argues that most developing countries are not ready to implement performance management. The World Bank *Public Expenditure Handbook* (1998) echoed this argument, stating that performance management will only succeed if it is built on, or builds in, the basics (p. 82). In an article titled 'Why Most Developing Countries Should Not Try the New Zealand Reforms', Schick (1998) outlines his argument. Developing countries have to follow a 'logic of development', and performance-oriented reforms are only the last step.

First, progress in the public sector requires parallel advances in the market sector. As long as the economy operates according to informal norms and property rights are defined more by practice than by contract, the government is not likely to make much headway in installing rule-based public management. Formalizing the market sector does not ensure reciprocal changes in public institutions, however.

Second, modernizing the public sector means establishing reliable external controls. As old-fashioned as external controls may seem to be, they are building blocks for a formal, rule-based, honest public sector. Operating in an externally controlled environment is an essential phase in the development process. It gives managers the skills to manage on their own, builds trust between central controllers and line managers and confidence between citizens and government, and encourages managers to internalize a public ethic of proper behaviour. As these basic conditions of formal management take root, it should be possible for central controllers to ease the regulations by giving line managers broader discretion in operating their programmes.

Third, politicians and officials must concentrate on the basic process of public management. They must be able to control inputs before they are called upon to control outputs; they must be able to account for cash before they are asked to account for cost; they must abide by uniform rules before they are authorized to make their own rules; they must operate in integrated, centralized departments before being authorized to go it alone in autonomous agencies.

**167**

The bipolar representation of the power struggle between managers and politicians is deceitfully simple. In reality, performance indicator regimes play a role in at least five power games. Performance indicator regimes potentially shift the balance of power between:

1   the executive and legislative;
2   executive politicians and administration;
3   staff and line agencies;
4   tiers of government;
5   leadership and front-line workers.

(2)   Normative institutions are the values, norms and roles that guide behaviour (Scott, 2001). *Values* are the conceptions of the desirable and standards to which existing structures and behaviour can be assessed. *Norms* specify how things should be done and reflect opinions about proper means and ends. *Roles* are the values and norms for specific persons or classes. March & Olsen (1989) talk about the logic of appropriateness. Unlike for coercive institutions, there is no rational calculation. The normative institutions constrain and enable rational calculations because they set the rules of the game and they structure choice. Normative institutions are identity based instead of preference based.

Professional identity is mainly shaped through education. Doctors, lawyers, anthropologists and engineers, to name a few, acquire the values, norms and roles typical of the profession. The normative pressure of a professional group can explain the non-use of performance information. The question thus is whether performance indicator regimes align with the norms and values of the profession or infringe on them (Abbott, 1988; Troupin, 2012). It can be hypothesized that:

1   Highly technocratic professions will be able to use their technical compe-
    tence as a line of defence against in their view too simplistic performance
    indicators.
2   Professions that are measurement-minded may have fewer problems with
    performance indicator regimes.
3   Professions that are well organized in professional associations will have better
    opportunities to voice their disagreement with the managerial doctrine.

## 3 CONSEQUENCES OF NON-USE

The explanations for the non-use of performance information can be manifold. Yet, we believe that the theories discussed above are useful to make a diagnostic of dwindling performance information use. To conclude this chapter, we discuss

 **168**

some of the effects of the non-use of performance information. This is somewhat of a lacuna in the performance literature. Many studies are concerned with the dysfunctional, perverse effects of the *use* of performance information, often (implicitly) assuming that non-use is preferential. The dysfunctional effects of the *non-use* however remain out of scope. Two consequences are discussed: over-claiming on the 'best practices' in reforms and the 'shortening of institutional memories'.

## 3.1 Over-claiming on 'best practice'

One of the most notable lacunas of performance information in the public sector concerns public management and governance. In policy sectors such as environmental policy, employment and education, much more information is available. This leads the OECD to conclude that there is a paradox at the heart of the international movement in favour of performance-oriented management reform (OECD, 2006).

> The reformers insist that public sector organisations must reorient and reorganise themselves in order to focus more vigorously on their results. They must count costs, measure outputs, assess outcomes, and use all this informa-tion in a systematic process of feedback and continuous improvement. Yet this philosophy has clearly not been applied to many of the reforms themselves, which have thus far been evaluated relatively seldom and usually in ways that have some serious methodological limitations.
>
> (quoted in Pollitt & Bouckaert, 2011: p. 140)

In absence of performance data on what works, reformers develop an almost religious belief in the 'best practice', with a substantial risk of context reduction as a consequence.

Concerns about inappropriately enthusiastic and uncritical acceptance of managerial and policy reforms are echoed within policy sectors such as health, where Marmor *et al.* (2005) find that

> There is . . . a considerable gap between promise and performance in the field of comparative policy studies. Misdescription and superficiality are all too common. Unwarranted inferences, rhetorical distortion, and caricatures – all show up too regularly in comparative health policy scholarship and debates.

They warn for costly policy errors based on misconceptions of the experience abroad (Marmor *et al.*, 2005: p.343).

## 3.2 Weak institutional memories

A review of US government reforms suggests that

> the deluge of recent reform may have done little to actually improve performance. On the contrary, it may have created confusion within government about what Congress and the president really want, distraction from needed debates about organisational missions and resources, and the illusion that more reform will somehow lead to better government.
>
> (Light, 2006, p. 17)

Others might strongly challenge these propositions. However, with limited time series data, it is all but impossible to determine the degree to which such alleged reversals or reform overloads have occurred. Mobility of staff and structural reforms lead to institutional memory loss.

Pollitt (2000) sees a role for record keeping in avoiding such memory loss. Record keeping can reinforce organizational memories under the condition that, first, significant data or decisions are documented; second, records do not get lost; third, they can be quickly accessed; and fourth, someone thinks of using them. If records are not limited to inputs (e.g. budgets and staff) or decisions, and include performance, institutional memory is without a doubt reinforced.

## 4 CONCLUSION

The question of why performance information is not used, notwithstanding its availability, provides some interesting insights into how performance information is processed by users. This chapter suggested various theoretical approaches to grasp these dynamics: truth and utility testing, bounded rationality, cultural theory and institutionalism. A good understanding of the theory behind the use of performance information is not only of academic interest, but also vital for designing successful measurement systems in practice.

## FURTHER READING

Non-use has not been studied extensively. Some surveys on use may give indications on non-use (Government Accounting Standards Board, n.d.; Berman & Wang, 2000; Melkers & Willoughby, 2005). A start for further reading on the suggested theoretical explanations would be Weiss & Bucuvalas (1980) on truth and utility tests, Simon (1976) on the psychological barriers, Hood (2000) for an application of group-grid theory to public administration, and March & Olsen (1989) on different institutional logics. Pollitt (2000) is a good reference on institutional memory and amnesia.

# REFERENCES

Abbott, A. (1988). *The System of Professions: An Essay on the Division of Expert Labor.* University of Chicago Press.

Bendix, R. (1974). *Work and Authority in Industry.* Berkeley: University of California Press.

Berman, E., & Wang, X. (2000). 'Performance Measurement in U.S. Counties: Capacity for Reform'. *Public Administration Review,* 60, 409–20.

Brignall, S., & Modell, S. (2000). 'An Institutional Perspective on Performance Measurement and Management in the "New Public Sector"'. *Management Accounting Research,* 11, 281–306.

Douglas, M. (1996). *Natural Symbols: Explorations in Cosmology.* London: Routledge.

Government Accounting Standards Board (n.d.). *Performance Measurement at the State and Local Levels: A Summary of Survey Results.* Washington, DC: GASB.

Hofstede, G. J. (2005). *Cultures and Organizations: Software for the Mind.* New York: McGraw-Hill.

Hood, C. (2000). *The Art of the State: Culture, Rhetoric, and Public Management.* Oxford: Oxford University Press.

Johnsen, A. (1999). 'Implementation Mode and Local Government Performance Measurement: A Norwegian Experience'. *Financial Accountability & Management,* 15, 41–66.

Kettl, F. D. (2002). *The Transformation of Governance.* Baltimore: Johns Hopkins University Press.

Laegreid, P., Roness, P. G., & Rubecksen, K. (2008). 'Performance Information and Performance Steering: Integrated System or Loose Coupling?'. In Van Dooren, W., & Van de Walle, S. (eds) *Performance Information in the Public Sector: How It Is Used.* Basingstoke: Palgrave Macmillan.

Light, P. C. (2006). 'The Tides of Reform Revisited: Patterns in Making Government Work, 1945–2002'. *Public Administration Review,* 66(1), 6–19.

Maggetti, M., & Verhoest, K. (2014). 'Unexplored Aspects of Bureaucratic Autonomy: A State of the Field and Ways Forward'. *International Review of Administrative Sciences.* doi:0020852314524680

March, J. G., & Olsen, J. P. (1989). *Rediscovering Institutions: The Organizational Basis of Politics.* New York: The Free Press.

Marmor, T., Freeman, R., & Okma, K. (2005). 'Comparative Perspectives and Policy Learning in the World of Health Care'. *Journal of Comparative Policy Analysis: Research and Practice,* 7, 331–348.

Melkers, J., & Willoughby, K. (2005). 'Models of Performance-Measurement Use in Local Governments: Understanding Budgeting, Communication, and Lasting Effects'. *Public Administration Review,* 65, 180–90.

Mintzberg, H. (1975). *The Nature of Managerial Work.* New York: HarperCollins.

Moynihan, D. P. (2008). *The Dynamics of Performance Management: Constructing Information and Reform*. Washington, DC: Georgetown University Press.

OECD (2006). *Issues in Output Measurement for Government at a Glance*. Paris: OECD.

Orton, J. D., & Weick, K. E. (1990). 'Loosely Coupled Systems: A Reconceptualization'. *The Academy of Management Review*, 15, 203–23.

Osborne, D., & Gaebler, T. (1993). 'Reinventing Government: How the Entrepreneurial Spirit Is Transforming the Public Sector from Schoolhouse to State House'. Reading, MA: Addison Wesley.

Pollitt, C. (2000). 'Institutional Amnesia: A Paradox of the "Information Age"?' *Prometheus*, 18, 5–16.

—— (2006). 'Performance Information for Democracy: The Missing Link?' *Evaluation: The International Journal of Theory, Research and Practice*, 12, 39–56.

Pollitt, C., & Bouckaert, G. (2011). *Public Management Reform: A Comparative Analysis* (3rd ed.). Oxford: Oxford University Press.

Sartori, G. (1969). 'Politics, Ideology, and Belief Systems'. *American Political Science Review*, 63, 398–411.

Schedler, K., and Proeller, I. (2007). *Cultural Aspects of Public Management Reform*. Amsterdam: Elsevier.

Schick, A. (1998). 'Why Most Developing Countries Should Not Try New Zealand's Reforms'. *World Bank Research Observer*, 13(1), 123.

Scott, W. R. (2001). *Institutions and Organizations*. Thousand Oaks: Sage Publications.

Simon, H. A. (1976). *Administrative Behavior: A Study of Decision-Making Processes in Administrative Organization*. New York: Free Press.

—— (1979). 'Rational Decision Making in Business Organizations'. *American Economic Review*, 69, 493–513.

—— (1997). *Administrative Behavior: A Study of Decision-Making Processes in Administrative Organizations*. New York: The Free Press.

Taylor, J. (2011). 'Factors Influencing the Use of Performance Information for Decision Making in Australian State Agencies'. *Public Administration*, 89(4), 1316–34.

Ter Bogt, H. J. (2004). 'Politicians in Search of Performance Information? Survey Research on Dutch Aldermen's Use of Performance Information'. *Financial Accountability & Management*, 20, 221–52.

Troupin, S. (2012). 'Professionalizing Public Administration(s)? The Cases of Performance Audit in Canada and the Netherlands'. Dissertation. Leuven, Belgium: KU Leuven. Retrieved from https://lirias.kuleuven.be/handle/123456789/349837.

Van de Walle, S., and Bovaird, T. (2007). 'Making Better Use of Information to Drive Improvement in Local Public Services: A Report for the Audit Commission'. Birmingham: School of Public Policy.

Van de Walle, S., and Van Dooren, W. (2010). 'How Is Information Used to Improve Performance in the Public Sector? Exploring the Dynamics of Performance Information'. In Walshe, K., Harvey, G., and Jas, P. (eds) *Connecting Knowledge and Performance in Public Services: From Knowing to Doing*. Cambridge: Cambridge University Press.

Van Dooren, W. (2008). 'Performance Indicators: A Wolf in Sheep's Clothing?' Paper presented at the symposium 'Changing Educational Accountability in Europe' (24/25 June 2008). Berlin: Wissenschaftszentrum Berlin für Sozialforschung.

Van Wart, M. (2003). 'Public-Sector Leadership Theory: An Assessment'. *Public Administration Review*, 63, 214–28.

Weiss, C. H. (1979). 'The Many Meanings of Research Utilization'. *Public Administration Review*, 39, 426–31.

Weiss, C. H., & Bucuvalas, M. J. (1980). 'Truth Tests and Utility Tests: Decision-Makers' Frames of Reference for Social Science Research'. *American Sociological Review*, 45, 302–13.

Wholey, J. S. (2002). 'Making Results Count in Public and Nonprofit Organizations'. In Newcomer, K., Jennings, E. T., Broom, C., & Lomax, A. (eds) *Meeting the Challenges of Performance Oriented Government*. Washington, DC: ASPA.

World Bank (1998). *Public Expenditure Handbook*. Washington, DC: World Bank.

# Chapter 9

# The effects of using performance information

## LEARNING OBJECTIVES

■ To have an insight into the dynamics that bring about effects of using performance information.

■ To develop a theoretically grounded and nuanced opinion on the effects of measurement.

## KEY POINTS IN THIS CHAPTER

■ The use of performance information can have functional and/or dysfunctional effects.

■ The manifestation of effects depends on the way performance information is used: learning, steering & control, or accountability.

■ Strategies to tackle dysfunctional effects should focus on the motive and/or the opportunity of dysfunctional behaviour.

## DISCUSSION QUESTIONS

■ Assume the role of a counsellor in an employment agency. You are evaluated based on the number of unemployed you counselled for. What would you do to get a favourable evaluation?

■ Assume the role of an advisor in an oversight agency that has to define some indicators for a broadcasting company. Which indicators would you define? Can they be manipulated?

■ Is it realistic to develop a functional performance accountability regime?

In conjunction with the NPM reform agenda, performance management acquired some faddish traits. Public managers jumped the bandwagon while management consultants further paved the way. The global management consulting market was worth $51 billion in 1996. In 2002, this figure rose to $119 billion (Saint Martin, 2005). The study of the effects of performance measurement has polarised around the proponents and critics of the broader New Public Management agenda. In this chapter, we will not take sides. We start with the observation that measurement is seldom unobtrusive and thus changes behaviour. The question that follows is whether these behavioural effects are functional or dysfunctional for performance. After reviewing functionality, we summarize the *conditions* under which functional and/or dysfunctional effects are likely to occur. We end with some thoughts on how to remedy dysfunctional effects.

## 1 MEASUREMENT CHANGES BEHAVIOUR

Performance measurement in organizations affects the behaviour of its members in a fundamental way. A study of the effects of performance measurement thus has to include the impact on the behaviour of managers, professionals, front-line workers, clients and stakeholders. Performance measurement is seldom unobtrusive.

This should however not come as a surprise. Social sciences have long established the behavioural effects of measurement. In the 1930s, Elton Mayo (1933) showed that the mere fact of being observed does influence behaviour. This effect, later coined as the Hawthorne effect, was discovered in a research project that was initially staged to study the impact of illumination on workers' productivity in an industrial plant. It showed that productivity rose in both the higher-light and the lower-light conditions, but in both conditions it dropped again after some time. The Hawthorne research team tested the effect of other variables such as maintaining clean workstations and clearing floors of obstacles. The same pattern was found. It was concluded that the mere fact of being observed does, at least in the short term, change behaviour and performance. In 1956, Berliner studied the production cycles in the planned economy of the Soviet era (1956). The uneven production patterns were a behavioural effect of measurement and targets. Typically, Soviet plants produced more than 50 per cent of their production in the last ten days of the month. Such 'production spurts' caused inefficiencies and coordination problems. Yet, the central administration did not manage to control the problem. Berliner demonstrated that monthly production targets combined with strong performance incentives for managers caused the spurts. Managers of local plants received considerable bonuses of up to 100 per cent of the base wage for meeting targets. Additional bonuses were provided when targets were surpassed. However, in the latter case, the next production target would be set at a higher level ('the ratchet effect'). As a result of this system, managers were inclined to do everything they could to meet targets without surpassing them too much. Therefore, they put pressure on all production factors (personnel, machines, etcetera) at the end of the month to reach the targets. The first weeks of the next month were used to maintain machines, allow for vacation of staff, and the like. Measurement and the essentially arbitrary choice of the accounting period (i.e. monthly targets) fundamentally altered the business cycle.

The behavioural effects of performance measurement are essential for performance-based NPM applications. For NPM, the informational value of performance measurement is overshadowed by the value for steering behaviour of organizations and individuals (see chapter 6). As a result, NPM assesses the functionality of performance measurement based on the behavioural effects that follow from performance information use rather than the information performance information yields.

## 2 FUNCTIONAL BEHAVIOURAL EFFECTS

In general terms, we define a phenomenon as being functional if its consequences attribute positively to a larger structure (Merton, 1949). Performance measurement thus would be functional when it contributes to the goals of a larger structure such as the organization, the policy sector, the whole of government or even society at large. Functionality of performance measurement is an empirical question that can be answered differently at different levels. The functional behavioural effects we discuss below mirror the three uses of performance measurement we identified in chapter 6. The effects could be seen as criteria for successful use of performance information. We therefore ask three questions for which a positive reply would point to a functional behavioural effect.

### 2.1 Does the use of performance measurement trigger learning and innovation?

Much of the evidence of learning effects is case based. Moynihan (2008) finds some evidence in the states of Vermont and Virginia of benefits of performance management in the respective Departments of Corrections. Basic goals and philosophies of programmes were questioned, an employee-centred culture was reinforced, communication between community and institutional staff was improved, and new leaders were socialized. Moynihan notes that although the performance management handbooks do generally not prescribe these effects, they are nonetheless important. Moynihan also assesses the Programme Assessment and Rating Tool (PART). The US Office of Management and the Budget (OMB) was the nucleus in this performance management initiative. The aim of PART was to assess the performance of federal programmes on a regular basis. Evidence suggests that PART is having an influence on decision-making within the OMB, albeit minor. The main critiques on PART, that is, its ambiguity and partisan nature, are at the same time its main strengths. PART allows different parties with different ideologies to come to different logic conclusions. These rationales are the core of the policy dialogue that is triggered by the process. Richard Nathan of the Rockefeller Institute is quoted saying that PART should not be seen as a tool to simplify the policy world. Instead, it should be seen as a way of complexifying decisions – prompting a serious dialogue about performance.

Benchmarking groups are another seemingly successful and upcoming practice. The idea is relatively simple. A number of organizations decide to get together in order to compare their performance. The first sessions are used to define the subject and to define indicators. Next, every organization gathers the information. A third party, usually a consultant or an academic, analyses the information and draws some tentative conclusions. In the final sessions, the results are discussed and matched to good practices within the organizations. At the end of the process, the benchmarking group decides which results can be released.

There are several examples. The Kommunale Gemeinschaftsstelle für Verwaltungsmanagement (KGSt), the largest German local government association, has a project to foster benchmarking groups amongst its members. Participation is voluntary and participants pay a fee for the KGSt guidance that covers the costs. Since its inauguration in 1996, more than 200 benchmarking groups were formed and almost 1,000 different municipalities participated. In 2002, 28 of the largest Dutch executive agencies – they handle 50 per cent of the public budget – formed a formal benchmarking organization, the Rijksbrede Benchmarking Group. Over the last years, the number of benchmarks and benchmark providers (read consultants) has boomed. The proliferation has led the Dutch local government association to award a hallmark for those providers that meet certain standards (Box 9.1). Recently, the target-driven English performance management regime also seems to have turned towards learning benefits. In response to the audit commission's abolition, the Local Government Association has launched the 'peer challenge' programme for local authorities, which is essentially a benchmarking group.

Benchmarking groups use performance information for learning, and nothing else. Other approaches suggest that accountability regimes should be more learning-like. Examples of *accountability-as-learning* are evaluation committees and assessment reports on the performance of public institutions (Lewis & Triantafillou, 2012). This model is for instance widely distributed in higher education. Most continental European universities undergo accreditation processes for research and education. In the UK, Australia and New Zealand, governments tend to rely on quality audits to assess performance. While the ultimate purpose of these efforts generally is accountability, the tone is softer compared to a hard-edged performance indicators regime. Learning and improvement are propagated as an important purpose besides accountability. The UK Research Excellence Framework (2014) for instance

## BOX 9.1 QUALITY CRITERIA FOR PROVIDERS OF BENCHMARKS ACCORDING TO THE DUTCH LOCAL GOVERNMENT ASSOCIATION (VNG)

*Requirements for a benchmark provider*

1 The provider establishes (with the participants) the objective of the benchmark and integrates it in the design of the benchmark.
2 The data remains the property of the participants.
3 The indicators are selected in cooperation with the participants.
4 The inputted data is checked for validity.
5 The benchmarks process schedules meetings with the participants.
6 The provider offers the opportunity to participate for several years.
7 The benchmarking exercise is evaluated.
8 The provider pays ample attention to improvement and performance of the participants.
9 The provider allows for interpretation of the data by participants.
10 The participants evaluate the process and the benchmark in a positive way.
11 The provider takes into consideration that participants have to ask for high-level commitment.
12 There is a willingness to disclose the methodologies and definition of the indicators.
13 Different points of view on the organizational processes are considered.
14 There is attention to the coordination of different benchmarks.
15 The provider is willing to align his approach with the methodology and definitions of the innovation monitor (a VNG project to coordinate benchmarks).

*Source:* www.vng.nl

announces that the results will be used for funding and for showing the benefits of public investment, as well as for the provision of benchmarking information. Lewis & Trianfillou (2014) critique the accountability-as-learning approach. They argue that accountability-as-learning is more likely to supplement than to replace existing performance indicator regimes of accountability; that it is likely to demand more not less data; that it requires extensive participation and dialogue; and that it may reinforce the logic of constant organizational change in the name of improvement. They warn that accountability-as-learning may simply increase administrative overload rather than reduce it.

In chapter 6, we discussed the difficulties of designing multi-purpose performance management systems. Accountability-as-learning will often give confusing signals to users of performance information. For learning purposes, they will need to take risks by exposing the weaknesses of the organization or programme. The incentives that follow from accountability guide the organization towards a performance beauty contest in order to secure future funding and development. It is difficult to do both accountability and learning. Since short-time organizational survival and growth is on the line in accountability regimes, it seems fair to expect that hard use for accountability will drive out soft use for learning.

## 2.2 Does the use of performance measurement improve steering & control in the organization?

Management in a public sector organization is fundamentally different from management in a private company. While private managers are mainly concerned about the bottom line of making sustainable profits, public managers are confronted with a top line of regulation, political interference and budget constraints (Wilson, 1989). As a result, public managers can only to a limited degree let performance indicators drive the decisions on how to steer & control their operations.

Nevertheless, there are many cases where steering & control did improve thanks to performance management initiatives. Let us first review some cases beyond the Anglo-Saxon world using the *PA@Babel database* (which holds English abstracts of non-English journals). Performance budgeting is implemented and used in the Belgian social security administration. Some significant improvements in service delivery were reported that could be largely attributed to performance management. Waiting times between the first day of unemployment and the disbursement of the first unemployment benefit were reduced from several months to a few weeks, which makes a big difference for claimants who have just lost their job (Baeck & Van Neyen, 2003). Bräunig (2007) demonstrates the benefits of benchmarking for controlling purposes in German social security. In France, the performance budgeting initiative (LOLF) has led to centralization in the justice sector, but also to budget cuts (Marshall, 2008). Lumijärvi (2001) points to the utility of the balanced scorecard in managing police units, provided that the scorecard is tailored to the context and needs of the organization. Vitezic (2007) as well as Verheijen & Dobrolyubova (2007) point to the benefits of performance management in developing countries, respectively Slovenia and the Baltic states. Further evidence of positive impacts of performance-based steering & control is found in the New York school system. Sun & Van Ryzin (2012) found that schools using performance management (setting goals, making plans, modifying practices) are performing better on test scores.

One of the best-documented performance management success stories is the New York Police Department's CompStat programme. In Box 9.2, Mayor Giuliani of New York explains how the system helped reduce crime through better allocation of resources. The system was perceived to be so successful that other NY city departments implemented similar systems for public parks and recreation (parkStat), for health (healthStat) and for the corrections department (O'Connell, 2001). Philadelphia has a schoolStat system and the city of Baltimore implemented a citywide system (Citistat). At the federal level, there is FEMAstat for emergency planning, HUDstat for housing policy and many more. Behn (2013) gives an overview of this performance-stat movement and argues that it is a unique performance management strategy. It is not budget-driven, not purely punitive, more enduring and embedded in routines, not non-committal and shared between top and middle management. In the terminology of our book, the performance-stat approach is a blend of steering & control and learning.

Again, difficulties of multi-purpose performance management systems may arise. Since media and top officials use most performance-stat systems for evaluating public policy, the accountability dimension can quickly gain the upper hand over other uses. Here, too, harder uses drive out softer ones. *Chicago Magazine* for instance published an extensive report on the manipulation of the crime statistics in the city (Bernstein & Isackson, 2014). The article observes:

> Of all index crimes (these are the crimes in the measurement system, red), motor vehicle thefts have plunged most. Over the past three calendar years, they're down 35 percent, again according to the department's own statistics. (They fell 23 percent last year alone.) Over that same three-year period, burglaries fell 33 percent; aggravated batteries, 20 percent; robberies, 16 percent. Current and former officers and several criminologists say they can't understand how a cash-strapped and undermanned department – one that by its own admission has been focusing most of its attention and resources on combating shootings and murders and protecting schoolchildren in a few very violent neighborhoods – could achieve such astounding results. 'God Almighty! It's just not possible,' opines a retired high-ranking officer who reviewed the department's statistics.

The authors explain this remarkable result by looking into the measurement system. Indexed crimes are counted differently or not counted at all. Also the lauded New York CompStat system was critiqued on the same grounds (Eterno & Silverman, 2012).

## 2.3 Does the use of performance measurement shape accountability based on performance?

The success of performance measurement for accountability rests on the pressure that measurement puts on organizations to critically assess their operations, to put established routines into question and to search for innovative solutions.

## BOX 9.2 MAYOR RUDOLPH GIULIANI ON COMPSTAT

The CompStat programme is . . . [a] programme that has had a big impact on the level of crime. I used to be the associate attorney general. I was in charge of dissemination of national crime statistics. So, I've been involved in crime numbers for 20 years. And it seemed to me that we were doing something wrong in the way in which we measured police success. We were equating success with how many arrests were made. A police officer was regarded as a productive police officer if he made a lot of arrests. He would get promoted. A police commander in a precinct would be regarded as a really good police commander if his arrests were up this year. This wasn't the only measure of success, but it was the predominant one.

Arrests, however, are not the ultimate goal of police departments or what the public really wants from a police department. What the public wants from a police department is less crime. So it seemed to me that if we put our focus on crime reduction and measured it as clearly as we possibly could, everybody would start thinking about how we could reduce crime. And as a result, we started getting better solutions from precinct commanders. We have 77 police precincts. Every single night they record all of the index crimes that have occurred in that precinct and a lot of other data. We record the number of civilian complaints. We record the number of arrests that are made for serious crimes and less serious crimes. It's all a part of CompStat, a computer-driven programme that helps ensure executive accountability. And the purpose of it is to see if crime is up or down, not just citywide, but neighbourhood by neighbourhood. And if crime is going up, it lets you do something about it now – not a year and a half from now when the FBI puts out crime statistics. After all, when you find out that burglary went up last year, there's nothing a mayor can do about it because time has passed and the ripple of criminal activity has already become a crime wave.

Now we know about it today. And we can make strategic decisions accordingly. If auto theft is up in some parts of the city and down in others, then we can ask why. And that will drive decisions about the allocation of police officers, about the kinds of police officers. This is one of the reasons why New York City has now become city #160 on the FBI's list for crime. Which is kind of astounding for the city that is the largest city in America. Think about the other 159 cities: many of them have populations that are 300,000, 400,000, 500,000. And on a per capita basis, some of them have considerably more crime.

*Source: quoted in O'Connell, 2001: p. 9*

The reasoning is that accountability should be based on performance rather than on inputs or mere compliance with rules and regulation.

This pressure can emanate from the general public and the media, from the political principals or from both. Without any doubt, the publication of performance information increases pressure on organizations. The next section will discuss several instances where this pressure has proved to be dysfunctional. Empirical evidence of whether accountability schemes really lead to better accountability is scarce. Yet, some cases are documented.

- A survey of performance practices in US counties by Berman & Wang (2000) found that an increased awareness about the need for accountability was one of the major outcomes of performance measurement schemes. Perhaps building *awareness* for accountability is what performance measurement efforts should hope for.
- Brezzi, Raimondo & Utili (2008) report on a financial performance incentive in a programme to develop the depressed regions of southern Italy. Regions that score well on 12 performance indicators could get financial rewards. A total of € 2.6 billion, accounting for 6 per cent of the programme's resources, was allocated in this way. It is assessed that significant results and modernizations can be attributed to the incentive system.
- Also in Italy, local governments can voluntarily engage in social reporting, which is seen as a means of democratic accountability. According to Marcuccio & Steccolini (2005), these efforts do lead to more transparency, although authorities tend to overstress their strengths and are inclined to play weakness down by referring to the unique context they operate in.
- Leighton (2008) argues that the call for performance-based accountability is inescapable. The spill-over of private sector scandals such as Enron and WorldCom has affected public trust. Hence, credible performance reporting is key. He argues that the quality of the reporting in Canada has improved over the last years in response to these challenges. The guidelines and audits of the Treasury Board and the Office of the General Auditor have reinforced this development.

Overall, it seems that better accountability is the least promising prospect for performance measurement. Full accountability, according to Thomas (2008), requires not only transparency, but also positive or negative sanctions. The OECD provides an overview of the potential positive or negative consequences of accountability for results (Table 9.1). Many of the proposed incentives however either are not realistic or may inhibit improvement rather than bring it about. Is it reasonable to stop funding a regional hospital when no other hospitals are nearby? What will be the consequences of cutting staff budgets of a school that failed to improve teaching methods? Probably, it means a higher pupil/teacher

**Table 9.1** *Incentives based on accountability for results*

| Mechanisms | Positive incentives | Negative incentives |
|---|---|---|
| Funding | − Increase funding<br>− Maintain status quo<br>− Provide bonuses<br>− Increase staff budget | − Reduce funding<br>− Eliminate funding<br>− Cut salaries<br>− Cut staff budgets |
| Flexibility | − Allow retaining and carrying over of efficiency gains<br>− Allow flexibility to transfer funds between line items in the budget<br>− Exempt agency from reporting requirements | − Return funding to the centre<br>− Restrict the ability to transfer funds<br>− Increase reporting requirements<br>− Order audits |
| Reputational | − Public recognition of performance | − Public criticism |

Source: based on OECD, 2008: p. 174

ratio that further diminishes the capacity for change. What happens if management of a badly performing immigration service is confronted with additional reporting? Probably, managers will have to lock themselves in their office to fulfil reporting obligations, and as a consequence, they are further alienated from what happens on the floor.

The hesitation to use incentives for performance is therefore not surprising. OECD surveys (2008: p. 162) found that ministries of finance hardly ever eliminate programmes when performance targets are not met. Moreover, between 2005 and 2007, the number of countries that claimed to do this further declined. Accountability failures are dependent on many factors that are often not included in the measurement system and that go beyond the reach of the organization that is held accountable. The main limitation of performance measurement is its inability to provide a conclusive answer to the performance question. In most cases, further interpretation is required. As a consequence, performance measurement and performance accountability may prove to be incompatible in many cases.

## 3 DYSFUNCTIONAL BEHAVIOURAL EFFECTS

In the previous section, we discussed some of the functions of performance measurement. The dysfunctions refer to those effects that undermine the goals of the larger structure. The literature on the dysfunctions of performance measurement is much richer than that on the functions. A multitude of effects of performance measurement has been described. Before we discuss a number of them in more detail, a categorization of the dysfunctional behavioural effects is proposed.

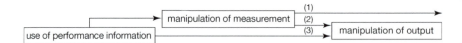

**Figure 9.1** *Effects of the use of performance information (Van Dooren, 2006)*

Dysfunctional effects are caused by either manipulation of the measurement process or a manipulation of the organizational output (Figure 9.1). The first set of effects mainly leads to measurement that is not a good representation of reality. Yet, the real quantity, quality and nature of the output of the organization are not affected. When measurement is pure window dressing, skewed measurement will not impact the day-to-day operations of the organizations. This category is represented by (1) in Figure 9.1.

Some dysfunctions do alter the daily operations of the organization through the behaviour of organizational members. In this case, outputs of a different quantity, quality or nature are pursued. These dysfunctions may materialize even with a perfect measurement system – category (3) in Figure 9.1. However, with an imperfect measurement system, the chances of such operational dysfunctions are higher – category (2) in Figure 9.1. Flawed measures may indeed be a catalyst for distorted operational practices

We now have a classification of measurement dysfunctions as well as a first scheme of how dysfunctions might interact. Before we discuss the effects, a final word on the intentionality of the occurrence of the effects is needed. Are these effects just 'happening', or are they the result of deliberate tactics of those who are confronted with performance information? The term 'manipulation' of measurement suggests the latter, and all the effects described below can be planned for. However, this does not exclude the possibility that some effects are unplanned side effects rather than the result of a grand manipulative design.

## 3.1 Distortion of performance information

Manipulation of measurement comes in many guises. There are at least seven ways of manipulating the measurement process (Smith, 1988; Bouckaert & Balk, 1991; Smith, 1995b).

1   *Over- and underrepresentation.* The measured value may not correspond with the real value and may provide a perception of more or less performance. Examples of both can be found in bibliometric analysis, which attempts to measure scientific impact through citation analysis (Garfield & Welljams-Dorof, 1992). On the one hand, the phenomenon of citation circles – academics that strategically decide to cite each other's work – may lead to overrepresentation. It brings about an overestimation of the impact of those authors. On the other hand, the obliteration

phenomenon leads to underrepresentation. This phenomenon refers to a process in which breakthrough advances – for example Einstein's theory of relativity – are cited less frequently over time. These landmark discoveries are incorporated into the generally accepted body of scientific knowledge. They are assumed, and therefore no longer cited. The measured value underestimates the real impact.

2   Bouckaert & Balk (1991) refer to the *Mandelbrot disease* as a second instance of failing measurement (see chapter 2). By looking at increasingly finer resolutions, more and more lengths are approximated, and the total estimate of length appears to increase to infinity. This process also takes place in performance measurement. More measurement may lead to higher values because phenomena are observed that were not seen before. The number of violations of human rights reported by Amnesty International may rise because of a real deterioration of the situation in the field. Yet, the establishment of new observatories may also cause a higher number. Similarly, homicide statistics – although hopefully not approaching infinity – may be higher in countries that routinely perform more post-mortem investigations. Whenever the magnitude of the underlying phenomenon is unknown, Mandelbrot is watching.

3   Third, the number of indicators in a set often risks inflating. This process is often termed as the 'mushrooming' of indicator sets. Too many indicators may indeed be problematic since the users of the information can no longer see the wood for the trees. In principal–agent relations, the creation of such an information overload may be a tactic of an agent to obfuscate real performance for the principal. Agents then exploit the information asymmetry that is typically in their advantage in principal–agent relations. For principals, this tactic is very difficult to counter. After all, the agent *is* providing huge amounts of information. The indicators are however only one, and not even the most important component of the information asymmetry. The capacity to make sense of the performance indicators is a more significant dimension of information asymmetry than the indicators themselves. Hence, the agent erodes the principal's sense-making capacity by providing more indicators than a principal can handle, while maintaining the image of cooperation and transparency. Moreover, a large indicator set conveniently raises the chances of excelling at least at some dimensions. This is particularly problematic for accountability purposes. Box 9.3 describes the case of the Lisbon process of the European Union. In a very explicit way, it is shown that too many indicators erode their regulatory capacity.

Notwithstanding the potential problems, the addition of increasingly more indicators is often a remedy for at least two other dysfunctional effects that we will discuss below: cream skimming (selecting the intake) and tunnel vision (focusing on the measured activities only). As a result, the definition of an optimal number of indicators is pointless. Organizations need to find this out through experience.

## BOX 9.3 TOO MANY INDICATORS? THE CASE OF THE LISBON PROCESS OF THE EUROPEAN UNION

At the Lisbon European Council in spring 2000, the European Union set the 'strategic goal for the next decade: to become the most competitive and dynamic knowledge-based economy in the world capable of sustainable economic growth with more and better jobs and greater social cohesion' (Paragraph 5 of the Council conclusions) (European Commission, 2000). This agenda has been monitored following the Open Method of Coordination (OMC). Each year, member states are held accountable for the progress as measured by means of a set of indicators. It is expected that these progress reports will push countries in the right direction. The indicator set started off with 35 indicators covering employment, innovation, economic reform and social cohesion. Soon, the set expanded to 42 indicators that now also cover environment as well as some general economic indicators. Besides the selection of structural indicators, hundreds of other indicators are collected in complementary processes.

After three years, the EU commissioned a mid-term review of the process, led by former Dutch minister-president Wim Kok. The proposal was to reduce the number of indicators to 14 in order to increase their ability to put pressure on nations. The mid-term review report states that

> more than a hundred indicators have been associated with the Lisbon process, which makes it likely that every country will be ranked as best at one indicator or another. This makes the instrument ineffective. . . . The European Commission should present the Heads of State or Government and the wider public annual updates on these key 14 Lisbon indicators in the format of league tables with rankings (1–25), praising good performance and castigating bad performance – naming, shaming and faming.
>
> (European Commission, 2004: p. 43)

For accountability, too many indicators are clearly a problem.

4    Performance information that is intensively used may get *polluted* (Bouckaert & Balk, 1991). This mainly refers to the terminology of the indicators. Different people interpret the concepts and definitions (slightly or substantially) differently. For some, performance refers to output, for others, performance is outcome and for still others it means both. The notoriously nebulous measure of public trust

for instance has been interpreted as a measure of openness (OECD, 2005), of performance (Afonso *et al.*, 2006) and of integrity (Pope, 2000), while in essence it only measures the disposition of people towards government (Van de Walle & Bouckaert, 2003). As a consequence, people talk at cross-purposes and the effectiveness of performance measurement erodes significantly. Although this dysfunction may well be the result of a spontaneous social mechanism, it is not unthinkable that actors deliberately create terminological confusion.

5   Performance information may be manipulated by *unjustifiable aggregation or disaggregation* data (see chapter 6) (Perrin, 1998). Composite indicators have the benefit of simplicity. Decision-makers with limited time or the general public with limited insight into complex policy matters are helped with a universal assessment of performance. Yet, by choosing and weighing the measures, organizations may hide problematic aspects of their performance. The reverse scenario is to look for more detail when aggregate measures are not satisfactory. For example, pointing to an improvement in a previously troubled quarter can divert attention from an overall increase in crime rates.

6   *Misrepresentation* is the deliberate manipulation of data – ranging from creative accounting to fraud (Smith, 1995a). There is a thin line between under- and overrepresentation on the one hand (point 1 above) and misrepresentation on the other. The distinction lies in the illegal character of misrepresentation as opposed to under- and overrepresentation. A public theatre is cheating when it deliberately counts more visitors than in reality attended a performance. Financial information systems combat misrepresentation by installing extensive internal control systems, supplemented by internal and external audit systems (Raaum & Morgan, 2001). For non-financial information, there is usually not such an extensive control structure. Misrepresentation thus has to be prevented in a different way. Some authors propose to rely more on trust-based systems (Grizzle & Pettijohn, 2002; Power, 1999).

7   *Misinterpretation* is the incorrect inference about performance brought about by the difficulty of accounting for the full range of potential influences on performance (Smith, 1995a). This dysfunction is particularly applicable to outcome measures. The ultimate impact of government output in society is often only visible in the long term. Moreover, societal change is seldom brought about by one single agency or department. Low unemployment figures for instance may be the result of a good training programme. Yet, the economic climate is without doubt also an important determinant. Moreover, tough inspection on moonlighting may add to the overall result of declining unemployment. Although this complexity is generally accepted, it is often forgotten about when indicators need to be interpreted.

**187**

## 3.2 Distortion of output

Manipulation of output is a second category of behavioural responses to the use of performance information. Unlike the manipulation of measurement, the manipulation of output alters the daily operations of the organization. Measurement is not (necessarily) skewed, but the underlying reality changes. This set of dysfunctions has an effect on what citizens directly or indirectly experience from public services. Therefore, the impact of manipulation on the nature, quality or quantity of outputs is more far-reaching than that of manipulating the statistics. In recent years, some dramatic cases of perverse effects have been documented (see Box 9.4).

1  *Measure fixation* is the pursuit of success as measured rather than as intended. Smith (1995a) gives the example of the 'hello' nurse in English hospitals. A nurse at the counter had to make a first contact with patients in order to meet a five-minute waiting time requirement, after which the patient was guided to another waiting room. Although the target is being met, this is clearly not an improvement of service delivery. University rankings are another example (Gormley & Weimer, 1999; Best, 2001). To obtain good rankings, universities may primarily try to improve prestige and not programme quality. Measure fixation may be avoided by including more indicators. However, by adding indicators, the risk of mushrooming crops up. Measure fixation may have two consequences: oversupply of services and/or a decline in quality.

(a)  Oversupply is the provision of more products and services than needed. Oversupply of measured activities is reinforced by the incentive structure of measurement. This is especially the case when unit costs are calculated in order to reimburse producers – as is the case in several European health systems. The medical accounting system stimulates medical overproduction. When fixed costs are considerable, as is the case for medical equipment, it usually is easier to reduce cost per unit by increasing output rather than decreasing input. As a result, the total output inflates (Dawson & Street, 2000). Oversupply of certain outputs often goes hand in hand with the neglect of other, unmeasured outputs and activities. In particular intangibles such as training and advice may be ignored. Blau (1963) gives an example of an employment agency where interviewers were motivated to complete as many interviews as possible. While doing so, they paid insufficient attention to other activities such as locating new jobs.

(b)  A second consequence of measure fixation is the loss of quality. Qualitative aspects of public services are usually more difficult to measure and therefore risk receiving less attention. Heinrich (1999) for instance observed that robust attention for cost-per-placement considerations in a job-training programme had a negative impact on service quality. Another example is situated in a

## BOX 9.4 GAMING: A WAKE-UP CALL FROM THE HOSPITAL SECTOR

The hospital sector shows the impact of performance targets on services. In 2010, the English Mid Staffordshire hospital got embroiled in a media storm after stories of patient neglect. The commission that investigated the case attributed the problems to amongst other things the star rating, target regime (Mid Staffordshire NHS Foundation Trust Public Inquiry, 2013). The report notes,

> The story the report tells is first and foremost of appalling suffering of many patients. This was primarily caused by a serious failure on the part of a provider Trust Board. It did not listen sufficiently to its patients and staff or ensure the correction of deficiencies brought to the Trust's attention. Above all, it failed to tackle an insidious negative culture involving a tolerance of poor standards and a disengagement from managerial and leadership responsibilities. This failure was in part the consequence of allowing a focus on reaching national access targets, achieving financial balance and seeking foundation trust status to be at the cost of delivering acceptable standards of care.
>
> (p. 3)

A similar case surfaced in the US Veteran Health Affairs (VHA) medical centres that cheated with waiting times, which probably led to avoidable deaths. Donald Moynihan blames the target regime:

> Imperfect performance measures were tied to pay incentives. Such performance incentives have been portrayed as the best way to manage all kinds of public services, even as evidence of their problems mount. According to a 2012 VHA guideline on how to evaluate performance, being 'results driven' constituted half of the evaluation for VHA network directors. The only easily measurable factor listed under the 'results driven' category was that patients not wait more than 14 days from their desired date for an appointment.
>
> (Moynihan, 2014)

British hospital, where waiting-time targets led to cancellations, long waiting times before appointments could be made, and a lack of follow-up visits (House of Commons Public Administration Select Committee, 2003).

2    A second dysfunction is *myopia* (Bouckaert & Balk, 1991). The long-term view is excluded by an over-fixation on the short-term goals. A myopic strategy usually favours curative services above preventive services – for example crime solving rather than crime prevention. Prevention is an example of an activity with results that are per definition intangible. In fact, the results are what did *not* happen. Another example is Blau's (1963) study of a court where the target of eight cases a month per person leads to the adjournment of difficult cases in favour of easy cases. The initial prioritization criterion, relative urgency, was replaced by another criterion, relative ease of processing. In the long term, obviously, the difficult cases accumulate. This effect is also found in the private sector, where companies (and their top managers) are driven to constantly improve quarterly results under pressure of stock markets and short-term incentive schemes. The 2008 financial crisis has uncovered the neglect of the long-term risks.

3    Third, *sub-optimization* refers to a situation where an optimal situation at unit level leads to a sub-optimal situation at higher levels. The pursuit of local organizational objectives goes at the expense of more general objectives (Bouckaert & Balk, 1991; Hood, 1974). This dysfunction often shows when the attainment of an outcome is the responsibility of a sequence of actors. Public security is an example of such a chained outcome. The first step is prevention: public places need to be well lit at night, people in shopping areas need to be alerted to pickpockets and social workers have to locate and remedy social hardship. Next, the police need to patrol and make arrests. The public prosecutor has to institute legal action and the courts have to pass judgements. Finally, the prisons have to detain convicts and the social services have to run programmes to reintegrate detainees into society. A high number of arrests, including less important infringements, may be optimal for a police force but sub-optimal for the overall outcome of public safety. Since the public prosecution and the courts have to process all the arrests, the often-limited capacity of the judicial system may become inadequate, and the more serious crimes may remain unsolved.

4    A fourth dysfunction is *cream skimming* (also called *cherry picking*) (Behn & Kant, 1999; Grizzle & Pettijohn, 2002). When confronted with output measures, organizations may be tempted to select the intake. Job training programmes for instance have been demonstrated to select those unemployed that are most likely to find a job (Anderson *et al.*, 1993; Heckman *et al.*, 1997). Although this strategy may be economically efficient, it usually contrasts with the public goals of the programmes that propagate equity of access to services.

**190**

An extreme manifestation of selection of intake is a full disinvestment in the services for which the target will never be reached. Rather than attempting to make these worst cases as good as they can get, they are written off. We might call this dysfunction *adverse skimming*, since the worst are left out instead of the best being taken in. Timeliness statistics for instance typically assess the performance of railroad companies. Therefore, an operator might rather have one train being much too late or even cancelled than many trains being a little late. In terms of service delivery, the latter option may be more acceptable.

5    A fifth dysfunction of performance measurement is *complacency*. Organizations will often strive towards adequate performance rather than excellence, since excellence also implies risks. Typically, organizations fear two consequences of excellent performance. On the one hand, there is the threat of budget cuts. It is often difficult to demonstrate that good performance is the result of good management and policy, and not of excessive resources. On the other hand, excellence may trigger ratchet effects (Bevan & Hood, 2006). Exceptional performance levels in a certain year may be considered the next year. Because standards of assessment shift upwards, it will become more difficult to excel in the future. Fear of the ratchet effect may cancel out the incentives that a measurement system is believed to introduce (Courty, 2004).

6    An excessively rigid measurement system may finally lead to *organizational paralysis* (Smith, 1995a; Bouckaert & Balk, 1991). Performance measures potentially guide behaviour, and as such, they have regulatory power. In the same way that too detailed regulation may squeeze out all freedom of action and innovation, too rigid performance measurement systems may ostracize the necessary discretion in organizations. Too detailed time registration systems and performance contracts for instance may inhibit experimentation. Time registration systems that make every failure visible and its costs computable will run counter to demands for innovation, which inherently require some tolerance of failure.

## 3.3 Performance target paradox

The result of the behavioural effects – functional and dysfunctional – is that performance will cluster around the target. Throughout time, an indicator loses its capacity to discriminate between good and bad performers because organizations adapt their performance. Meyer & Gupta (1994) call this the performance paradox (see also Van Thiel & Leeuw, 2002). We will use the term 'performance *target* paradox', because the effect that Meyer and Gupta describe should be attributed to the practice of target-setting based on performance indicators. As we discussed above, target setting is a feature of the use for accountability, which is only one dimension of the use of performance information besides steering & control and learning.

Figure 9.2 graphically represents the performance target paradox. We assume that performance is normally distributed and that a target is introduced on the average. The performance target paradox predicts that underperformers will change their behaviour in a functional or dysfunctional way to meet the target, while those that are performing better than the target will lower performance levels in order to avoid the ratchet effect. Some worst cases even may be abandoned (adverse skimming). The distribution clusters around the mean, with a slight increase in worst cases to account for adverse skimming.

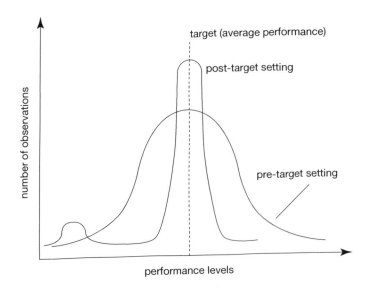

**Figure 9.2** *Performance target paradox – the tendency towards target*

## 4 CONDITIONALITY OF FUNCTIONS AND DYSFUNCTIONS

The sections above have put the functions and dysfunctions of measurement in a behavioural perspective. Individual behaviour however is encapsulated in a complex configuration of institutions that determine the conditionality of functions and dysfunctions. We limit the discussion here to the incentive structure that is embedded in the use of performance. It however goes without saying that other structural and cultural characteristics will also play a role. Since targets are often imposed in a hierarchical context, the acceptance of hierarchy might foster a culture where target-based performance measurement thrives well (Bendix, 1974). It seems plausible that cultures with a higher acceptance of hierarchy (such as England) will more quickly engage in target setting. Bureaucratic cultures

## BOX 9.5 ENGLISH EXCEPTIONALISM ACCORDING TO CANDIDE (VOLTAIRE)

Hood argues that the use of performance targets in England is rather exceptional (Hood, 2007). No other country in the world uses them with the same vigour. He refers to Voltaire's 1759 work *Candide ou l'optimisme* to illustrate the cultural background to this extraordinary position (Voltaire, 2006). Here, we include the translated excerpt of Voltaire's work.

> Talking thus they arrived at Portsmouth. The coast was lined with crowds of people, whose eyes were fixed on a fine man kneeling, with his eyes bandaged, on board one of the men of war in the harbour. Four soldiers stood opposite to this man; each of them fired three balls at his head, with all the calmness in the world; and the whole assembly went away very well satisfied.
>
> 'What is all this?' said Candide, 'and what demon is it that exercises his empire in this country?' He then asked who was that fine man who had been killed with so much ceremony. They answered, he was an Admiral. 'And why kill this Admiral?' 'It is because he did not kill a sufficient number of men himself. He gave battle to a French Admiral; and it has been proved that he was not near enough to him.'
>
> 'But,' replied Candide, 'the French Admiral was as far from the English Admiral.' 'There is no doubt of it; but in this country it is found good, from time to time, to kill one Admiral to encourage the others.'

such as France and Germany, on the contrary, may be less receptive to target-based governance arrangements (see Box 9.5).

In chapter 6, we identified three uses of performance information with different assumptions – to learn, to steer & control, and to give account. *Use for learning* assumes that people are intrinsically motivated to perform well and to seek responsibility. The use of performance information for research and learning has the lowest impact on the degrees of freedom of the organization. *Use for steering & control* is mainly about allocating resources and taking corrective actions when performance is lagging behind. The use for steering & control may have a significant impact on the degrees of freedom within an organization. However, the managers of an organization still control the performance information as well as the message that performance information gives to the outside world. The third purpose is *accountability*. The main proposition is that the public sector should be accountable

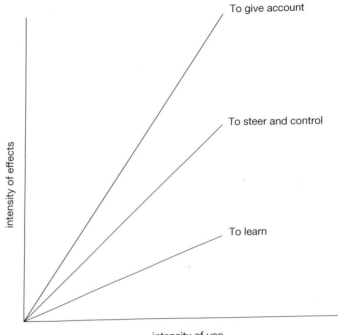

**Figure 9.3** *Central thesis of conditionality: use determines effects*

to the citizens/taxpayers and politicians and therefore performance of public bureaucracies should be disclosed to politics and the public.

It can be assumed that both functional and dysfunctional effects will be conditioned by the use of performance information. Figure 9.3 represents some rudimentary working hypotheses.

(a) There is linear relationship between the intensity of use and the intensity of effects.
(b) The gradient is steeper for higher pressure uses; accountability > learning; and accountability > steering and control.
(c) No use implies no effects (the curve starts in the origin).
(d) The function is similar for different kinds of behavioural effects.

Empirical evidence for these relations is limited. Research comparing different uses of performance information is virtually absent. Nonetheless, some counter-hypotheses can be formulated vis-à-vis the working hypotheses.

(a) The relation may not be linear. In the case of very intense uses of performance information, measures may run down more quickly (see the performance

 **194**

target paradox), and therefore the intensity of the effects may decline since measurement no longer shows variation. If this were the case, the relation would be parabolic rather than linear.

(b) The gradient may not necessarily be steeper for accountability use than for steering & control, since both uses potentially have high stakes. Use for learning may be fundamentally different in this respect.

(c) Measurement without use may nonetheless trigger effects when people believe that the information *can* be used. This will again mainly be the case for accountability and steering & control and less so for learning. If this is the case, the curve does not start in the origin.

(d) The relation between effect and use may be different depending on the particular use and effect under study. It may well be that intensive use for learning triggers very intense functional effects without having the dysfunctional effects.

## 5 HOW TO REMEDY DYSFUNCTIONAL EFFECTS?

The description of the dysfunctions of measurement raises the issue of how to remedy these effects. As anyone who every now and then watches a detective film is perfectly aware, committing a crime requires an opportunity and a motive. Up to this point, the line of reasoning has been that use for accountability and/or steering & control has a more pressing and direct impact on the organization than use for learning. The direct stakes in terms of budget allocations, bonuses and sanctions are higher. Therefore, the hard uses provide a *motive* for altering behaviour as purposed by the indicators. A motive for dysfunctional behaviour however needs to be combined with an *opportunity* for altering output. It is not always possible to manipulate performance indicators.

Table 9.2 provides constraints that may limit the propensity of dysfunctional behaviour, as well as some counteracting strategies. The analysis is mainly based

**Table 9.2** Constraints and counteracting strategies for dysfunctional behaviour

| A. Opportunity – constraints | B. Motive – constraints |
|---|---|
| No control over intake | Habit formation and predictability |
| Characteristics of the service | Consequential loop (boomerang effect) |
| Administrative and sectorial networks | Intrinsic motivation |

| C. Opportunity – counteracting strategies | D. Motive – counteracting strategies |
|---|---|
| Control and standardization through ICT | Abandon targets |
| Double-checking (of a sample) | Absolute targets |
| Qualitative assessment | Flexible dealing with targets |

on interviews with middle managers in regional government administration (Van Dooren, 2006). The constraints that limit opportunity and motives are to a large extent givens that cannot be influenced in the short term. The counteracting strategies are deliberate actions that aim at taking away opportunity and/or motives for dysfunctional behaviour.

## 5.1 Constraints on the opportunity for dysfunctional behaviour

First, organizations need to have an impact on the intake. Only in this case, effects such as cherry picking will be possible. Schools for instance that are obliged to enrol students on a first-come-first-served basis will not be able to hunt for pupils with strong socio-economic profiles. An emergency unit of a hospital is not supposed to control its intake when ambulances pull up with heavily injured patients. Similarly, courts cannot refuse persons seeking justice.

Second, the characteristics of the service may limit the opportunity for gaming. This is for instance the case for adverse skimming. A complete disinvestment in a service will only be possible when the importance for individual beneficiaries of that service is limited. Delaying an already delayed train more will meet less resistance than setting aside a dossier for subsidising a school. In the latter cases, the disadvantaged will almost always appeal to the courts. Similarly, a decline in quality of services as a result of number fixation will be noticed more quickly in face-to-face services than in for instance road construction.

A third limitation is caused by exposure of the production process to peers in administrative and sectorial networks. Dysfunctional behaviour may be quickly identified by other organizations within administrative and social networks. In general, public organizations are embedded in a web of relations within the administration as well as within politics and society. In some policy sectors, the social distance between societal actors, politicians and the administration is closer relative to others. This is particularly the case when a policy sector is highly institutionalized with strong umbrella organizations. In this case, the opportunity to alter output to obtain favourable scores is reduced because of peer insight into the production function of the organization.

## 5.2 Constraints on the motive for dysfunctional behaviour

First, increasing experience in working with performance information leads to habit formation. The use of performance information becomes more predictable over time, and as a result it may also become less threatening. Obviously, predictability may also increase the opportunity for dysfunctional behaviour, since actors learn how to play the game. Opportunity and motive work against each other in this case.

Second, the motive may be affected because of the consequential loop of dysfunctional behaviour. A public organization, or even the individual employee, may be directly affected in a later stage by gaming in an earlier stage. For instance, pursuing quantity at the expense of quality may result in a higher workload because more appeals are lodged with administrative courts. Inferior quality may return like a boomerang. Obviously, this is not always the case. A noteworthy counterexample is low quality in paying allowances or tax inspections. When low quality means that decisions are made in favour of the beneficiary, cases will not return.

Third, there is substantial evidence that intrinsic motivation in public bureaucracies is still substantial (Perry & Hondeghem, 2008). In particular in highly professionalized services, professional standards outweigh the pressure to obtain high performance scores.

## 5.3 Strategies to reduce the opportunity for dysfunctional behaviour

First, information and communication technology (ICT) may strongly reduce the opportunity for skewing performance measures. ICT is increasingly used for process management. Since all dossiers need to be inserted in computers, data can be broken down to the individual employee and the individual dossier. Control and audit opportunities are much stronger. In addition, standardization of online forms reduces the opportunity for misclassification – deliberate or not.

Second, traditional control techniques may be employed. A common technique is to double-check a sample of registrations in the measurement system. In addition, analysis of outliers or unlikely results may be a useful approach. The perceived probability of being controlled may strongly affect the opportunity for dysfunctional behaviour. In this respect, a certain reverberation of the controls being executed in the organization makes sense.

Third, in addition to measurement, public organizations may resort to qualitative assessments. This can be done through focus groups and conversations with staff and stakeholders. Corroboration of measurement results with other sources of knowledge can be a very effective way to uncover gaming. Note that such corroboration is already built into the use for learning.

## 5.4 Strategies to take away the motive for dysfunctional behaviour

The strategies for taking away the motive are all directed towards target setting. The most obvious strategy is to abandon targets, and to primarily aim at triggering dialogue and learning effects. This is a good strategy if learning is the purpose of

**197**

measurement and the measurement system is designed along these lines. If not, without a target people will often rely on other ways of sense-making when confronted with the data. The most likely point of reference will then be last-year performance or performance of comparable units. If this is the case, the motive gets back in by the backdoor, but remains implicit.

Another strategy is to formulate an absolute standard (e.g. 100 per cent precision, zero tolerance for corruption). There is usually a strong symbolic dimension to an absolute target. The message is that the organization for instance does not tolerate corruption, even when corruption levels are low. In this sense, the target is mainly used to set the agenda. However, as a yardstick, an absolute target is not useful, and again, the implicit standard is not clear.

Still another strategy is to phrase the targets in general terms. Rather than a precise number, the targets are formulated in terms of an increase or decrease of the results. There is a target, but not as strict as a numerical standard. Here, too, it is better to be roughly accurate than precisely wrong. In addition, the standard is made explicit, which should build trust in the system.

## 6 CONCLUSION

The use of performance information influences behaviour in functional and/or dysfunctional ways. The dysfunctional effects usually get more airplay in the academic field than the functional ones. A balanced view however takes both into account. The occurrence of effects depends on the way performance information is used, besides some general cultural and institutional variables. Finally, it is argued that dysfunctional effects can be tackled by taking away the motive or the opportunity to behave dysfunctionally.

## FURTHER READING

In the 1990s, Bouckaert & Balk (1991) and Smith (1995a) pointed to the dysfunctional effects of performance measurement. One of the most cited recent studies of the dysfunctional effects of performance management is Bevan and Hood's analysis of the British healthcare sector (Bevan & Hood, 2006). See also Van Thiel & Leeuw (2002) on the performance paradox. A recent study that documented some functional effects of performance management is Moynihan (2008). Cases of functional effects can also be found under the best practice banner on for instance the website of the IBM Centre for the Business of Government. From the canon, the case studies by Blau (1963) should have priority on reading lists.

# REFERENCES

Afonso, A., Schuknecht, L., & Tanzi, V. (2006). *Public Sector Efficiency: Evidence for New EU Member States and Emerging Markets*. Lisbon: Technical University of Lisbon.

Anderson, K. H., Burkhauser, R. V., & Raymond, J. E. (1993). 'The Effect of Creaming on Placement Rates under the Job Training Partnership Act'. *Industrial and Labor Relations Review*, 46, 613–24.

Baeck, K., & Van Neyen, S. (2003). 'Risicobeheer bij de Rijksdienst voor Arbeidsvoorziening. Een nieuw element binnen het geïntegreerd beheersmodel'. *VTOM*, 8.

Behn, R. D. (2013). *The PerformanceStat Potential: A Leadership Strategy for Producing Results*. New York: Brookings Institution Press.

Behn, R. D., & Kant, P. A. (1999). 'Strategies for Avoiding the Pitfalls of Performance Contracting'. *Public Productivity and Management Review*, 22, 470–89.

Bendix, R. (1974). *Work and Authority in Industry*. Berkeley: University of California Press.

Berliner, J. S. (1956). 'A Problem in Soviet Business Administration'. *Administrative Science Quarterly*, 1, 86–101.

Berman, E., & Wang, X. (2000). 'Performance Measurement in U.S. Counties: Capacity for Reform'. *Public Administration Review*, 60, 409–20.

Bernstein, D., & Isackson, N. (2014). 'The Truth about Chicago's Crime Rates: Part 2'. *Chicago Magazine*. 19 May. Retrieved from http://www.chicagomag.com/Chicago-Magazine/June-2014/Chicago-crime-statistics/.

Best, J. (2001). *Damned Lies and Statistics: Untangling Numbers from the Media, Politicians, and Activists*. University of California Press.

Bevan, G., & Hood, C. (2006). 'What's Measured Is What Matters: Targets and Gaming in the British Health Care Sector'. *Public Administration*, 84, 517–38.

Blau, P. (1963). *The Dynamics of Bureaucracy: A Study of Interpersonal Relationships in Two Government Agencies*. Chicago: University of Chicago Press.

Bouckaert, G., & Balk, W. (1991). 'Public Productivity Measurement: Diseases and Cures'. *Public Productivity & Management Review*, 15, 229–35.

Bräunig, D. (2007). 'Benchmarking als sachzielorientiertes Controllinginstrument am Beispiel von Sozialversicherungsträgern'. *Zeitschrift für öffentliche und gemeinwirtschaftliche Unternehmen*, 30.

Brezzi, M., Raimondo, L., & Utili, F. (2008). 'Using Performance Measurement and Competition to Make Administrations Accountable'. In Delancer Julnes, P., Berry, F. S., Aristigueta, M., & Yang, K. (eds) *International Handbook of Practice-Based Performance Management*. Thousand Oaks: Sage.

Courty, P. (2004). 'An Empirical Investigation of Gaming Responses to Explicit Performance Incentives'. *Journal of Labor Economics*, 22, 23.

**199**

Dawson, D., & Street, A. (2000). 'Comparing NHS Hospital Unit Costs'. *Public Money and Management*, 20(4), 58–62.

Eterno, J. A., & Silverman, E. B. (2012). *The Crime Numbers Game: Management by Manipulation*. Boca Raton, FL: CRC Press.

European Commission (2000). 'The Lisbon European Council – An Agenda of Economic and Social Renewal for Europe'. Contribution of the European Commission to the Special European Council in Lisbon, 23–24 March 2000. Brussels: European Commission.

European Commission (2004). *Public Finances in EMU*. Brussels: Office for Official Publications of the European Communities.

Garfield, E., & Welljams-Dorof, A. (1992). 'Citation Data: Their Use as Quantitative Indicators for Science and Technology Evaluation and Policy-Making'. *Science and Public Policy*, 19, 321–321.

Gormley, W. T., & Weimer, D. L. (1999). *Organizational Report Cards*. Cambridge, MA: Harvard University Press.

Grizzle, G. A., & Pettijohn, C. D. (2002). 'Implementing Performance Based Budgeting: A System Dynamics Perspective'. *Public Administration Review*, 62, 51–62.

Heckman, J., Heinrich, C., & Smith, J. (1997). 'Assessing the Performance of Performance Standards in Public Bureaucracies'. *American Economic Review*, 87, 389.

Heinrich, C. J. (1999). 'Do Government Bureaucrats Make Effective Use of Performance Management Information?' *Journal of Public Administration Research and Theory*, 9, 363–93.

Hood, C. (1974). 'Administrative Diseases: Some Types of Dysfunctionality in Administration'. *Public Administration*, 52, 439–54.

—— (2007). 'Public Service Management by Numbers: Why Does It Vary? Where Has It Come From? What Are the Gaps and the Puzzles?' *Public Money and Management*, 27, 95–102.

House of Commons Public Administration Select Committee (2003). *On Target? Government by Measurement*. London: House of Commons.

Leighton, B. (2008). 'Recognizing Credible Performance Reports: The Role of the Government Auditor of Canada'. In Delancer Julnes, P., Berry, F. S., Aristigueta, M., & Yang, K. (eds) *International Handbook of Practice-Based Performance Management*. Thousand Oaks: Sage.

Lewis, J. M., & Triantafillou, P. (2012). 'From Performance Measurement to Learning: A New Source of Government Overload?' *International Review of Administrative Sciences*, 78(4), 597–614.

Lumijärvi, I. (2001). 'Tasapainoitettu mittaristo (BSC) poliisitoiminnan arvioinnin ja kehittämisen työkaluna'. *Hallinnon Tutkimus*, 20, 72–80.

Marcuccio, M., & Steccolini, I. (2005). 'Nuovi modelli di accountability nelle amministrazioni pubbliche: un'analisi empirica del contenuto del bilancio sociale degli enti locali'. *Azienda Publica*, 18, 665–88.

Marshall, D. (2008). 'L'impact de la loi organique relative aux lois de finances (Lolf) sur les juridictions'. *Revue Française de l'Administration Publique*, 125.

Mayo, E. (1933). *The Human Problems of an Industrial Civilization*. New York: Macmillan.

Merton, R. K. (1949). *Social Theory and Social Structure: Toward the Codification of Theory and Research*. New York: Free Press.

Meyer, M. W., & Gupta, V. (1994). 'The Performance Paradox'. *Research in Organizational Behavior*, 16, 309–69.

Mid Staffordshire NHS Foundation Trust Public Inquiry (2013). *Report of the Mid Staffordshire NHS Foundation Trust Public Inquiry: Executive Summary*. London: The Stationery Office.

Moynihan, D. (2014). 'Op-Ed: The Problem at the VA: "Performance Perversity"'. *Los Angeles Times*. Retrieved from http://www.latimes.com/opinion/op-ed/la-oe-moynihan-va-scandal-performance-perversity-20140602-story.html.

Moynihan, D. P. (2008). *The Dynamics of Performance Management: Constructing Information and Reform*. Washington, DC: Georgetown University Press.

O'Connell, P. E. (2001). 'Using Performance Data for Accountability: The New York City Police Department's CompStat Model of Police Management'. *The PricewaterhouseCoopers Endowment for the Business of Government*. Washington, DC: PricewaterhouseCoopers.

OECD (2005). *Strengthening Trust in Government*. Paris: OECD.

—— (2008). *OECD Public Management Reviews: Ireland*. Paris: OECD.

Perrin, B. (1998). 'Effective Use and Misuse of Performance Measurement'. *American Journal of Evaluation*, 19, 367.

Perry, J. L., & Hondeghem, A. (2008). *Motivation in Public Management. The Call of Public Service*. Oxford: Oxford University Press.

Pope, J. (2000). *Confronting Corruption: The Elements of a National Integrity System*. Berlin: Transparency International.

Power, M. (1999). *The Audit Society: Rituals of Verification*. Oxford: Oxford University Press.

Raaum, R. B., & Morgan, S. L. (2001). *Performance Auditing: A Measurement Approach*. Altamonte Springs, FL: Institute of Internal Auditors.

Saint Martin, D. (2005). 'Management Consultancy'. In Ferlie, E., Lynn, L. E., & Pollitt, C. (eds) *The Oxford Handbook of Public Management*. Oxford: Oxford University Press.

Smith, P. (1988). 'Assessing Competition among Local Authorities in England and Wales'. *Financial Accountability and Management*, 4, 235–51.

—— (1995a). 'On the Unintended Consequences of Publishing Performance Data in the Public Sector'. *International Journal of Public Administration*, 18, 277–310.

—— (1995b). 'Performance Indicators and Outcome in the Public Sector'. *Public Money and Management*, 15(4), 13–16.

Sun, R., & Ryzin, G. G. V. (2012). 'Are Performance Management Practices Associated with Better Public Outcomes? Empirical Evidence from New York Public Schools'. *American Review of Public Administration*, 44, 324–38.

Thomas, P. G. (2008). 'Why Is Performance Based Accountability so Popular in Theory and so Difficult in Practice?' In KPMG (ed.) *Holy Grail or Achievable Quest? International Perspectives on Public Sector Performance Management.* KPMG.

Van de Walle, S., & Bouckaert, G. (2003). 'Public Service Performance and Trust in Government: The Problem of Causality'. *International Journal of Public Administration*, 26, 891–914.

Van Dooren, W. (2006). 'Performance Measurement in the Flemish Public Sector: A Supply and Demand Approach'. Leuven, Belgium: Faculty of Social Sciences, Leuven University.

Van Thiel, S., & Leeuw, F. L. (2002). 'The Performance Paradox in the Public Sector'. *Public Performance & Management Review*, 25, 267–81.

Verheijen, T., & Dobrolyubova, Y. (2007). 'Performance Management in the Baltic States and Russia: Success against the Odds?' *International Review of Administrative Sciences*, 73, 205–15.

Vitezic, N. (2007). 'Beneficial Effects of Public Sector Performance Management'. *UPRAVA: mednarodna znanstvena revija za teorijo in prakso*, 5, 7–27.

Voltaire (2006). *Candide*. Project Gutenberg.

Wilson, J. Q. (1989). *Bureaucracy: What Government Agencies Do and Why They Do It*. New York: Basic Books.

# Chapter 10

# The future of performance management

It is always somewhat venturesome to title a text 'The future of . . . '. What we present here is a somewhat tendentious extrapolation of current trends. More so than in other chapters, we take positions which are often hypothetical. The function in the context of a textbook is to trigger debate while making use of the frameworks and concepts of the previous chapters. We first outline some paradoxes in performance measurement and management, which at the same time echo some of the challenges for performance management. The second part asks the question how we can do better in the future. Argyris & Schön's (1996) distinction between single- and double-loop learning is used to categorize the character of the proposed solutions to the challenges (Van Dooren, 2011). Single-loop solutions try to mitigate the implementation problems of performance management. The main argument is that better results in performance management can be obtained by better implementation. Single-loop solutions propose to have a *second go* with an essentially good system. In contrast, the double-loop cluster of responses proposes to change (parts of) the system. The message is not just to try it again, but also to do it differently. Rather than focusing on the nuts and bolts of implementation, this section suggests a more fundamental redesign of performance management in a complex environment that is in permanent flux.

## 1 PARADOXES IN PERFORMANCE MEASUREMENT AND MANAGEMENT

In recent years, research has uncovered some paradoxes in the current practice of performance management. Some of these paradoxes are discussed below: (1) the counting of the uncountable, (2) relying on but not trusting professionals, (3) paralysis by too much analysis, (4) the difficulty of accountability arrangements in collaborative settings, and (5) the hope for better performance that performance management often cannot meet.

### 1.1 Counting the uncountable

Allegedly, in Albert Einstein's office at Princeton University there hung a sign stating that 'Not everything that counts can be counted, and not everything that can be counted counts'. Performance measurement adepts sometimes forget about this insight. Managers and politicians inferred from the conviction that *what gets measured, gets done* that *what does not get measured, does not get done*. This incorrect logical inference was reinforced by management consultants advocating the quest for the ultimate set of key performance indicators (KPIs) (see for instance Kaplan & Norton, 1996, on the Balanced Score Card). Many employees inferred that services not subjected to a KPI are not that important. Divisions in large organizations often lobby to get their activities into the KPI set. They know that what is counted, counts.

 **204**

In the last decade, several performance management experts have pled for a focus on measuring outcomes instead of outputs or processes (Hatry, 2002; Perrin, 2003). The argument is that only outcomes are 'real' key results. Real equals results that matter for society. It does not matter how many police patrols are negotiating the streets (which is an output); citizens want safety (which is an outcome). Therefore, performance measurement should primarily focus on outcomes. Yet, and herein lies the paradox, outcomes are in many instances very hard to count. We know that what is measured gets attention, but we also know that many important dimensions are immeasurable. A key issue thus is how to cope with the uncountable in performance management systems.

## 1.2 Distrusting professionals, but relying on them

Performance management doctrine has an ambiguous attitude towards expertise and professionals.

On the one hand, professionals are the key to better performance. In fact, the NPM phrase 'let managers manage' reflects a confidence in the professionalism of managers. Similarly, it is expected that managers are entrepreneurs and leaders that bring about the best in the staff under their supervision. Not in a command and control style, but by empowerment. On the other hand, the performance movement expresses a certain distrust in professionals. Davies & Lampel (1998), assessing performance management in the British National Health Service, argue that managers needed performance information in order to intervene successfully in the doctor–patient relationship. Hence, a plethora of indicators has been developed in order to counterbalance doctors' professional knowledge. Radin (2006) provides the example of the British Research Assessment Exercise (RAE), which audited the research quality of universities based on a number of performance indicators such as the number and type of publications. Rather than trusting the professional researcher, quality is counted. Similarly, Radin (2006) points to the No Child Left Behind initiative in public schools in the USA. She asserts that the standardized tests do not leave enough room for teachers' discretion.

There is a clear paradox. On the one hand, trust in professionalism is vital in an increasingly complex society. On the other, performance management systems are reluctant to grant this trust and hence fall back on control and audit. In circles of auditors, the adage 'In god we trust, the rest we audit' is well appreciated. According to Power (1999) these audits are to a large extent ceremonial – he speaks of rituals of verification. Many audits are mainly about creating an illusion of control. Similar arguments can be made for other performance measurement initiatives in both public and private sectors. The challenge for performance management lies in allowing for trust and professional discretion while agreeing on definitions of performance indicators.

## 1.3 Paralysis by analysis

Decision-makers have to process a lot of information: budgets, audits, impact analyses, evaluation studies, memoranda from interest groups, laws and jurisdiction, personal communication, and so on. An almost superhuman analytical capacity is required to process all these sources. Performance information comes on top of this pile, and for this reason, the risk of an information overload increases even more. Although performance management is devised to improve decisions, it may also lead to paralysis. It should thus not come as a surprise that practitioners consider selectivity in measurement to be one of the key challenges for implementing performance management (Mayne, 2007). Before, we discussed how bounded rationality leads to coping strategies (chapter 8, on non-use) in information processing. We also discussed evidence of middle managers making more use of performance information than senior officials (Taylor, 2011). The key challenge for performance management is digesting performance information into a decision-relevant format for top decision-makers (Kroll, 2013).

## 1.4 Collaboration and performance: if everyone is accountable, no one is

There is increasing awareness that public organizations cannot be effective on their own. Actors from all spheres – the executive, legislature, the citizen and the administration – are expected to share responsibilities.

A considerable literature on collaboration, partnerships and networks has developed (see for instance Milward & Provan, 2000; Vangen & Huxham, 2001; Koppenjan & Klijn, 2004; Agranoff, 2005; and a recent special issue of *Public Management Review* on network effectiveness: Mandell & Keast, 2008). As a result of collaboration, the responsibilities for performance are shared as well. Hence, when many organizations participate, it becomes more difficult to hold a single organization accountable for results. And if many are accountable, the risk occurs that no one is taking responsibility for failure and everybody for success.

Should we then stick to traditional accountability schemes with one principal and one agent? Probably not. The willingness to collaborate can erode when one-to-one accountability schemes are maintained. Denhardt & Aristigueta (2008) demonstrated that typical approaches to performance management are impacting partnerships and collaborations. Performance-based accountability systems tend to undermine collaborative efforts unless they are accompanied by other strategies for providing an impetus for alignment and collaboration across agencies.

## 1.5 Attribution bias: what can performance management do to improve performance?

The evidence on whether performance management actually contributes to better performance is not overwhelming (see chapter 9 for a discussion on the effects of performance). Indubitably, other organizational factors besides performance management do have an impact on performance. A literature study of the OECD assesses the drivers of performance (Van Dooren et al., 2007). Decentralization for instance appears to be a structural feature of public administration that positively influences performance. Attention to the soft dimensions of HRM is an example of a management practice that influences performance. Performance pay systems on the contrary mostly seem to have a negative effect. Other variables such as budgeting flexibility, coordination efforts, unionization and openness of the recruitment system can be expected to have an influence on performance as well. Finally, and maybe blindingly obviously, lacking resources may affect the performance of public organizations.

We do not argue that performance management does not lead to performance. Evidence is mostly lacking to substantiate either a positive or a negative relation. Research in this area faces the challenging task of not only collecting empirical evidence on the relation between performance management and performance, but also contextualizing empirical evidence. Practitioners should be wary of an attribution bias and develop a realistic perspective of what can be expected from a performance management system. If resources for services are below threshold, a performance management system will not fix it.

## 2 SINGLE-LOOP LEARNING: TOWARDS BETTER IMPLEMENTATION

Few argue against the *aims* of performance management. Hatry (2008) for instance finds it hard to believe that performance management will not continue far into the future. Nonetheless, as we argued in other chapters in this book, performance management is not without its problems. Practitioners, management consultants and academics have sought solutions in response to the paradoxical and often problematic nature of performance management. Yet, the solutions that are proposed do have a different bearing on performance measurement and management. We first discuss some single-loop solutions that propose to continue with the current performance regimes.

### 2.1 Improve the quality of performance information

We argued in this book that quality of performance information alone does not guarantee the use of performance information. Yet, it definitely *can* be an important factor. Research suggests that often only modest attention is paid to quality assurance practices in the area of performance measurement (Mayne, 2007). Hatry (2008) argues that an investment in the many dimensions of quality can ratchet up the use of performance information.

- *Validity of the performance indicators.* Do the indicators measure what is relevant and important about the particular issue or service?
- *Quality of the data.* Is the data collected for each of the performance indicators of sufficient accuracy?
- *Timeliness of the data.* Are the performance data collected and reported in a sufficiently timely fashion so the information is available when needed?
- *Analysis of the data.* Has at least some basic analysis been undertaken of that data to put it into meaningful form, such as by providing breakouts of the aggregate data and by providing legitimate comparisons so that users can interpret the extent to which the measured levels of performance represent good or poor outcomes?
- *Presentation of the performance information.* Is the information presented in a form that the user groups can understand and interpret and in an easy-to-read format?

Besides these punctual criteria, quality may also refer to the ethical attitude of measuring bodies (Bouckaert & Halligan, 2008). Integrity, independence and transparency relate to the quality and integrity of performance information and the institutions responsible for them. Credibility of performance information is in the eye of the user related to the credibility of the provider. There are two major institutions responsible for safeguarding integrity: the audit offices and the statistical offices. The cascade of a solid internal control system, which is assessed by an internal audit office under the guidance of an internal audit committee, which itself is assessed by an external audit office, sometimes even a Supreme Audit Institution, is designed to provide assurance about the quality of performance information. In some instances the cascade is successful, while in other cases quality assurance is mainly a bureaucratic snowball. The role of statistical bureaus will become more important. Statistical agencies are recognised as having the capacity to look beyond single organizations. With an increasing span and depth of performance information, there is a need to look beyond outputs to societal outcomes. A key issue for the future is the combination of audit standards and statistical standards and making these useful for managing performance.

## 2.2 Leadership

An OECD 2005 survey (Curristine, 2005b) found that strong leadership (also politically) is key to explaining success in performance management. Someone has to put his or her shoulders under a performance management effort and develop a measurement strategy. Preferably, this person carries some weight. However, leadership as a concept is ill specified, and hence the interpretation of the OECD survey results is more complicated. The issue of leadership raises a host of questions: who should the leader be? What traits are important for performance leadership? Where does leadership in performance come from and how can it be sustained?

Behn (2004) regards performance leadership as a capacity of public managers. He opposes the performance leadership model to a focus on performance systems and structures. He writes that 'rather than develop public managers with the leadership capacity to improve the performance of their agencies, we have sought to create performance systems that will impose such improvements' (p. 3). This approach echoes the need to trust public managers as management professionals. Performance leadership, in this view, aligns best with the managerial and learning perspectives on the use of performance.

## 2.3 Ownership

Another magical word in the management discourse is *ownership*. Implementation failures are regularly said to be caused by a lack of it. Mayne (2007) for instance notes that a system built on filling in performance information forms for others, with no apparent use for those down the line, is unlikely to be robust and survive over time. Better implementation of performance measurement and management requires that those who are affected by the system have to accept and internalize the system.

Different uses suggest different challenges in creating ownership. High-stakes use such as performance contracts and league tables necessitate a thorough ex ante dialogue with the *owners-to-be* in order to define indisputable and robust indicators. Inevitably, such hard uses will feature relatively more top-down implementation characteristics. Softer uses such as benchmarking circles and other learning efforts require an effort to avoid a non-committal attitude. Bottom-up processes will be relatively more important in these instances.

## 2.4 Setting realistic expectations

Performance management reforms are often victims of over-commitment. Many people need to be convinced in order to introduce a performance management system: politicians, top and middle managers, professionals and front-line workers. Hence, an understandable strategy is to create high expectations and to play down the costs. Yet, although this strategy may prove successful in the short term, it almost definitely will boomerang in the medium term. Typically, costs of a performance management system are tangible and become apparent relatively shortly after the introduction of the system. They mainly include the costs of building a data infrastructure. Benefits on the other hand are intangible and may only appear in the longer term. Disillusionment with performance systems that do not (yet) deliver may undermine confidence, and hence the failure of the performance management effort may become a self-fulfilling prophecy.

## 2.5 Adequate training and skills development

A next strategy to improve implementation is to provide training and to develop skills of both producers and consumers of performance information (Wholey, 1999). Training efforts that provide statistical and design skills are oriented towards producers of performance information. These courses mainly seek a better crafts-manship in measurement. Two additional training needs however need to be met. First, producers of performance information should not only be good at measurement. They also need to be able to communicate measurement to different audiences. A good understanding of the needs of these audiences is required. Second, we can also envisage skill development at the receiving end. Users of performance information such as politicians, top managers and even citizens could be target groups. Obviously, the nature of such training courses needs to be different. They should primarily focus on the capability to recognize credible performance information and to understand the ways in which it can be sensibly put to use. They should also focus on the limitations of performance information.

## 2.6 Integration

Integration, coordination, formalization, consistency, coherence, routine-build-ing and alignment are some of the most common keywords for those who want to fix performance management without questioning its blueprint. Although the importance of integration and coordination is undeniable, we should also acknowledge the limitations. Complexity and change regularly tear carefully coord-inated systems apart. The desire to coordinate all efforts in advance may lead to delay and even deadlock. In some instances, it may make more sense to remedy the consequences of ill-coordinated performance efforts than to embark on excessively ambitious coordination efforts (see also Laegreid *et al.*, 2008).

## 3 DOUBLE-LOOP LEARNING: RETHINKING PERFORMANCE MANAGEMENT

In 2003, the UK House of Commons (2003) investigated English performance management practices. The conclusion was that the English public sector had to move from a measurement culture towards a performance culture. Too often, performance management is devised following *a machine-based engineering logic.* Performance management is locked into formal systems and is expected to steer

 **210**

behaviour like the controls of a factory robot. At the same time, performance management has slipped through the fingers of those managers, officials and professionals that are supposed to benefit from it. In many instances, perverse behavioural effects ensued. Future performance measurement and management will need to move away from systems thinking and engineering logics in order to facilitate a performance rather than a measurement culture. How then could the next generation be conceived? We first argue that a reconsideration of the assumptions of performance management is needed. Next we discuss the implications for performance management founded on this alternative set of assumptions.

## 3.1 Rethinking the assumptions of the performance movement

The context of public administration is complex and ambiguous. Kravchuk & Schack (1996) explain what complexity means: indeterminate objective functions, multiple administrative layers, collective action problems, system overloads and information overloads, and an increasing scope and scale of operations. Noordegraaf & Abma (2003) add that current performance management, which they label as management by measurement, only fits the rare unambiguous contexts of public administration. There are many sources of ambiguity: history (what has happened?), intentions (what must be done?), technology (what can be done?) and participation (who is present?) (March & Olsen, 1976). Defined as such, not many unambiguous contexts will be found. Since ambiguity is everywhere, the prospects for performance management in this view are rather limited.

An alternative approach is to rethink performance management to make it 'ambiguity proof'. This can only be done by taking complexity and ambiguity as a given, and rebuilding performance management on this foundation. Complexity should be the assumption of performance management, and dealing with complexity should be its ambition. Radin (2006), analysing performance management in the USA in the last decades, concludes her insightful study with a plea to rethink the assumptions of the performance movement. Many problems with performance measurement and management can in her view be attributed to these faulty points of departure. Six issues need reconsideration to better fit with real-world experience (Table 10.1).

Taking complexity seriously also has benefits. Not only because performance management systems may be more useful, but also because they may drive innovation. Public innovation has been one of the main agendas in public sector reform (Hartley, 2005). Conditions for learning include cross-sectoral and cross-disciplinary approaches as well as front-level discretion and responsibility (Albury, 2005). Performance indicators that challenge disciplinary boundaries rather than reconfirm them may provide evidence for innovative dialogue and ultimately foster change (Osborne & Brown, 2005).

**Table 10.1** Rethinking the assumptions of the performance movement

| Issue | Classic assumptions | Alternative assumptions |
|---|---|---|
| Intelligence | – Clarity, universal principles, literal meanings | – Multiple sources, situational knowledge, literal and symbolic meanings |
| How the world works | – Linear cause–effect relations<br>– Clear (or at least clarifiable) goals<br>– Planned | – Complexity, inter-dependence and unplanned change |
| Organizational theory | – Generic principles, internal focus | – Focus on the environment of the organization |
| Professionalism | – Distrust<br>– Control is needed | – Essential to programme operation<br>– Discretion is needed |
| Values, politics and power | – Value-neutral, apolitical, widely shared | – Value-laden, highly political and controversial |
| Information | – Information is available, neutral and conclusive | – Information is partially available and often costly, value-laden and mostly inconclusive |

Source: based on Radin, 2006: pp. 241–2

## 3.2 Rethinking performance management

The review of the assumptions requires a rethinking of the blueprint of performance management. Three implications are discussed below: performance management needs to be more agile, closer to the action and more political.

### Performance management needs to be agile in order to deal with complexity

Kravchuk & Schack (1996) refer to Ashby, a cybernetics scholar, who posited that only complexity can absorb complexity. Rigid information systems will not be able to apprehend and understand rising complexity in the environment. In the most extreme cases, chaos will appear to reign due to the ever-increasing gap between experience and the knowledge base as provided by the information system. Information (what we believe to know) and practice (what we experience) risk becoming separated worlds: one orderly, where objectives are set and performance targets are reached, and one chaotic, where people are mainly concerned to muddle through the day. The 2008 crisis in the financial sector demonstrated the consequences of rigid performance management in increasingly complex settings. The panic was total when the financial sector started to realize that the information system of the rating agencies did not at all reflect real risks.

The main implication would be that performance information should be used for learning, and less so for accountability. Performance-based accountability requires stability for the period for which targets are set. Not many fields remain stable for three to six years. Research in New Zealand has proved that it is very difficult for governments to live up to the stability requirement and that accountability erodes accordingly (Gregory & Lonti, 2008; Carlin, 2006). In addition to stability, accountability requires relatively univocal performance measures that do not allow for much interpretation. The performance indicators have to be accurate reflections of performance. Learning does not require the same stability and robustness. On the contrary, performance measurement is part of a permanent dialogue in order to make sense of complexity. Hence, indicators can and should be adjusted in response to contextual changes and new insights.

If performance management were to move away from accountability, other forms of organizational control would need to be reconsidered. A well-established distinction is between market-, hierarchy- and network-based systems (Bradach & Eccles, 1989). Performance-based accountability aligns itself with either hierarchical or market-based control. League tables that attempt to provide quasi-markets are an example of the latter. Performance targets are an example of hierarchical rule.

There are three alternatives to performance-based accountability. The most obvious alternative is to revert to the administrative default mode, which is traditional regulation. Second, market-based control can be instituted by competitive tendering or competition-based on process or input specifications. Third, trust-based control systems can be a good alternative to performance-based accountability. Trust-based systems rely on traditions, on professions and on standard operating procedures. They are very cost-effective and there is a

**Table 10.2** *Alternatives for performance-based accountability*

| Mode of organization | Performance-based control | Alternative modes of control |
| --- | --- | --- |
| Markets and prices | – Performance indicators as currency in quasi-markets, competition based on performance specifications | – Competitive tendering, competition based on process or input specifications |
| Hierarchy and authority | – Performance indicators as coercive rules | – Traditional regulation |
| Networks and trust in professionalism | – Incompatible | – Custom, tradition, reciprocity, professionalism, trust |

considerable ownership within the vertical responsibilities. However, trust is difficult to build and to maintain.

## Performance management needs to be closer to the action

Kettl (2002) argues that the traditional US public administration boundaries of mission, resources, capacity, responsibility and accountability must be managed in an increasingly complex and political context, necessitating additional negotiation and collaboration between systems and agencies. These complex parallel processes are in a unique way shaped by situational requirements of time and place.

Organizations typically have an undercurrent of repeated decisions they have to make. Recurrent financial, HRM and contract cycles have been the main vehicle for incorporating performance information in decision cycles (see chapter 5). Without doubt, these cycles will remain the foundation of performance management in the future as well. To these recurrent cycles, a constant stream of unique one-off decision processes is added. In recent decades, the weight of stable, recurrent processes has decreased. Top-down performance management on a yearly basis (as in the budget cycle) or monthly basis (as in many Balanced Score Card systems) will need to be supplemented by flexible efforts to provide performance information on demand. Since complex, unique processes will gain importance, the timing and ownership of performance measurement will be challenged.

- Timing – 'guerrilla tactics': in complex policy and management processes, the demand for performance information can arise relatively unexpectedly. At the same time, it can fade away as quickly as it came about. In such a context, expert staff are needed to quickly infuse complex processes with performance information. It is vital that they are able to both capture the need for and understand the availability of performance information. Rather than technical experts, the measurement professionals need to become information brokers.
- Ownership – 'decentralization of performance management': rather than devising top-down systems, performance management needs to be in the hands of middle managers and front-line supervisors who understand the situational requirements best.

For budgeting, this approach would suggest infusing performance information into budget negotiations on an *ad hoc* basis rather than systematically reporting performance in the budget document voted in parliament. Since the budget document is mainly an after-the-fact codification of political processes of negotiation that have taken place before, performance budgets risk becoming a purely bureaucratic exercise. Some confirmation is found in an OECD survey on performance budgeting showing that countries use performance information to inform, but not to determine, budget allocations (Curristine, 2005b). Furthermore, it is argued that much 'linking' of this performance and financial information has been simply providing them in the same report.

## Performance management needs to be political

Some time ago, Innes (1990) observed that the only way to keep data-gathering out of politics is to collect irrelevant data. Performance management, including the use of performance information for policymaking, *has* to be political. Good performance information should strengthen the evidence base for solving political problems of who gets what, when and how (Lasswell, 1936). Such issues are relevant from micro to macro levels: in government-wide policymaking, in policy sectors and networks, in organizational management and in micro-management. We thus do not imply that the political institutions (ministers, parliament, parties . . . ) have to interfere with all performance issues at all levels. Rather, the political nature of performance management needs to be recognized.

- A first implication is that performance management should involve more, rather than fewer, actors. Performance learning, the preferred use in agile performance management systems, will have the highest impact when different perspectives are drawn into the analyses.
- A second implication is that performance management should deal with controversy rather than suppress it. Performance information should not be an authoritative argument to end conflicting views on where to allocate resources. Rather, it should underpin a careful argumentation of causes, consequences and priorities.

The previous paragraphs dealt with the political nature of performance management, and not so much with the political system. There are some efforts however to strengthen the role of performance information in the political system as well. Such initiatives will only be successful however when they acknowledge the different values and positions that political players assume. Performance information that promises to end political debates, to get political argumentation out of the political system, is irrelevant at best, and harmful at worst. Conflict is essential for the functioning of democracy, and therefore performance information should primarily refocus political debate rather than curb it.

## 4 CONCLUSION

This chapter discussed some of the challenges performance management faces. The way performance management is practised is not always consistent with the demands of professionals and networks. In order to be relevant, performance management systems need to be able to deal with the complexity in the environment. Part of the solution can be found in improving the current performance management system. These single-loop changes essentially propose to do the same, but better: better quality data, more ownership, stronger leadership, integration, training and expectations management. The single-loop solutions may not be enough though to cope with increasing complexity. We suggest some double-loop solutions that alter the way performance management is done. Performance management systems should facilitate learning.

## FURTHER READING

Three texts that suggest more fundamental ways to rethink performance management are by Kravchuk & Schack (1996), Moynihan (2008) and Radin (2006). The report of the UK House of Commons Public Administration Select Committee is also worth reading (House of Commons Public Administration Select Committee, 2003). *Public Performance & Management Review* devoted a special issue to the future of performance management with relatively short and provocative contributions by key authors (volume 25, issue 4). Hatry for instance discusses the fashions and fallacies in the field (2002). A special issue of *Public Management Review* (Mandell & Keast, 2008) discusses performance of networks. Exemplary studies that focus on implementation are by Mayne (2007) and Curristine (for performance budgeting) (Curristine, 2005a).

## REFERENCES

Agranoff, R. (2005). 'Managing Collaborative Performance'. *Public Productivity & Management Review*, 29, 18.

Albury, D. (2005). 'Fostering Innovation in Public Services'. *Public Money & Management*, 25(1), 51–6.

Argyris, C., & Schön, D. (1996). *Organizational Learning: A Theory of Action Perspective*. Reading, MA: Addison-Wesley.

Behn, R. D. (2004). *Performance Leadership: 11 Better Practices That Can Ratchet Up Performance*. Washington, DC: IBM Center for the Business of Government.

Bouckaert, G., & Halligan, J. (2008). *Managing Performance: International Comparisons*. London: Routledge.

Bradach, J. L., & Eccles, R. G. (1989). 'Price, Authority, and Trust: From Ideal Types to Plural Forms'. *Annual Review of Sociology*, 15, 97–118.

Carlin, T. M. (2006). 'Victoria's Accrual Output Based Budgeting System – Delivering as Promised? Some Empirical Evidence'. *Financial Accountability & Management*, 22, 1–19.

Curristine, T. (2005a). 'Government Performance: Lessons and Challenges'. *OECD Journal on Budgeting*, 5, 127–51.

—— (2005b). 'Performance Information in the Budget Process: Results of OECD 2005 Questionnaire'. *OECD Journal on Budgeting*, 5, 87.

Davies, H. T., & Lampel, J. (1998). 'Trust in Performance Indicators?' *Qual Health Care*, 7, 159–62.

Denhardt, K., & Aristigueta, M. (2008). 'Performance Management Systems: Providing Accountability and Challenging Collaboration'. In Van Dooren, W., & Van de Walle, S. (eds) *Performance Information in the Public Sector: How It Is Used*. Basingstoke: Palgrave Macmillan.

Gregory, R., & Lonti, Z. (2008). 'Chasing Shadows? Performance Measurement of Policy Advice in the New Zealand Government Departments'. *Public Administration*, 86, 837–56.

Hartley, J. (2005). 'Innovation in Governance and Public Services: Past and Present'. *Public Money & Management*, 25(1), 27–34.

Hatry, H. P. (2002). 'Performance Measurement: Fashions and Fallacies'. *Public Performance & Management Review*, 25, 352–8.

—— (2008). 'The Many Faces of Use'. In Van Dooren, W., & Van de Walle, S. (eds) *Performance Information in the Public Sector: How It Is Used*. Basingstoke: Palgrave Macmillan.

House of Commons Public Administration Select Committee (2003). *On Target? Government by Measurement*. London: House of Commons.

Innes, J. E. (1990). *Knowledge and Public Policy: The Search for Meaningful Indicators*. New Brunswick: Transaction Publishers.

Kaplan, R. S., & Norton, D. P. (1996). *The Balanced Scorecard: Translating Strategy into Action*. Boston, MA: Harvard Business School Press.

Kettl, F. D. (2002). *The Transformation of Governance*. Baltimore: Johns Hopkins University Press.

Koppenjan, J. F. M., & Klijn, E. H. (2004). *Managing Uncertainties in Networks: A Network Approach to Problem Solving and Decision Making*. London: Routledge.

Kravchuk, R. S., & Schack, R. W. (1996). 'Designing Effective Performance Measurement Systems under the Government Performance and Results Act of 1993'. *Public Administration Review*, 56, 348–58.

Kroll, A. (2013). 'The Other Type of Performance Information: Nonroutine Feedback, Its Relevance and Use'. *Public Administration Review*, 73(2), 265–76.

Laegreid, P., Roness, P. G., & Rubecksen, K. (2008). 'Performance Information and Performance Steering: Integrated System or Loose Coupling?' In Van Dooren, W., & Van de Walle, S. (eds) *Performance Information in the Public Sector: How It Is Used*. Basingstoke: Palgrave Macmillan.

Lasswell, H. (1936). *Politics: Who Gets What, When and How?* New York: Whittlesey House.

**217**

THE FUTURE OF PERFORMANCE MANAGEMENT

Mandell, M., & Keast, R. (2008). 'Introduction'. *Public Management Review*, 10, 687.

March, J. G., & Olsen, J. P. (1976). *Ambiguity and Choice in Organizations*. Bergen: Universitetsforlaget.

Mayne, J. (2007). 'Challenges and Lessons in Implementing Results-Based Management'. *Evaluation*, 13, 87–109.

Milward, H. B., & Provan, K. G. (2000). 'Governing the Hollow State'. *Journal of Public Administration Research and Theory*, 10, 359–80.

Moynihan, D. P. (2008). *The Dynamics of Performance Management: Constructing Information and Reform*. Washington, DC: Georgetown University Press.

Noordegraaf, M., & Abma, T. (2003). 'Management by Measurement? Public Management Practices amidst Ambiguity'. *Public Administration*, 81, 853–71.

Osborne, S. P., & Brown, K. (2005). *Managing Change and Innovation in Public Service Organizations*. London: Routledge.

Perrin, B. (2003). *Implementing the Vision: Addressing Challenges to Results-Focused Management and Budgeting*. Paris: Organisation for Economic Co-operation and Development.

Power, M. (1999). *The Audit Society: Rituals of Verification*. Oxford: Oxford University Press.

Radin, B. A. (2006). *Challenging the Performance Movement: Accountability, Complexity, and Democratic Values*. Washington, DC: Georgetown University Press.

Taylor, J. (2011). 'Factors Influencing the Use of Performance Information for Decision Making in Australian State Agencies'. *Public Administration*, 89(4), 1316–34.

Van Dooren, W. (2011). 'Better Performance Management'. *Public Performance & Management Review*, 34(3), 420–33.

Van Dooren, W., Lonti, Z., Sterck, M., & Bouckaert, G. (2007). *The Institutional Drivers of Efficiency*. OECD/GOV technical papers. Paris: OECD.

Vangen, S., & Huxham, C. (2001). 'Enacting Leadership for Collaborative Advantage: Uncovering Activities and Dilemmas of Partnership Managers'. *British Journal of Management*, 14, 61–76.

Wholey, J. S. (1999). 'Performance-Based Management: Responding to the Challenges'. *Public Productivity and Management Review*, 22, 288–307.

# Index